lumbar;-6 | sacral;-5 | coccygeal vertebrae
mach | small intestine
iaphragm | small colon
spleen | large colon
kidney | caecum
rectum
pelvic girdle
bladder
femur
urethra
stifle joint
tibia
hock
nt bones
non bone
moid bone
pastern bone
pastern bone
l bone

PONY CLUB MANUAL
NUMBER TWO

This is the second of three manuals commissioned by the New Zealand Pony Clubs Association. The first two books cover the whole of the Pony Club syllabus. They must be read in conjunction, as the basis of most of the work in this book is explained in *Manual One*. *Manual Two* is a more technical book, covering the requirements for the more advanced certificates — C+ (13 years+), B (15 years+), A and H (17 years+). All necessary information for these tests is contained herein. *Manual Three* is for instructors and administrators.

Apart from certificates, this book should be a valuable guide for all riders and horse owners from early teenage to adult. The more specialised dressage and jumping chapters, and those dealing with the conditioning and care of the horse, will be of great assistance to the competitive rider. Those people who just enjoy riding and being with their horses will find all the information they require to ensure that they and their mount enjoy a safe and rewarding pastime.

Manual Two is well illustrated throughout, and has been compiled with the assistance and approval of Pony Club's national and senior instructors, as well as other professionals — veterinarians, farrier and saddler.

These manuals are unique in that all stages are clearly set out in a progressive manner. They not only provide complete instruction for the young rider, but are also essential for instructors, examiners, parents and other supportive adults. In fact, with their aid, everyone should be absolutely sure as to what to expect from horse and rider, at any given stage of what is undoubtedly a demanding and somewhat complex sport. Nowhere else in the world has the Pony Club syllabus been set out in this progressive fashion.

Manual Three, how to teach what is contained in *Manual One* and *Two*, completes the series.

While these manuals were initially for New Zealand riders, their content applies equally well in other countries. The manuals are also being used for the instruction of Pony Club riders in Australia, Canada, the United States and South Africa.

Books by Elaine Knox-Thompson
and Suzanne Dickens

Guide to Riding and Horse Care (Lansdowne/Weldon 1977,
1979, 1984, 1988: Orbis UK 1981, Merehurst UK 1985,
Howell US 1985)

The Young Horse (Collins 1979, 1985)

Horses and Ponies (Shortland 1989)

Pony Club Manual No. 1 (1981, 1982, 1984, 1986, 1988, 1990)

Pony Club Manual No. 2 (1985, 1988, 1990)

Pony Club Manual No. 3: For Instructors (1989)

The three manuals are published by
Ray Richards Publisher
in conjunction with the
New Zealand Pony Clubs Association Inc.

Horse Sense (TVNZ 1982)
Television Series by Elaine Knox-Thompson
and Suzanne Dickens

PONY CLUB MANUAL
Number Two

by

Elaine Knox-Thompson
BHSI, IIH

and Suzanne Dickens
BHSI, IIH

Drawings by Megan Harvey
Photographs by Suzanne Dickens

Auckland
RAY RICHARDS PUBLISHER

First published 1985
Revised edition, 1988, reprinted 1990

RAY RICHARDS PUBLISHER
49 Aberdeen Road, Auckland 9
in conjunction with
NEW ZEALAND PONY CLUBS ASSOCIATION

© Elaine Knox-Thompson and Suzanne Dickens

ISBN 0-908596-22-7

Designed by Don Sinclair
Typeset by Linotype Service (PN) Limited
Printed by Colorcraft Limited

CONTENTS

FOREWORD

MANUAL 2 is the second of a series of three manuals produced for the Pony Clubs Association. This second manual has been widely researched and offers an invaluable source of knowledge and information. It completely defines the syllabus and training techniques for the more advanced levels of Pony Club. C+ on to B, H, and A Certificates are comprehensively covered, yet the simplicity of the manual makes it a unique reference book for any equestrian enthusiast.

The authors, Elaine Knox-Thompson and Suzanne Dickens, spent the first part of their lives riding, training and instructing in the United Kingdom. They came to New Zealand in 1956 and established a reputation for the thoroughness and quality of their work in instruction and examination. This dedicated experience, supported by overseas travel, has given them a comprehensive understanding of the world of the young rider and the international Pony Club movement.

The equestrian experience of the two authors, along with assistance from fellow members of the Pony Clubs National Instructor panels, and their knowledge and life-long involvement in Pony Club, have resulted in three manuals that have gained world-wide recognition and which are the invaluable companion of many thousand young riders, Pony Club instructors, examiners and administrators.

We have always placed great emphasis on the Pony Club branch working rally and on the manuals as the complete base for all Pony Club instruction and learning. The Pony Clubs Association proudly acknowledges the improved standards being established at all levels since the releasing of the manuals, with greater equestrian abilities and depth of knowledge being shown by our riding members and instructors.

The 1988 edition of *Manual 2* has been revised and updated.

Roland R. Matthews
President — N.Z. Pony Clubs Association

INTRODUCTION

THIS IS the advanced manual of the New Zealand Pony Clubs Association. It continues from the point reached by *Manual One*. Between them, the two books cover the whole range and system of Pony Club instruction. They define the syllabus and training programme for each of the certificates, from D and C (*Manual One*) to the C+ Certificate and certificates, B, A, and H (*Manual Two*).

The Objects of This Book Are:

1. To provide instruction in as practical a way as possible, and all the information needed for C+, B, A and H certificates. There are, of course, immense difficulties in learning any physical subject from a book. All top riders find it necessary to receive regular instruction, or at least to have somebody to watch and comment. Pony Club members are fortunate that help is always available. For them, the manuals should complement the instruction at rallies, providing immediate reference and assistance in pinpointing faults before bad habits become established.

2. To give younger and less experienced riders an introduction to more advanced work generally. It is appreciated that many people don't want to reach the heights, but simply wish to enjoy riding as a social activity and a pleasant form of exercise, shared with an animal. Some, especially in town areas, have limited scope and facilities. But, as with any sport, the more you know about it, the more you can get out of it. It is hoped that the ideas herein will prove interesting, improve understanding and increase appreciation of the problems and achievements of top competitors.

3. To provide all riders, whether Pony Club members or not, with a reliable course of riding instruction and an authoritative source of information on the care of horses and ponies. The book is not intended purely as a textbook for the passing of certificates. If it can help **ALL** horses and ponies to be better ridden, better understood and better cared for, and conditioned for the work required of them, it will have been well worthwhile.

Riders must remember to refer to *Manual One* for the start of each subject — bitting, shoeing, paces of the horse, etc. *Manual One* is the foundation book, and, while it is true to say that the majority of those using it belong to a younger age group, it is nevertheless 'essential reading' for all riders, whatever their age or standard. Unless you have a sound working knowledge of *Manual One*, you will not derive full benefit from *Manual Two*.

Pony Club aims to give its senior members a good grounding on orthodox lines in all branches of riding and horse management. This will enable them subsequently to specialise in whatever branch appeals to them. The great majority of riders of international standard started their training in Pony Club.

Training methods may appear to be many and various, but top instructors are remarkably similar in their teaching. Everybody is aiming for the same goal of a happy and successful partnership between horse and rider — variations are not so much a question of different methods as of slightly different slants on the approach to that goal. In controversial areas, *Manual Two* tries to give different ideas, for and against, as impartially as possible. While all instruction and examinations are based on the two manuals, Pony Club is prepared to consider other methods, provided they are safe, efficient and humane.

But do bear in mind that when things don't work, this may be due to a correct method misunderstood or misapplied, or to previous work being hurried or insufficiently established. Changing the method without clear understanding may lead to complete confusion for horse and rider. If in doubt, seek advice.

To Parents

By the time your child reaches the stage of *Manual Two*, you will probably already be an experienced Pony Club parent, able, and hopefully willing, to pass on to others the advice and knowledge that you yourself gained as a newcomer.

From the teenager's point of view, the post-C period is often a time of decision as to whether or not to continue with riding. Many are just starting secondary school with its increasing pressures of work and recreation and widening interests.

Then there is the often traumatic experience of changing from a well-loved and familiar pony to a horse, which can seem a totally different animal with its long stride and unpredictable strength and reactions. Understandably, many riders pale (inwardly, if not outwardly) at the thought of going over the ground work again, especially if the new horse is young or insufficiently schooled. This applies particularly to less adventurous or less skilled riders.

If you are by now convinced of the advantages of riding for your offspring, this is a time for tactful encouragement without pushing. Assistance with feeding, and possibly exercising the horse, may be appreciated at times, but the important thing is to show interest without interference — a thin line indeed! Probably the greatest material help at this time, apart from acting as chauffeur, will be in providing financial backing to meet the weekly feed and other bills, at least until the rider is able to provide, and drive him/herself.

There will inevitably be increasing expense, especially with the real enthusiasts who want to travel to shows, trials or hunts. Horses cost more to keep than ponies, especially the larger thoroughbreds. (A point to bear in mind when buying.)

One thing is certain, and that is that riding and Pony Club still have much to offer teenagers — the continuity of their club affairs and a feeling of belonging and being needed — not only by their horse, but by others in the club. Instructors and committee members rely on them for some assistance and leadership, the younger ones look up to them and follow their example and an hour or so on a horse in the fresh air is a wonderful let-up in the midst of swotting for examinations.

ACKNOWLEDGMENTS

OUR THANKS to the New Zealand Pony Clubs Association for their continued faith and encouragement. Their patience and lack of pressure for quick results have shown a real appreciation of the complex problems involved in compiling this manual.

Thanks also to Janey Fisher, Margaret Harris, Cheryl Monds, Errol O'Brien, and Jennifer Stobart (all BHSI), our colleagues on the National Instructors panel — once again, our thanks and appreciation for the willingness to discuss and share ideas and training methods. It is rare indeed for seven professionals to reach such amicable agreement.

And thanks to all the Pony Club members in different parts of the country who worked so hard for the photographs, even if not finally included. It was decided that to be authentic each level, B or A, should be shown by riders of that standard, to give a clear idea of what can reasonably be expected. The efforts and good spirit of all involved, as well as their well turned-out and co-operative ponies and horses, were a great incentive.

There has been encouraging feedback from Pony Club instructors for *Manual Two*. Some, including our president, Virginia Johnson, and Tony St John, chairman of Training Committee, have taken considerable time and trouble to read and comment on the text. Many of their suggestions have been incorporated. Some members have assisted greatly with comments as to the suitability of the text for the different levels.

A book of this nature requires much research and assistance from people who are experts in the horse-related aspects of their particular professions or trades:

Megan Harvey has responded in her usual clear style of illustration to the often difficult demands made upon her. Her determination that every drawing should be correct has meant many hours of work.

Deciding exactly how much to include on veterinary matters is always difficult. We are much indebted to John Noble BVSc, and Peter Marshall BVSc, for their assistance in consultation and in reading and approving the veterinary chapters.

Brian McDonald, master farrier, checked the shoeing sections. His advice and clear explanations have been invaluable.

Trevor Brown, of Taupo Saddlery, also gave us valuable information and advice in his field. We thank him for this, and for the loan of equipment used in photographs.

Our thanks also to: Tauhara branch of Taupo District Pony Club for the use of their grounds and equipment. And: Wills National Equestrian Centre for the use of their horses and facilities, and the working pupils (all Pony Club members) for their assistance in the lunging and stabling photographs.

Finally, to Ray Richards, our publisher. We cannot thank him enough for his patience and tolerance. Our thanks also to his wife and daughter, Barbara and Nicki, whose meticulous editing have greatly improved the text, and to Don Sinclair, designer, who has once again 'put it all together'.

STRUCTURE OF PONY CLUB ADMINISTRATION

Members 15,000 approximately — junior, associate, senior, life.

Branches 350 approximately. Belong and send delegates to —

Clubs 83, including Suva, and the Chatham Islands. Send delegates to —

Areas 16. Send delegates to —

Committee of Management — comprising —

Executive — the president, immediate past president, vice-presidents, treasurer and secretary. The 16 area delegates and one representative each from the National Instructors and Technical Delegates panels, the New Zealand Horse Society and National Youth Council.

Sub-committees — formed from within the Committee of Management — Training, Championships, Inter-Pacific, Games, Finance and Rules.

Representatives are sent to — Royal Agricultural Society of New Zealand, New Zealand Horse Society, Riding for the Disabled and the Accident Compensation Corporation.

Annual Conference — two voting delegates from each club, open to all members.

1
PONY CLUB AND THE OLDER MEMBER

NEW ZEALAND PONY CLUBS ASSOCIATION

For details of the foundation and objects of the New Zealand Pony Clubs Association, see *Manual One*, page 7.

Structure of Administration (opposite)

The line of communication goes from the individual member through the branch, club and area to the Committee of Management. This committee meets three times a year and is responsible for the general running of Pony Club affairs. Sub-committees deal with their respective spheres, but their decisions must be approved by the Committee of Management. The Executive meets when necessary to deal with matters of an urgent nature only.

Activities administered or instigated by the association, and of special interest to older members and associates include:

Conference, held annually in a different area, by invitation of the host club. All members are welcome to attend. Remits submitted by clubs lead to debate on many topics, and decisions are taken here which may affect everybody in Pony Club. An instructors' demonstration or discussion is also held at conference time.

Inter-Pacific exchange. A biennial rally of teams from all the 'Pony Club countries' bordering on the Pacific (plus Great Britain), who take it in turns to act as host. Includes competitions for both national and 'scrambled' teams, but the main object is to meet and get to know one another over a period of about a month. A wonderful experience. Candidates for selection must hold B Certificate, be good riders on unknown horses and good ambassadors for their country.

The Pony Club team championships. Held annually by areas, in rotation. Teams consist of the three top scorers in the D.C. (Dorothy Campbell) section for junior members, and the A.1. section for associates, in the Area Trials. Good fun for those who enjoy a challenge, and are ready for this level of eventing. Horses and ponies must be at least five years old, and riders should not enter until they have had considerable experience in novice and club competition.

A and H certificates. Examination dates and venues are set for the coming year by the Committee of Management.

RESPONSIBILITIES OF A PONY CLUB MEMBER

As a more senior member, you have an increasing responsibility to uphold the good name of Pony Club by showing courtesy and consideration to other road-users. Uneducated or unthinking riders may cause accidents and/or create ill-feeling towards all horse people. *Manual One*, Chapter 5, sets down the Road Code and guidelines for riding on farmland, beaches and other places. Of course, these rules still apply, and a few basic reminders and suggestions may not go amiss.

At Pony Club

An organisation such as ours depends on teamwork for its survival. Because you pay a subscription, it does not mean that you should expect to be waited on, and you will find that the sense of 'belonging' is far greater if you are prepared to lend a hand. Naturally, you will be involved in your own rally activities for most of the time, but there are still several ways in which you can assist such as:

Arriving in good time and helping to set out jumps and other equipment — also putting things away at the end.

Being quick to help the instructor alter fences during a lesson.

Making new members welcome. (Remember how you felt at your first rally?)

Helping younger members all you can — e.g. checking tack — especially girths, stirrups and bits; escorting to and from rallies; answering questions patiently. (Or finding out the answers if you don't know!)

Whatever you do, you set an example. Help by making it a good one, most of all if things are not quite going your way. Swearing, sulking or showing-off do not improve your image or the atmosphere at rallies. Rudeness, to instructors or anyone else, is inexcusable. Your regular attendance should be of mutual benefit to you and your club.

For the Sake of Other People

Keep off footpaths, berms and cultivated roadsides. Droppings and hoofprints in such places make all riders unpopular, whether Pony Club or not.

Walk your horse among people on foot, wherever you are.

Never dash off suddenly when riding with others, particularly if beginners, nervous riders or young horses are in the party.

Show appreciation of any act of courtesy towards you — e.g. motorists slowing down or pulling out.

For the Sake of Your Horse

Don't treat him as a machine. Make his life varied and interesting, with a good balance between work, play and exercise.

Make sure he gets sufficient of the right kind of food and exercise to make him fit enough for the work you expect from him.

Make sure that his tack is comfortable and well-fitting. By now, it is up to you to check everything and either tell your parents when repairs are needed, or to arrange and pay for them yourself. Don't use severe bits or gadgets unless your instructor agrees that they are necessary, and never use any gadget just because it is new, or because somebody else does.

Never ride him when he is tired, sick, lame or out of sorts — find out what is wrong and do something about it. Don't sit around on his back for long periods.

If you lose your temper — get off and cool off! Never hit him when you are angry. Punishment, if deserved, must be administered objectively and without malice, and only when you are sure he understands what you want and is capable of doing it.

Take a pride in him. Naturally, he must be well enough cared for to prevent injury, but try to go a little further than this!

For Your Own Sake

Always wear your helmet and suitable footwear when riding.

Observe normal safety rules — run up stirrups when dismounted, check girths and pick up reins before mounting. Check your tack frequently, for your own safety as well as your horse's comfort, especially girths and girth-straps, size of stirrup irons, all stitching and buckles. Reins not properly joined in the centre are dangerous.

On the road, obey the Road Code. Don't ride a young horse or one you know to be nervous in traffic on your own.

The following are all potentially dangerous:

Sitting sideways on the horse with one foot in the stirrup — you could easily get dragged if he moved suddenly.

Swimming or jumping your horse when on your own.

Attempting to jump anything beyond your own or your horse's ability.

Putting on or taking off a raincoat, jacket or jersey when mounted.

Riding your horse in a halter. NEVER do this on the road.

Going off on your own without telling anyone where you are going or how long you expect to be away.

Most accidents are avoidable. Lack of attention to these common-sense rules can injure, or even kill, your horse or pony, or you. Form the habit of doing things correctly — bad habits have a nasty knack of surfacing in moments of stress.

Apart from the activities mentioned above, Pony Club still has much to offer, on a give-and-take basis. Companionship, instruction, discussion and mutual assistance with horse problems, plus the opportunity for social service in returning to others some of the pleasure and knowledge you have gained. Ways you can help:

Instructing. From age 16 onwards, you can attend instructors' courses and start as an assistant instructor. You will be surprised how much this helps with your own riding.

Examining. From age 18, you can, if invited, examine for D Certificate.

Supervising games and play activities for younger members.

Coaching. A and H Certificate holders, in addition to the above, can be of the greatest assistance in helping other candidates.
On the administrative side:

Serving on your branch or club committee.

Attending conference as a club delegate.

Assistance with:

a. the club grounds and grazing arrangements. Checking horses and paddocks, organising rosters, facilities, etc.

b. running of rallies, camps, competitions, treks, etc.

You should, of course, still receive advice and instruction yourself, although in smaller branches the latter may have to be arranged at club level.

SENIOR MEMBERS

Pony Club in New Zealand has senior members, over 21.

These members make a tremendous contribution to the movement, and form the great majority of administrators and instructors at all levels. Few associate members have either the time to cope unaided with the necessary organisation, or the experience that comes with age and is often required to deal with the inevitable domestic problems. A good committee and a well-organised team of instructors are the making of any club — rewarding to belong to and ensuring enjoyment and success for all.

While many clubs include senior members in their riding activities, this depends entirely on the available instructors and facilities, and is left to the discretion of individual clubs to decide.

Pony Club is one of the biggest youth movements and *the* biggest riding organisation in the world. Only by mutual co-operation and assistance can it continue to expand and develop the great work it does for young riders and their mounts.

2

TEST SHEETS: C+ CERTIFICATE AND B CERTIFICATE

C+ CERTIFICATE

This test has been introduced to bridge the big gap between C and B certificates. It is not compulsory as a qualification for B. Its purpose is to provide an incentive for members who, having achieved C, would value an interim test to check progress and maintain interest, or for those who would like to go a little further than C, but do not feel confident enough to think of B at this stage.

C+ is not intended to be an 'in depth' examination, but rather to show that the candidate's ability, and his/her understanding of riding and the care and conditioning of the pony are developing on sound lines.

A certificate and clip will be awarded for C+, as for the other tests.

TEST SHEET: C+ CERTIFICATE

Minimum age: 13 years

This is an official required test of a standard halfway between C and B certificates. Candidates must hold C Certificate, and must pass C+ before attempting B Certificate.

OBJECTIVES

To become an active, all-round rider, with knowledge of the aids and ability to apply them effectively.

To ride over simple show jumping and cross country fences at trot or canter.

To be capable of joining in any suitable Pony Club activities.

To gain practical experience and knowledge of the care and conditioning of a pony at grass.

To have a thorough knowledge of the Road Code as it applies to ridden horses. Ride safely and sensibly on the roads or in the country.

RIDING

Turnout of pony and rider.

Position, at walk, trot, canter and gallop, becoming steadier and showing that the rider is progressing on sound lines. Sitting trot, rising trot on either diagonal, change of diagonal. Understand the horse's action (footfalls) and rhythm in all paces. Show practical knowledge of even paces and of the pony accepting the bit. Know what is meant by 'on the bit'. Know the aids for, and be able to carry out, the following movements:

Circles — 10m in walk, 15m in trot, 20m in canter.

Serpentines or loops, at candidate's choice.

A few lengthened strides in trot.

Turn on the forehand.

Change of leg through trot.

Gallop.

Show that the jumping position is becoming better established.

Understand what is meant by correct contact in jumping.

Ride correctly over trotting poles or cavalletti.

Jump a variety of fences and simple combinations at trot and canter. Up and down hill, drop fences, banks and ditches may be included.

How to walk a jumping course.

Maximum height for C+ Certificate, 75cm.

Candidates are *not* required to change ponies.

ROAD CODE — RIDING OUT AND ABOUT

Know the Road Code as applied to ridden horses.

Show understanding of the requirements for riding alone or in company, on the roads or in the country.

PONY MANAGEMENT

Paddocking

Daily check of pony and paddock.

Recognise these poisonous plants — ragwort, hemlock, tutu, castor oil plant (northern New Zealand).

Feeding, Exercising, and Conditioning

Understand the principles of watering and feeding.

Recognise good and bad hay.

Recognise the following feedstuffs and explain their uses: pellets, oats, barley, maize, bran, linseed, chaff, molasses, salt.

Understand the principles of getting a pony fit, up to a 'good working condition' level.

Describe own mount's feeding programme at different times of the year.

Handling

Handle a pony safely and efficiently at all times.

Lead a pony in and out of a yard or through a gateway.

Grooming and Clipping

Groom a pony efficiently. (Wisp not required.)
Know the names and uses of different types of clips.
How to prepare the pony for clipping.

The Foot and Shoeing

Name the parts of the foot, and parts of the shoes.
Know the names of the farrier's tools.
Discuss own mount's shoeing — type of shoes used.

Travelling

Be able to put on travel boots or bandages at candidate's choice.
Be able to load and unload a quiet pony, with help.

Health

Have knowledge of everything covered in 'Health, Ailments and Injuries', *Manual One*.
Know when to call the vet, and what to have on hand when he comes.
Carry out prescribed treatment for wounds, lameness or ailments.
Some knowledge of internal parasites affecting horses.
Describe own mount's worming programme.

SADDLERY AND EQUIPMENT

Be able to fit a saddle and a snaffle bridle.
Knowledge of types of bits in everyday use, any 3, candidate's choice.
Care and cleaning of equipment.

NOTE. The syllabus for C+ Certificate includes all work for previous certificates, whether or not it is specified on this Test Sheet.
Read: *Manual One*, and *Manual Two* as appropriate.

TEST SHEET: B CERTIFICATE

Minimum age: 15 years
Candidates must hold C Certificate

OBJECTIVES

To become an active, all-round rider, who knows the reasons for what he is doing, and is able to assess results.
To ride over different types of fences at specified paces.
To be capable of riding and jumping any well-mannered horse or pony and commenting on his way of going.

To be capable of joining in any suitable Pony Club activities of interest to the rider (e.g. eventing, hunting, treks, gymkhanas, etc.) and of looking after the horse before, during and after the day's activity.

To gain knowledge and practical experience of the care and conditioning of horses, and to be able to look after a temporarily stabled horse.

To ride intelligently and with due regard for others on the roads and in the country, with a knowledge of pace and distance.

RIDING

Turnout of horse and rider.

Position at all paces, well established and showing some depth, enabling the rider to apply aids smoothly and accurately.

Have knowledge of physical exercises to improve the rider's position.

Use diagonals correctly at all times.

Understand the horse's action (footfalls) and rhythm in all paces.

Show working trot and canter, and understand the difference between the horse 'accepting the bit' and being 'on the bit'.

Perform the following movements:

Circles down to 10m in walk and trot, 15m in canter.

Serpentines.

Lengthening of stride in trot and canter.

Turn on the forehand.

Riding in position (placing the horse).

Canter from walk.

Change of leg through trot.

Demi-pirouette at walk — early stages.

The candidate must be able to explain the aids for each movement and its objects.

Ride with a double bridle (or pelham) and understand its action.

Gallop.

Ride and jump a different horse.

Show a balanced jumping position, with steady lower leg and independent hands.

Understand the importance of correct contact in jumping and be able to demonstrate this.

Jump a variety of fences and combinations at all paces.

Jump up and down hill, drop fences, banks and ditches.

Show use of poles and/or cavalletti and exercises to improve a horse's jumping.

Have some basic knowledge of building simple schooling fences, combinations and exercises.

Know how to walk a jumping course.

(Maximum height for B Certificate fences, 90cm.)

Know the names of the president of the New Zealand Pony Clubs Association, and of the club chief instructor.
Some knowledge of the organisation of the NZPCA.
Know the objects of the NZPCA. (*Manual One*, page 7.)
Responsibilities of a Pony Club member.

HORSE MANAGEMENT

Paddocking

Daily check of horse and paddock.
Recognise the more common poisonous plants.
Knowledge of maintenance of own horse's paddock.

Feeding, Exercising and Conditioning

Understand the principles of feeding and watering, and be able to put these principles into practice.
Recognise good and bad hay — meadow, lucerne, clover.
Recognise the following feedstuffs and explain their uses: pellets, oats, barley, maize, bran, linseed, chaff — oaten, hay or lucerne — molasses, salt.
Understand the principles of conditioning and getting a horse fit.
Signs of fitness in a horse.
Bringing a horse up after a spell, and roughing off.
Describe own mount's feeding programme at different stages of fitness.

Handling

Handle a horse safely and efficiently at all times.
How to hold a horse for shoeing, clipping or veterinary treatment.
Running up in hand for lameness or action.

Grooming, Clipping and Trimming

Understand the terms 'quartering' and 'strapping' (or 'stropping').
Strap a horse efficiently.
Cooling down after work, including washing down and drying off a wet or sweating horse.
How to pull the mane.
Plait the mane and tail.
Trim heels with scissors and comb.
Know the names and uses of different types of clips.
How to prepare the horse for clipping.

The Foot and Shoeing

Name the parts of the foot, the parts of the shoe and the different types of shoes used.
Name the farrier's tools and know their uses.
Recognise good and bad shoeing.
Discuss own horse's shoeing — reasons for the shoes used.

Travelling

Prepare a horse for travel, showing knowledge of suitable clothing and protective bandages and boots.
Knowledge of loading and unloading.
Care of the horse during a journey, and while away from home.

Stabling

Points to check in a loose box.
Use of stable tools to muck out, pick up droppings, put down a bed.
Some knowledge of the use and maintenance of the following types of bedding — straw, sawdust, shavings.
Stable routine over a limited period — e.g. at shows, championships.
What to look for when inspecting a stabled horse first thing in the morning and last thing at night.
Lead a horse in and out of a loose box.
How to deal with a 'cast' horse.
How to deal with a horse who has 'broken out'.

Health

Have sound knowledge of everything covered in 'Health, Ailments and Injuries', *Manual One.*
Know the horse's normal temperature, pulse and respiration. Be able to take respiration.
Know when to call the vet, and what to have on hand when he comes.
How to report a sick or injured horse's symptoms to the vet.
Detection of heat, pain and swelling in a horse's leg.
Carry out prescribed treatment for wounds, lameness or ailments.
Have some knowledge of internal parasites affecting horses. Describe own horse's worming programme.
Some knowledge of 'tying-up'.
Some knowledge of sprains and splints.

Know the Horse

Good and bad points of conformation — terms in common use.

Good and bad action. Recognise faults in action — dishing, brushing, etc.

Some knowledge of the horse's teeth — names of the teeth.
Recognise permanent teeth, milk teeth, tushes.

SADDLERY AND EQUIPMENT

Check fitting of saddlery, including double bridle or pelham, martingales, nosebands, breastplates, surcingles.
Types and fitting of brushing boots, bell boots, bandages, covers.
Types of bits and their action.
Care, cleaning and storage of equipment.
Inspection of saddlery for soundness.

NOTE. The syllabus for B Certificate includes all work for previous certificates, whether or not it is specified on this Test Sheet.

3
RIDING: B CERTIFICATE

Training Objectives

1. To become an active and thinking rider, able to assess results.
2. To produce a horse or pony who is a pleasant ride and a good all-rounder.
3. To gain experience in riding different horses and ponies.

As a start to achieving these objectives, it will help if you understand more about the horse's paces and the terms which are used to describe his way of going.

PACES

You already know (*Manual One*, page 62) that each of the horse's paces has its own rhythm. As your 'feel' develops, a knowledge of the horse's action and footfalls at each pace will help you to apply the aids at the best moment in his stride, for any particular purpose.

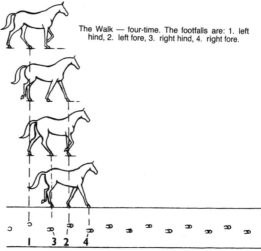

The Walk — four-time. The footfalls are: 1. left hind, 2. left fore, 3. right hind, 4. right fore.

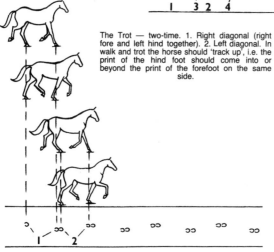

The Trot — two-time. 1. Right diagonal (right fore and left hind together). 2. Left diagonal. In walk and trot the horse should 'track up', i.e. the print of the hind foot should come into or beyond the print of the forefoot on the same side.

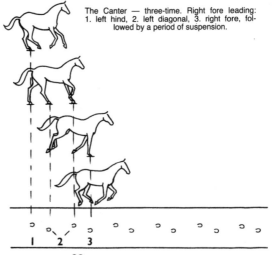

The Canter — three-time. Right fore leading: 1. left hind, 2. left diagonal, 3. right fore, followed by a period of suspension.

The Walk

In dressage, several variations of each pace are recognised by the F.E.I. (Fédération Equestre Internationale).

At the walk, these are: medium, free, extended and collected.

There is no 'working walk'. We shall be concentrating on the medium and free walks at this stage.

Faults in the walk. 'Pacing' or 'ambling', when the two feet on the same side come down together, giving a two-time beat.

Not 'tracking up', as explained above, with the hind feet. This shows lack of impulsion, the forward drive from the hindquarters. (See page 26.)

The pace being hurried or irregular.

The Trot

Recognised trots are: working, medium, extended and collected. Our present aim will be to establish a good working trot with some lengthening and shortening of the stride, though not yet to the extent of medium or collected trot. These advanced paces are dealt with in 'Riding: A Certificate'.

Faults in the trot. 'Running', when the speed is too fast, with short, hurried strides.

Lack of impulsion or of balance, not bringing the hind legs sufficiently under the body, so that the steps become heavy and lacking in spring and the horse fails to track up.

Any irregularity in the pace.

The Canter

Recognised canters are the same as for the trot: working, medium, extended and collected. Here again, we shall aim to establish a good working pace, with some lengthening and shortening.

Faults in the canter. 'Disunited'. Footfalls in this case could be, for instance, left hind, right lateral, left fore. A very uncomfortable pace, easily recognised!

Four-time beat. Shows stiffness and lack of impulsion; the horse does not bring his hind legs sufficiently under him, so that the two legs of the diagonal do not come down together.

Cantering on the 'wrong' or outside leg on a turn or circle.

In more advanced dressage the horse is sometimes deliberately asked to canter on the outside leg as a suppling and obedience exercise. This is called 'counter canter' or 'contra-lead'. (See page 154.)

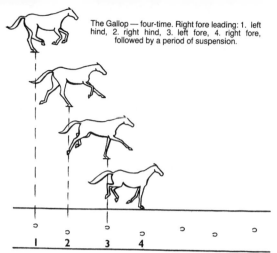

The Gallop — four-time. Right fore leading: 1. left hind, 2. right hind, 3. left fore, 4. right fore, followed by a period of suspension.

The Gallop

The main fault in the gallop is failing to stretch out, not achieving a clear, four-time beat.

Footfalls in the paces. An excellent way of seeing the footfalls in the paces is to put different coloured bandages on the diagonal pairs of legs. Two people can do this together, taking turns to ride and to watch.

The Halt

In a 'working halt' the horse must be attentive and motionless, standing straight and square and remaining on the bit.

TERMS
BALANCE

A horse is well balanced, or 'in balance', when his own weight and the weight of his rider are distributed in such a way that he can use himself to the best advantage for whatever he is doing.

However good his natural balance when at liberty, a young horse, when first ridden, tends to be 'on the forehand'. He goes with a very low head-carriage, trying to get the additional weight of the rider forward over his shoulders, where he can carry it most easily. This makes him heavy and unresponsive to ride for most purposes, and puts extra strain on his forelegs.

On the forehand.

24

In the course of training, the horse must develop his muscles, especially those of the back and hindquarters, and supple all his joints, so that he can bring his hind legs further under his body, thereby taking more weight on the hindquarters and lightening the forehand.

Improvement of balance is one of the main objects of our training. The average Pony Club mount has to be very versatile — dressage, jumping, games, even to be a good ride, all require good balance.

The better his balance, the easier it will be for the horse to achieve:

1. Light and rhythmic paces.
2. Smooth changes of pace and direction.
3. Lengthening and shortening of the stride.
4. Adjustment of balance for all phases of a jump.

Good balance, hindquarters well engaged. The rider's knee is a little stiff, but the overall impression is of harmony. Photo: J. M. S. Galbraith.

A beautifully balanced combination.

25

Factors which adversely affect balance:
1. Poor conformation.
2. Training — a. lack of or incorrect.
                    b. hurried — expecting too much too soon, especially from a young or unfit horse.
3. The rider — a. just being there!
                   b. too far forward, overweighting the forehand.
                   c. too upright on a young horse — forcing.
                   d. not straight, leaning, or collapsing hip or shoulder.
                   e. stiff or unsteady.
                   f. poor co-ordination of aids.
                   g. pulling the head up, instead of bringing the hocks under.

IF THE RIDER IS NOT BALANCED, THE HORSE CANNOT BE BALANCED

Balance is improved by appreciating the problems and following a progressive programme of dressage, gymnastic jumping exercises and riding out, especially on hills.

IMPULSION

Controlled energy. The thrust comes mainly from the hindquarters, and will increase as the horse becomes more supple and muscular. You will feel this in the swing and movement of the horse's back, as his hind legs come further under him.

RHYTHM

The regularity of the hoofbeats, maintained at all times.

TEMPO

The speed of the rhythm.

STRAIGHTNESS

The hind feet should always follow in the tracks of the forefeet — on straight lines, the whole horse must be straight, on curves he must be bent so that his body forms a segment of the curve. Otherwise the impulsion from the hindquarters will not go 'through' the horse.

OUTLINE OF THE HORSE

The picture in silhouette. Depending on the state of training:
1. The quarters should appear level with, or possibly lower than the withers.

2. The back and the top line of the neck rounded, never hollow.

3. The forehand should be light, free and unrestricted.

The general impression should be of roundness and elasticity.

OUTLINE OF THE RIDER

The picture in silhouette:

1. Should always appear supple and in balance with the horse.

2. The body should be erect (ear, shoulder, hip and heel in line) at halt, walk, sitting trot and canter, and slightly forward in rising trot.

3. The rider's back should be straight, neither hollow nor rounded.

4. There should be a straight line from elbow to bit, the thumb the highest point of the hand.

ACCEPTING THE BIT

The horse going freely forward, calm and attentive, with a steady head and even contact on the bit. At this stage, he may be a little heavy and on the forehand, either owing to lack of muscular development or because he is not being asked to do anything else! He should, however, accept *all* the rider's aids without resentment or evasion.

ON THE BIT

The horse is accepting the bit, but shows improved balance, with better use of the hocks and a well-rounded outline. His neck should be flexed just behind the poll and his lower jaw relaxed. The poll should be the highest point.

Many people have the mistaken idea that putting a horse on the bit is concerned only with his head carriage, and that it is a matter of inducing him to arch his neck and bring his nose in towards his chest. Not so! He will gradually come on the bit himself when he is ready and able to, if he is ridden and trained correctly. He cannot come on the bit until he accepts it, and until his balance has developed sufficiently to enable him to carry himself lightly and easily.

On the bit.

Accepting the bit.

WORKING PACES

(See *Manual One,* page 106.) The horse is ridden forward with seat and legs into a responsive hand, so that he is not allowed to go faster or to drop behind the bit, but is asked to engage his hocks and relax his lower jaw. He should either hold the bit softly in his mouth or gently chew on it, and his mouth should be moist. The pace should feel light and springy. He should be calm and attentive to your aids, and sufficiently balanced to be able to obey them promptly.

For true working paces, the horse must remain on the bit consistently throughout his work. However, at B Certificate level it is adequate if he accepts the bit at all times, and shows himself capable of coming on it intermittently.

ABOVE THE BIT, BEHIND THE BIT

These and other 'bit evasions' are described in 'Bits and Bitting' page 262. If your horse does not accept the bit, refer to this section.

HALF-HALT

This is a 'calling-to-attention', mentally and physically. The rider sits taller and lifts the diaphragm, as when taking a deep breath, at the same time lightly closing both legs. It is a momentary aid, sending the horse forward into a closed hand. It helps to lighten and balance the horse, and to prepare him for transitions and other movements.

THE RIDER

By now, you will realise that the way a horse goes depends greatly upon his rider. You must strive constantly to improve yourself, because there is no way that you can make the horse better than you are.

There are three main areas to work on:

1. Your seat, position and balance.
2. Your 'feel' for the way the horse is going, and whether he is correctly balanced and placed to carry out whatever you are asking of him.
3. The way in which you apply your aids.

SEAT, POSITION AND BALANCE

Your first aim must be to sit deeper and steadier in the saddle. You must be supple if you are to remain in balance with the horse, but should try to avoid all unnecessary movement. The steadier you are, the better your 'feel' and the more clearly and accurately you can apply your aids.

A workmanlike position in sitting trot. Good back and use of lower leg. Hands not quite level.

Sitting trot. As much of the more advanced work is done in sitting trot, it will be necessary to practise this until it becomes easy and comfortable. The biggest enemies are stiffness and grip, often caused by trying too hard to prevent yourself from bouncing. Slow the pace a little at first, and just let yourself move softly in rhythm with the two-time beat of the trot.

You should continue to practise the suppling and agility exercises — especially those that help to supple any part of your anatomy that you know to be stiff.

Here are four other useful exercises at this stage. At trot, without stirrups:

1. 'Relaxed' and correct position. Jog round slowly at first, reins in one hand, other hand on the pommel, elbow relaxed. Let your legs flop, toes dangling. You should feel quite relaxed and easy, seat remaining in contact with the saddle. Now take your riding position — toes to the front, knees and ankles supple, heels slightly down, inside of the calf in contact with the horse's side. You will have to bend the knee more as you take this position, but be sure you don't pull it up. Practise riding position — relaxed position several times alternately, and keep your legs 'long' throughout. As you get steadier, take the hand off the pommel and let it hang loosely down from the shoulder, and ask a little more activity from the horse.

2. Reins in one hand, riding position. Hold the 'spare' hand at shoulder height, with a straight arm, palm down, either in front or to the side. See how still you can keep *both* hands.

3. Tap on your thigh in rhythm with the horse's step. This is particularly good as your seat becomes steadier and you are asking a more active trot from the horse. Be sure to keep the hand holding the reins still.

4. At the canter — probably best done on a large circle in the open. Reins in the outside hand, inside arm swinging pendulum fashion — in rhythm with the horse's stride, so that you touch him either on the shoulder or behind the saddle each time the leading leg comes down. Excellent for improving the rhythm of the canter, and helping you to relax your back and hips at this pace.

Exercises are an essential part of training for almost any sport. They develop balance, suppleness, co-ordination, muscle control and general physical fitness — qualities just as vital to the rider as to any other athlete.

As you improve, it is a good idea to do some of your school work without stirrups. Steady yourself with a hand on the pommel when necessary, especially during transitions.

FEEL

Since you cannot see yourself, a sense of feel plays a big part in riding. To develop this, begin with the halt. Are the horse's forefeet 'square'? If you can't feel it at first, glance down at his shoulders. It is easy to see if they are level. You can soon tell if he is resting a hind leg, but are they even? It takes considerable practice to feel this.

Then try to count the hoofbeats at the walk. Shutting your eyes can make this easier. Count the hoofbeats out loud, and get somebody to tell you if you have got it right. (Another thing two people can practise together.)

At the trot, can you tell by feel, without looking down, whether you are using the correct (outside) diagonal on a circle? Can you *start* rising on either diagonal, at will? Concentrate on feeling the movement of the diagonals and it will come with practice. By the time you sit your B Certificate the correct use of diagonals should be second nature, and you should feel at once if you are wrong.

At canter, you should be able to feel which is the leading leg as the horse strikes off. If you can't, practise canter strike-offs with your eyes shut, on a straight line. (Choose a safe place for this.) It won't matter which leg is leading, but try to feel which it is before you look down to check.

Shutting your eyes can be very helpful at all paces, because it forces you to concentrate on the feel of what the horse is doing.

THE AIDS AND THEIR APPLICATION

Natural and artificial aids are explained in *Manual One*, pages 54-62.

With a deeper seat, plus increased feel and knowledge of the horse's paces, you should now be able to apply these aids with more understanding and accuracy.

Natural Aids

Back and seat. You *must* be straight on the horse's back at all times, shoulders parallel with the horse's shoulders, hips with his hips, otherwise you will put him off balance. The use of back and seat as aids will gradually evolve as the correct position and use of the legs become established. This is an aid that belongs to more advanced riding; it is not used continuously, but momentarily when balancing and preparing the horse for any change of pace, direction or movement. (See 'Half-Halt', page 28, and, 'Riding: A Certificate', page 151.)

Legs. The inside leg (the one on the inside of the horse's bend) creates impulsion. It is used at (i.e. *just* behind) the girth, or occasionally *very* slightly further back. It normally acts inwards with a light nudging or tapping action, never with a tight squeeze or a backwards and forwards kicking movement.

The outside leg supports and controls the hindquarters. It should maintain contact on the horse's side, about 10cm behind the girth, so that it is ready to act instantly when needed.

When riding on a straight line, the legs act evenly at the girth.

Hands. The inside hand asks for the placing of the horse's head by the 'take and give' action of the fingers. This hand must be still in relation to the horse's mouth.

The outside hand allows the required amount of bend, and controls the speed. You may be able to achieve this control of speed by closing the hand, but sometimes a stronger action from the shoulder blade through the arm will be needed. Never use more strength than is absolutely necessary and never use a continuous pull on the rein. It needs skill to maintain the placing of the head with the inside hand while controlling the speed with the outside one.

Once the pace is established, impulsion is maintained by riding the horse forward from the inside leg to a steady contact on the outside rein.

The whole art of training lies in the co-ordination of these aids. It is important to use them in the right order — seat and/or leg must always precede hand. Prepare yourself and the horse in plenty of time, so that you never apply aids abruptly or roughly, even though you may have to use them strongly at times.

Voice. Your voice is more important than ever when your horse is learning new movements — letting him know the *exact moment* when he is doing well and pleasing you, correcting him quietly but firmly when he is mistaken, and helping to maintain his concentration throughout.

Artificial Aids

Dressage whip. You will probably find it useful at this stage to use a long dressage whip (90cm approximately) when schooling on the flat. The extra length enables you to reinforce your leg aids by using the whip close behind your leg, while keeping both hands on the reins. If you try to do this with a short whip you will jerk the horse's mouth. A dressage whip is only to be used to draw attention to, and, if necessary, to reinforce, your leg aids. It must *never* be used for punishment, or when jumping.

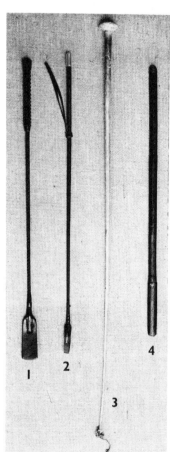

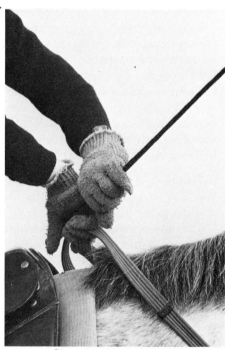

Changing the dressage whip, from right hand to left.

Whips. 1. Good, general purpose whip. Easy to hold, ideal length (maximum 75cm) and wide flapper. 2. No knob, difficult to hold, flapper too narrow. 3. Dressage whip (only). Good knob, not too flexible. 4. Showing cane. Correct for showing classes. Held in the centre, in the outside hand in the show ring.

Spurs. Spurs should *never* be used on a horse who does not understand basic leg aids, or by a rider with unsteady seat or legs, who might use them unintentionally.

Spurs. Use only blunt spurs, without rowels. The shank must always point downwards, and the spur be well up on the heel — on the spur block, if available. Straps must match colour of boots, and buckle on the outside.

Martingales, nosebands, etc. (See 'Auxiliary Saddlery', page 269.)

PLANNING A PROGRAMME

At this stage, it will be helpful to work out a long-term programme covering all aspects of training and enjoyment with your horse. There will be times when, owing to other commitments, the time of year or the state of the ground, you may not have the opportunity or inclination to train at all. At other times, when preparing for shows or trials (or for B Certificate) quite intensive training will be essential for several months beforehand. Between these two extremes, aim to keep a balance between work and play.

Try to make an honest assessment of your own and your horse's good and bad points. You may have good feel and quick reactions, but be unable to make full use of them because you are not steady enough in the saddle. Your horse may have a great 'pop' in him, but be headstrong and difficult to turn. Plan to tackle and improve the weak points, and to strengthen the partnership between you.

Planning is especially important if you are a competitive person. Competition can be a great incentive, but it can also lead to a narrow approach to training, and to short cuts and over-facing due to the constant pressure to produce a winning performance. This is less likely to happen if you have a long-term goal. You should regard the lesser competitions as stages on the way, to gain experience and test your progress, rather than to be won at all costs. Then there will be time for consolidation and general improvement, and to enjoy training in a more relaxed atmosphere.

If you are not competitive, motivation can be a problem. It is easy to get into the habit of drifting rather aimlessly from day to day, practising the things you already do fairly well, but not tackling faults or new movements. Once again, planning helps.

Think ahead. Training does not show instant results, it takes time to learn new exercises and establish a higher level of performance — approximately three years to cover the syllabus from C to B. Thought and application are vital, but training should now become increasingly interesting and enjoyable. If it is boring to either partner, it is high time to revise your programme — perhaps turn your horse out and have a spell!

When working out your overall programme, refer to 'Conditioning' (pages 88 to 92) and 'Jumping: B Certificate'.

DRESSAGE

When in full work, aim to train from three to five times a week for about thirty to forty-five minutes, including work-in. Two or three of these training sessions should take place in a school or dressage arena, which helps you to ride more accurately.

It is best to do your dressage at the beginning of your riding period. The horse must learn to settle down and behave himself even if he is feeling fit and fresh. In training, this freshness will give more sparkle to his work, and he will be less likely to become bored.

Each session starts with working-in, to warm the horse up, to settle or activate him (according to temperament) so that he is attentive, and to establish the regularity of the paces and the bend.

Begin in the open, with a few minutes walk on a long rein, asking for an energetic, even stride, checking your position and getting in the mood. Then trot on, still on a fairly long rein, using rising trot for at least the first five minutes. Make use of a large area, change direction frequently and insist on a regular pace, active but not hurried, throughout. After this, spend some time working on your position, usually without stirrups. Next, with or without stirrups, in the open or in the school, introduce circles (large to begin with), serpentines and other movements, changes of pace (including canter), gradually asking the horse to come on the bit and produce working paces.

The exercises and movements which follow will all help to give variety to the work, and improve the horse's balance, suppleness and responsiveness. Some of these, such as the turn on the forehand, are 'stepping stone' exercises which lead to more advanced movements. Others, such as smaller circles, lengthening of stride and demi-pirouette, will be used and developed throughout the horse's training.

Practise one or two exercises/movements from your programme

each time. Introduce the main object of the day's session after the horse has been well worked in, and try to make some improvement. You must be firm enough so that the horse listens to you and tries hard to please you, but sensitive enough to appreciate his problems and know when he is doing his best. Be generous with praise, and reward him frequently with a rest on a long rein. Only as his strength and understanding develop should you gradually ask him to maintain carriage and concentration for longer periods.

When the horse has tried hard and shown even a little improvement in something that he finds difficult, switch to one of his easier movements, so that you can finish on a good note.

Assess results frequently and honestly, always checking that your aids were clear and correct before blaming the horse if things went wrong. If you have real problems, it may be wise to wait until the next rally and consult your instructor.

CIRCLE EXERCISES

Circles are among the most useful balancing and suppling exercises at all stages of training, and should play an important part in every training session. At B level, you should be able to ride circles down to 10m at walk and trot, 15m at canter.

Aids for circles —a reminder. Sit straight and tall, shoulders square with the horse's shoulders, hips with his hips. Look where you intend to go.

The inside hand asks for the direction and the placing of the horse's head to the inside. An open rein would not normally be used at this stage of training.

The outside hand allows the required bend, and controls the speed.

The inside leg, used at the girth, maintains impulsion, keeps the horse out on the circle, and creates the bend in his body.

The outside leg, used about 10cm behind the girth, supports the inside leg and controls the hindquarters.

NOTE. Sitting trot should be used for all circles under 20m.

THE LARGE CIRCLE IN THE OPEN

This would usually be about 30m in diameter. It is useful when working in, and there are several exercises connected with it.

Change of rein through the circle. An excellent suppling exercise if the change is made in the form of a half figure eight, as shown, so that there is a clear change of bend in the centre. A good preparation for serpentines, where several changes of bend are required.

Change of rein into the circle — achieved by making a half circle inwards and returning diagonally to the large circle. The size of the half circle will depend on the pace and on the suppleness of the horse. Change the bend as you rejoin the large circle.

Change of rein out of the circle — the half circle is made to the outside — a more difficult exercise than the previous one. Change the bend as you leave the large circle.

A smaller circle — 10 to 20m diameter, depending on the horse's state of training — on the circumference of the large circle. In trot, do this smaller circle sitting. You should feel that the horse increases the bend, brings his hocks further under him and becomes lighter.

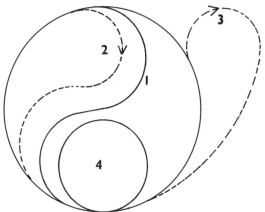

Exercises on the large circle.

This exercise is especially helpful when working on lengthening the stride at the canter (see page 40). Use the smaller circle to get the horse balanced and light, lengthen on for a few strides on the large circle, then make use of another smaller circle to bring him back and restore balance, particularly if he is inclined to fall on his forehand.

CIRCLES IN THE SCHOOL

A well marked arena will help you to ride circles and all other exercises more accurately. Ride any new movement at the walk until you are sure of the shape and the exact track to be taken.

Check that your 20 metre circles are correct before attempting anything smaller.

15m circles. It is easiest to begin these from B or E — the circle is three-quarters of the width of the school.

10m circles. A half-circle on to the centre line, returning to the quarter marker, as shown in the diagram, is a good way of introducing these, and also of changing the rein.

Do this exercise in reverse too, beginning with the incline to the centre line and finishing with the half-circle.

Or, half-circle on the centre line, continue down the centre for a few strides, then half-circle away, either to the same side or to the opposite one. When you feel the horse can maintain impulsion and bend, ask for the full 10m circle.

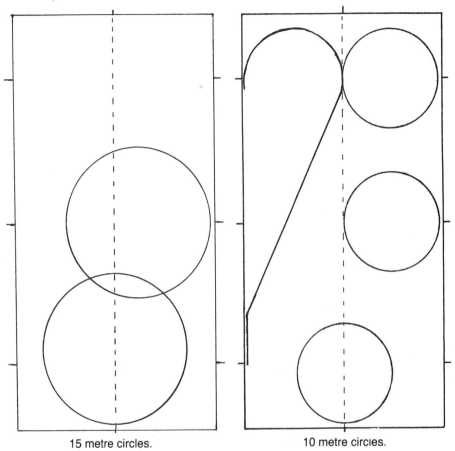

15 metre circles.   10 metre circles.

Variations in the size of the circle. Excellent for making the horse more attentive and responsive. These can be done in several ways — e.g. a 20m circle from B or E, followed immediately by a 15m circle from the same marker. In trot, do the larger circle rising, the smaller one sitting, aiming to maintain the rhythm while increasing the bend.

Decrease and increase of circle. This is a more advanced exercise in varying the size of the circle. Spiral inwards to reduce the size from, say, 20m to 15m. Then, by increased use of the inside leg in rhythm, ask the horse to move a few steps diagonally forwards and outwards, so that he returns to the 20m circle. The outside leg supports behind the girth, the hands maintain the placing of the head and control the speed. Sit straight, and try to stretch down into the inside heel, without collapsing either hip or shoulder. Looking over the outside ear helps to give the idea of direction.

Increasing the circle. Pony moving away nicely from the rider's leg. Her outside leg should be drawn back further to control the quarters in case of need.

How it should feel. The horse should feel light and active, and the crossing of his legs should be quite clear.

This is a 'leg yielding' type of exercise. Its advantages are:

1. It emphasises the action and importance of the inside leg in keeping the horse out on the circle and maintaining the bend.

2. It is an early 'lead-up' towards lateral work (see page 158).

Change of rein through the circle. As in the open, through a 20m circle. (Not smaller.)

The figure of eight. This is a change of rein out of the circle. Both circles must be the same size.

Many faults in circles arise from the horse not obeying the inside leg. The rider then uses the leg harder, often causing him to lean in and collapse the inside hip. Check your position and straightness, and that the outside hand is 'allowing' the bend, and reinforce the inside leg with the whip, when necessary.

SERPENTINES

Movements on curves, involving changes of direction and of the horse's bend.

Object. To supple the horse. He should change from one bend to the other smoothly.

Introduce when the horse is bending reasonably well to either side. Serpentines may be done in the open or in the school.

Pace. At this stage, walk and trot. Canter serpentines should not be attempted yet.

Method. A good way to start is by making a series of 20m half-circles in the open, initially going on a straight line between them while repositioning the horse, then gradually cutting down the number of straight strides.

Two useful types of serpentine in the school are shown below:

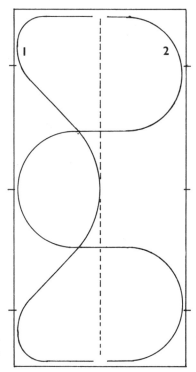

Serpentines. 1. A single loop. This may be made shallower at first. 2. Three loops.

Aids. The main point is the smooth change of aids from one side to the other, starting with the repositioning of the horse's head, followed immediately by the change of position and action of the rider's legs. Sit straight throughout, look along the track you intend to follow. In rising trot, change the diagonal at the moment of each change of direction.

How it should feel. Smooth and flowing — really 'curvy'!

Common Faults	Correction
1. Failing to change the bend, resulting in the horse falling in. Usually happens when changing to the horse's stiff side.	Go straight in between to allow time to reposition horse before taking new direction. Practise 'riding in position', (page 44).
2. Loss of rhythm, impulsion or balance.	Check smoothness of aids and action of lower leg.

LENGTHENING THE STRIDE

The horse should lengthen his stride while maintaining his balance and rhythm. His outline will be longer than in the working pace, because he will have to stretch his head and neck out a little to achieve this lengthening of stride. It is important that the lengthening comes 'from behind', the hindquarters driving more energetically forward. In trot, there should be a clear overstep, with the hind feet coming down beyond the prints of the forefeet. This exercise leads on to medium and, eventually, to extended paces.

Lengthened strides. Active, calm, well balanced. Some horses might need to stretch the head and neck out a little more, especially in the early stages.

Objects

1. As a balancing and suppling exercise. As circles and serpentines supple the horse laterally, so lengthening and shortening the stride supple him longitudinally (lengthways). The ability to adjust the length of stride is essential in jumping.

2. To increase the power of the hindquarters, and to maintain or re-establish impulsion when you are working on more restricted exercises.

Introduce when the working pace is reasonably well established, and the horse calm.

Pace. Trot and canter. Most horses will be ready to lengthen the trot before the canter, because it takes longer to establish a true working canter.

Method and aids. A good place to start in trot is on the long side of the school. In canter, it is generally better to begin on a large circle in the open.

In trot, in the school. Prepare the horse as you come round the end of the school. He should be on the bit and as light as possible, but full of energy and wanting to go forward. Make sure he is straight after the corner, half-halt to bring him to attention, then close both legs at the girth and steadily increase the drive. Be ready to allow the horse to take your hand forward a little as you feel him begin to lengthen. Only ask a few strides at first, then bring him back to the working pace. As he improves, you can gradually increase the distance until he can hold it for the whole long side, and can begin to ask for lengthening on the diagonal, but the side of the school will help to keep him straight in the early stages.

In canter, the aids are similar, but, as already mentioned, it is best to begin on the large circle in the open. (See 'Circle Exercises', page 36.)

How it should feel. Definitely increased power from behind, the horse covering more ground with each stride. As true lengthening develops, you will begin to feel more swing in the horse's back, especially in trot.

NOTE. As this is a 'change of balance' exercise, the 'coming back' is just as important as the lengthening. To bring the horse back: sit down, with a tall back, close both hands, lighten the action of the legs, then use hands and legs alternately. The aids will vary according to the balance and temperament of the horse — the aims are to prevent him falling on his forehand, or losing the impulsion that he gained from the lengthening. You have to find the correct balance of the aids, so that you don't create resistance, but make it easy for the horse to do as you ask. When it is right, you should feel that the horse still has the extra energy that he gained from the lengthening, as he returns to the working pace, but that he is now using it to bring his hocks further under him, and his steps should feel a little higher and lighter than they did before he lengthened.

COMMON FAULTS

1. 'Running' — increasing the speed with little or no lengthening. **Correction:** Bring the horse back to the working pace at once — ask again in the same place. Do this every time he tries to run on. Check preparation and co-ordination of aids. Could be due to loss of balance or misunderstanding.
2. Breaking into canter. **Correction:** Check at once, re-establish pace before trying again. Abrupt aids or loss of balance are common causes.
3. Nothing happens at all. **Correction:** Some horses find lengthening quite hard, and *must* increase the speed a little at first. Make sure that the horse is 'pushed together' and wanting to go forward, and that your hands allow him to stretch. In all these cases, praise enthusiastically at the least sign of correct lengthening. Don't ask too much too soon.

TURN ON THE FOREHAND

A turn from the halt (up to 180°) in which the horse's hind legs move in 'even, quiet and regular' steps round the forehand. The forelegs 'mark time', so that the horse appears to pivot on the inside foreleg.

Objects
1. To gain more control over the horse's hindquarters. It is another 'lead-up' exercise towards lateral work
2. It helps to improve the rider's co-ordination in applying the aids. You have to learn to 'act' with one leg while 'supporting' with the other. You have already felt this to some extent when you use the inside leg to maintain impulsion and bend the horse on a circle, while 'supporting' with the outside leg.
3. It is useful when opening and shutting gates.

Turn on the forehand should never be over-practised. There is little point in continuing with it once the horse will move freely away from the acting leg.

Introduce. When the halt is established. Attempting this before the horse will stand still will only make him more restless.

Right turn on the forehand. Hind leg crossing well, forelegs 'marking time', pony attentive. Rider's weight slightly to the right, otherwise aids correct.

Aids. For a right turn: sit straight and tall, have the horse standing square. The right hand may position his head very slightly to the right. Use the right leg, slightly drawn back, with a tapping action. This is the 'acting' leg, asking him to step away and move his hindquarters to the left. The left, 'supporting' leg is used as required, to maintain impulsion, or drawn back to regulate the steps and control the hindquarters, should they move away too fast. The left hand maintains contact to prevent the horse moving forward or bending his neck excessively. When he has completed one step, check with the left leg, pause and praise with voice before asking for another step. After two or three steps, walk forward immediately — there is no halt *after* a turn on the forehand. Reverse these aids for a left turn.

When practising this exercise, alternate the turns with a plain 'halt and walk on' to discourage the horse from anticipating the turn, and with brisk trots to maintain impulsion and interest.

How it should feel. The horse should feel calm and attentive, the steps measured, not hurried or dragging. The inside hind leg (the right one in a right turn) should cross in front of the outside one. With practice, you will be able to feel quite clearly whether or not this is happening.

COMMON FAULTS

1. Turning on the centre — moving forelegs as well as hind legs. **Correction:** Check that you are sitting straight — not dropping the inside shoulder. Don't over-position the head, increase the support with the outside hand.
2. Horse stepping back. **Correction:** Support with outside leg — check that hands are not too strong.
3. Horse stepping forward. **Correction:** Check with outside hand. Often caused by lack of balance in horse or rider, or by poor balance of aids.
4. Shuffling round, instead of crossing hind legs. **Correction:** Be sure to give a separate leg aid for each step. It must be clear and definite.
5. Horse resisting leg, even stepping towards it, instead of away. **Correction:** Check that supporting leg is quiet, and acting leg clear — back up with whip, if necessary. *Praise* when correct.
6. Horse 'running away' from the leg, or anticipating. **Correction:** Practise plain halts, then one step only on forehand. Emphasise pause between steps.
7. Head resistance. **Correction:** Check balance between hand and leg. Don't hurry.

The turn on the forehand has the great advantage from the rider's point of view of being a movement from the halt, which happens almost in slow motion, and therefore gives you time to observe the effect of your aids, and to adjust them as needed.

The Turn Around the Forehand

This is a similar movement, but the horse is taken straight into it from a half-halt, in walk. You could do this sometimes as a variation when you and your horse are familiar with the turn on the forehand.

RIDING IN POSITION (PLACING THE HORSE)

The horse's head is positioned slightly to one side, so that the rider can just see the eye and nostril on that side. The head is placed as for a circle, but the horse remains on a straight line. In the school, the horse may be positioned either to the inside or to the outside.

Objects

1. To prepare the horse and help to bend him for a circle or a corner in the school, or to place him for a canter strike-off.

2. To help to straighten the horse.

3. To keep the horse's attention.

4. To help to put the horse on the bit, particularly on his stiff side, by softening the muscles of the jaw, neck and shoulder.

5. As a preparation for demi-pirouette (page 48) and shoulder-in (page 162).

Riding in position, left rein. 1. Position left (inside), maximum degree of placing, horse has remained straight and light. 2. Position right (outside). Straight, not quite so light. Note rider's left leg controlling quarters. Her right hip has slipped a little, but she is looking ahead well.

Introduce when the horse is accepting the bit. On the long side of the school or against a fence line. It is best to begin with inside position.

Pace. Start at the walk, until the horse understands what is wanted. After this, it is better done in sitting trot, because there is more impulsion in trot. In canter, the horse should always be positioned towards the leading leg.

Aids — position right. Ask with the right hand for the placing of the head, use the right leg in rhythm for impulsion. The left leg controls the quarters and helps to maintain impulsion, the left hand allows the required placing of the head and controls the speed. Reverse these aids for position left. Only ask a few steps at first.

In outside position, the horse is positioned to the right when on the left rein, or vice versa. Be careful not to change from inside to outside position until you are past the first quarter marker on the long side, and change back again before the second quarter marker.

How it should feel. The horse should be straight and active. He should feel distinctly lighter and very attentive.

COMMON FAULTS

1. Horse comes out of track, in inside position. **Correction:** Check that inside hand is not too strong, support with inside leg. Sit straight.
2. Horse resists — comes off bit, or tilts head, usually to stiff side. **Correction:** Try to find correct balance between hand and leg to make him understand. Quiet praise when he is right. Very slightly open inside rein may help at first.
3. Loss of impulsion — slowing down. **Correction:** Check balance of aids — hand may be too strong, with too little drive. Overdoing the placing of the head, inside hand pulling back or crossing over the neck will all aggravate this fault.
4. Quarters swinging. **Correction:** Support with outside leg. Don't over-position.

CANTER EXERCISES

Objectives

1. To improve the sureness of the canter strike-offs on either leg, and the quality of the canter.
2. To be able to ride circles down to 15m diameter in canter. (See page 36.)
3. To be able to lengthen and shorten the canter stride. (Page 40.)

Aids for canter strike-offs are very individual. Even advanced riders agree that when riding an unknown horse 'finding the right buttons to press' can be quite difficult.

You will soon be asking for canter on a named leg on a straight line. Before attempting this, it is important to clarify your aids on a circle. There are two schools of thought, both of which are acceptable. The position of the rider and the placing of the horse are identical in both methods, it is the final application of the aids that varies.

Aids. In sitting trot, check that the horse is positioned to the inside, active and attentive. Check that the outside leg is drawn back, inside leg at the girth. From here:

Method A. Apply the outside leg behind the girth to activate the horse's outside hind leg (first beat of the canter), and follow with the inside leg to create impulsion. Reason: The horse's outside hind leg starts the canter, therefore this is the one to act on.

Method B. Maintain contact with the outside leg as a reminder to activate the horse's outside hind leg, and ask for the impulsion into canter with a distinct nudge from the inside leg. Reasons: It is generally accepted that the inside leg asks for impulsion. There is less risk of the quarters being displaced, especially when striking off on a straight line.

Find out which method suits your partnership and use it consistently. Be prepared to adapt when riding unknown horses.

Strike-off on a named leg on a straight line. A good place to start this is just before the quarter marker coming on to the short side of the school. Begin on your horse's best side. Correct placing is essential. Approaching the quarter marker, the horse must be on the bit, light and attentive. Use sitting trot, sit tall, and check that the horse is in inside position. Then apply canter aids, as above.

Strike-off from the walk. This will be one of the first exercises where you 'skip' a pace on a transition — trot, in this case. A splendid exercise for improving the balance of both horse and rider. The horse must bring his weight onto his outside hind leg if he is to achieve this strike-off. If you collapse forward or inwards you make it almost impossible for him — he will lose his balance and be forced to take one or two trot strides.

Begin on a corner or circle. The horse must be carefully positioned, light and attentive. Give a clear half-halt, making sure to lift the diaphragm, and follow immediately with your canter aid.

How it should feel. The horse comes back on his hocks, almost as though he were going to jump. The push-off into canter with the outside hind leg should be clearly felt.

Change of leg through the trot. This is not a 'simple change', which is made through walk. (See page 154.)

This change may be made in the school either: 1, on a large figure of eight, or 2, on a change of rein across the diagonal.

1. First practise the large figure of eight in sitting trot (see page 38). When the horse is changing the bend well, ask him to canter in the first quarter of the circle after X. Work on this until you are sure of the canter strike-off on either leg after the change of bend. Then

practise bringing him back to trot in the last quarter of the circle before X. Finally, put it all together — canter, trot, in last quarter circle, change bend in trot, strike-off in first quarter circle. But don't do the whole exercise every time, or the horse will soon begin to anticipate. Eventually, you should be able to do this very smoothly with only two or three trot strides through the change of bend.

2. The change on the diagonal. Don't try this one until you are sure of the strike-off on a named leg on a straight line.

First, get the strike-off after X. Leave it until you are quite close to the quarter marker to begin with. Then work on the canter-trot transition before X. When you can do them both separately, smoothly and with the horse remaining straight, put them together. Aim eventually to make the change with about two trot strides either side of X.

At this stage, the horse's balance in canter should be improving steadily, making the pace lighter and more vibrant. He should always lead on the correct leg, whether on the flat or jumping. If he is wrong at any time, you should notice and correct it at once.

In canter, your back should be straight but very supple, hands allowing the necessary movement of head and neck, legs always in contact to maintain impulsion. If you can feel the action of the canter, and use your inside leg lightly as the horse is coming on to the second beat (the outside diagonal), this will help tremendously in improving the rhythm of the pace and bringing the horse's hocks under him.

THE DEMI-PIROUETTE

This is a half turn (180 degrees) on the haunches at the walk. The hind legs make a small half-circle, the forelegs a bigger one round them. The outside foreleg crosses in front of the inside one. There is no halt, and the rhythm of the walk must be maintained throughout.

In advanced dressage, pirouettes may be performed at walk or canter — they are not done at trot.

Object. Another excellent balancing and suppling exercise, particularly encouraging the flexion and engagement of the inside hock.

Introduce when the walk is active and regular, the horse coming on the bit, and, as a result of the previous exercises, you have fairly good control over his hindquarters.

You are only expected to show the early stages of this movement for B Certificate, so don't be in a hurry.

Method and aids. It is easiest to begin this movement as you come into a corner in the school, at the end of the long side. As you pass the quarter marker, position the horse to the inside, half-halt, then lead

Starting demi-pirouette. 1. Rider's position good. Pony shows a little too much neck bend, but is maintaining forward movement well. 2. Pony rather unsure, but rider's aids very tactful — note outside hand and leg. Excellent results at this level.

him round with the inside hand, firmly supported by the outside one to prevent excessive neck bend. Use both legs to keep up the rhythm of the walk, the outside leg back to control the hindquarters, sit straight and tall, look over your inside shoulder.

It is far more important in these early stages to keep the rhythm than to make a 'tight' turn — at first, the hind legs may come as much as 2 metres out of the track. This would be quite acceptable at B Certificate level.

How it should feel. The four-time beat of the walk should remain clear throughout. The horse should feel calm and light, with a definite engagement of the hocks and a shifting of the balance towards the hindquarters.

COMMON FAULTS

1. Loss of rhythm, horse 'stopping' or even stepping back. **Correction:** Check balance between hand and leg — the former may be too strong. Use *both* legs, try to use them in rhythm.
2. 'Falling in', too much neck bend. **Correction:** Check that you are sitting straight and supporting with the outside hand.
3. Turning on centre, quarters swinging. **Correction:** Use outside leg more firmly, especially in latter half of turn. Always make use of the side of the school or a fence line to help control the hindquarters. Check the inside hand is not pulling back or crossing over.

Constant checking of your position and aids, letting the horse know the instant he succeeds, all improve performance. By now, this work should at least bring a sense of fulfilment, if not actual enjoyment. For most people, that comes with achievement and the partnership that develops between horse and rider.

RIDING WITH A DOUBLE BRIDLE OR PELHAM

The double bridle is used for advanced dressage tests and for showing, the pelham mostly for showing — it is never allowed for dressage. Both are occasionally used for hunting or jumping, but this is not generally recommended.

These bits should not be used on novice or maiden horses or ponies, but the double bridle, in particular, can do much to enhance the appearance and lightness of those of open or championship standard — *provided* they are fitted and used correctly.

If you wish to show your horse in a double bridle (or pelham) you should:

1. Study the section on 'Curb bits' (pages 265-9) where the action of these bits, and the assembly, putting on and fitting of the double bridle, are explained.

2. Learn to handle two reins. A good way of doing this is to put a second, narrower rein on to your snaffle bit. This represents the curb rein. Practise varying the contact between the two reins, always remembering to treat the 'curb' with the utmost respect and delicacy. This 'curb' rein is held on the inside.

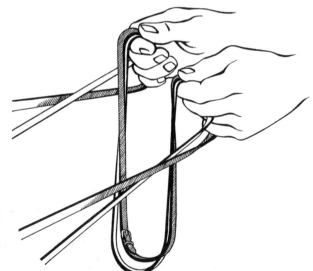

Holding the reins of a double bridle. Bridoon on the outside — one or two fingers divide the reins, which pass together over the first finger, with thumb on top.

3. Be sure that your horse is ready for it. He must at least be going freely forward and accepting the bit in a snaffle, otherwise he is more likely to be upset and spoilt by curb bits than to go kindly in them.

Work the horse in his snaffle bit, before putting on the double bridle. It is wise, when mounting, to leave the curb rein on the horse's neck, and just take up the bridoon. Also to use the bridoon rein only when holding or leading a horse in a double bridle.

The first time you use the double bridle, ride your horse in it for only a few minutes in the open, mainly in rising trot. Have the curb chain fairly loose and ride mostly in the bridoon rein. If he accepts the bridle happily, after a few days you can take up the curb chain to its correct length, and begin to make more use of the curb and to work at different paces. Danger signals are the horse losing impulsion and dropping behind the bit, becoming overbent, throwing his head about or becoming uneven in his paces, but these things should not happen if he is introduced to the new bits carefully and sympathetically.

Once the horse is familiar with it, the double bridle, or pelham, should not be used more than once or twice a week in training, and never when you are teaching him anything new.

From the rider's point of view, learning to handle the two reins makes you concentrate on your hands, and greatly develops their sensitivity. The art of it is to maintain the placing of the horse's head with a steady contact on the bridoon rein and to use the curb only when needed to give extra lightness and flexion of the lower jaw. You have to think hard about riding the horse forward and finding the right balance between hand and leg.

JUDGMENT OF SPEED AND DISTANCE

A knowledge of a horse's average speed at the various paces is useful for calculating the time that will be needed to ride a given distance — for treks, exercising or going to Pony Club, for example.

Average speeds on flat to undulating ground for a horse are: walk 6 km/h; trot 12 km/h; canter 20 km/h. Gallop can range from about 30 km/h to something over 60 for a Derby winner!

For road journeys, or for exercising a reasonably fit horse — where you would probably alternate walk and trot — you should allow for an overall average of about 9 km/h. If the horse is not very fit or the terrain is steep or rough, this could well be reduced to 5-6 km/h. Even when the occasional canter is possible, you should not try to exceed 9 km/h.

When learning to judge speed, start with the slower paces. Try to find a measured kilometre between signposts on a quiet road, or use the speedometer of the car to measure a kilometre between landmarks. See if your horse can actually walk a kilometre in ten minutes, or trot one in five. Then try timing yourself between power poles or pylons, which are usually evenly spaced, to test the regularity of your speed. You will need a digital watch for this, or at least one with a good second hand.

For faster paces, a large, flat paddock is ideal, or possibly the beach could be used at a quiet time. Ride beside a vehicle driven at the required speed — e.g. 20 km/h for canter.

In eventing, the speed for the cross country is given in metres per minute, which can easily be converted into kilometres per hour. For instance, if the speed is 455 metres per minute, this is 27.30 km/h — say 28 for timing purposes. This is a strong canter or a steady gallop. Practise until you really get the feel of this speed beside the vehicle — until you can tell the driver if it is correct. You should now be able to judge your speed over a measured distance without the aid of the vehicle.

This judgment of speed is essential for event and endurance riders.

THE GALLOP

An occasional gallop is good fun, and makes a welcome change from more restricted training. Apart from this, it is an essential part of getting a horse fit for hunting or eventing. It clears his wind, encourages the horse to lengthen his stride, and can be useful to sharpen up a lazy horse.

Too much galloping hots a horse up, runs condition off him, and can do great damage to his legs, especially on hard or heavy going.

Where to gallop. As suggested above for 'Faster paces'. If on the beach, check that the sand is firm over the whole distance — hitting a soft spot at speed could cause a severe sprain.

Never gallop on roadsides, even if there is a wide grass verge; on hard or rough ground; in long grass where holes or snags could be concealed; downhill, especially if the gradient is steep or the going slippery; or anywhere other people could be endangered.

When to gallop. Preferably, when you have done some pace work at the canter, as suggested above, and the horse will canter quietly in the open.

The horse must be well worked in, and thoroughly loosened up.

Never gallop with a totally unfit horse, or if there is any suspicion of unsoundness in the horse.

Method. Check your girth. It is normally best to use jumping length stirrups and a forward position. Steadily increase the speed from canter until you feel (and probably hear) the beat change from three- to four-time. Maintain the gallop for about 200-400m, then slow down through canter, trot, to walk, praise, long rein. Never pull up abruptly — it can cause strained tendons.

It is essential to have firm hand and leg contact at the gallop, to keep the horse balanced and under control. He should really stretch out, and there is more movement of the head and neck than at the canter. Your hands must follow to allow for this, while keeping an even contact.

If the horse is inclined to be hot and excitable:

1. Don't gallop until you have sure control at canter. Practise alternate periods of about 200m canter, progressive transition back to walk, long rein, calm down, canter again. Gradually increase the speed of the canter as the horse settles.

2. Go away from home, if possible slightly uphill.

3. Don't gallop with other horses until the horse is under control when galloping on his own.

4. If you have trouble in steadying, first use your voice quietly. Sit more upright and apply 'downward transition' aids — on no account lean back with your hands in the air. If the horse ignores your aids, fix the inside hand on his neck so that his head is placed *very slightly* in that direction, then use the outside hand and arm in a series of definite pulls (not jerks). Continue the quiet use of voice.

Steadying an impetuous horse. Rider is calm, strong, determined. Left hand fixed, right hand acting.

If the horse still won't slow down and you feel you are losing control, bring him on a large circle — if you pull him round sharply you may bring him down. Decide which way you are going and stick to it — don't suddenly change direction — and steadily reduce the size of the circle. If you use an open inside rein, firmly supported by the outside one to prevent excessive neck bend, and by the outside leg, the horse *must* come round. Keep calm, and when you have him on the circle, apply the strong aids as above. Always fix the inside hand and check with the outside one.

These aids can also be useful when steadying a strong horse in front of a fence in cross country.

For the lazy horse, or one who has difficulty in lengthening his stride:

1. Go towards home.

2. Go 'upsides' with another horse who has a good long gallop stride. This means that you keep the two horses level and really close — stirrup-irons just about touching. If you feel your horse begin to stretch out to go with the other one, praise him heartily and don't ask too much too soon. Galloping usually comes naturally to thoroughbred horses, but others often have to be taught to do it.

If you are asked to gallop in the show ring — in a hunter class, for example, you would retain your full-length stirrups and a more upright position.

RIDING UNKNOWN HORSES

This is a most important part of more advanced riding and of your development as a horseman or woman. Nobody ever learnt to ride on just one or two horses. Every horse is an individual, differing in temperament, physique and ability from every other. You have to learn to sum a horse up quickly, so that you can come to terms with him and he will work willingly for you.

Before you ride a strange horse, find out all you can about him — his age, state of training and any personal idiosyncrasies he may have. Try to see him ridden by his owner first, and watch carefully how he goes as compared to your own horse. If he appears to be quicker and sharper in his reactions, you must be especially quiet in your handling of him, at least until you get to know one another.

Before you mount, have a quick check of the fitting of saddle and bridle. Make sure the irons and leathers are of a suitable size for you — if not, take the ones off your own saddle. It is not wise to use spurs or a dressage whip on a horse you don't know — certainly not without asking his owner. Check the girth.

Insist that the horse stands still while you mount. This sets the tone for all future dealings. Even after you are mounted, stand still for a few moments, speak to the horse, give him a pat on the neck, then walk off on a light contact. Do one or two halts to test his responsiveness. Then trot on, and work in as you would with your own horse, even if this one has already been working. Change rein frequently, and notice if he is stiffer on one side than the other. Don't do any cantering or jumping until you feel you have really come to terms with the horse. This quiet approach will make all the difference to the way he goes for you, especially if he is a nervous or excitable character. As you work him, try to form your own opinion of the horse — a general impression of his way of going, balance and temperament.

Be even more careful, if that is possible, with someone else's horse than you are with your own. Keep him away from other horse's heels, don't gallop about unnecessarily or ask him to jump anything unless you know it is within his capacity. Bring him in cool. If you ignore any of these points, you won't get many further opportunities for riding unknown horses! One other thing — if you expect to ride other people's horses, you must be prepared to let them ride yours.

4
JUMPING: B CERTIFICATE

Training Objectives

1. To become a stronger and more adaptable rider over fences.
2. To develop judgment of pace and control over all types of fences.
3. To train your horse or pony to jump calmly and in good style.

POSITION

Length of stirrup. Stirrups should be shortened by at least two or three holes for jumping, depending on the saddle and on your build. If the saddle is forward cut with knee rolls and the stirrups are too long, you will not be getting the support from the saddle that it is designed to give. If it is cut fairly straight and you shorten the stirrups too much, your knee will come over the front of the flap. (See page 280 for types of saddles.)

Shortening the stirrups closes the angles at ankle, knee and hip, giving a broader base of support and a stronger and better balanced jumping position.

You should normally maintain a forward position — shoulder, knee and toe in line — over the fence and on the flat between fences. As your balance and suppleness improve, you may find it helpful, for greater control, to sit more upright between fences when working on jumping exercises and possibly in show jumping, provided you are agile enough to be 'with' the horse as he takes off. In cross country, it is essential to adopt a forward position between fences to lighten the weight on the horse's back and loins, but here, too, the position on the approach will vary according to circumstances.

Good, strong, basic jumping position.
Stirrups could be a hole shorter.

More upright position used to good effect in steadying a keen pony on approach to fence.

Over the Fence. The points to check are:

Head up, looking over the fence, over the last element of a combination or towards the next fence if a turn is involved.

Body forward from the hips — the 'shoulder, knee and toe' line should normally be maintained. **Back** flat.

Hands and arms. Reins held in the usual way, but shorter than for dressage. The straight line from elbow to bit should be maintained, the hands either side of the neck and independent of it, following the movement of the horse's head and neck and maintaining even contact.·

Thigh and knee in close contact with the saddle, taking more weight than on the flat.

Lower leg. Heels must be down firmly, toes may be slightly turned out. Otherwise the lower leg normally retains its usual position with the inside of the calf in contact with the horse's side, so that aids may be applied correctly and impulsion maintained. In cross country, it is permissible for the lower leg to move slightly forward when landing from a drop fence or into water.

Strong, well-balanced position, lovely contact.

COMMON JUMPING FAULTS AND THEIR EFFECTS

Head — looking down or back. Upsets balance and weakens position, as well as breaking concentration on the 'track' ahead.

Body. Too far forward — in front of the horse's movement. Weakens drive on approach and may cause rider to continue alone if

Left behind. Rider shows excellent reactions to avoid hurting horse's mouth and back.

horse stops! Affects the balance of both horse and rider on take-off, and often leads to 'collapsing' of body on landing, especially over drop fences.

Too far back — behind the movement or 'left behind'. Very uncomfortable for horse and rider — difficult or impossible to follow with hands. Must be prepared to let the reins slip through the fingers. Too much weight on the horse's loins and too little freedom of head and neck will make him jump with a flat or hollow back.

Shoulders hunched, back rounded. Not an effective position. Causes stiffness and makes you tire quickly when riding across country, owing to the difficulty of getting a good breath of air into your lungs.

Back hollow — makes for stiffness.

Hands and arms. Reins 'bridged'. Encourages the rider to lean on the horse's neck, instead of developing an independent seat and hands, and often prevents the hands from following correctly towards the horse's mouth.

Reins too long. Results in lack of control. Bringing the elbows back behind your body in an effort to maintain contact puts you in a weak position.

Reins too short. Loses the bend in the elbow and pulls you forward. Makes the hands heavy and prevents them following sufficiently over the fence.

Hands shooting up the mane, towards the horse's ears. Often goes with bridged reins and the body too far forward, 'lying' along the horse's neck. Upsets balance and contact.

Hands shooting up the mane. *Never* carry your whip like this.

Hands fixed, resting on neck. Horse cannot use his head and neck freely.

Hands shooting forward suddenly in the last strides before take-off, called 'dropping the horse'. Loses all control and puts the horse right off balance. Particularly dangerous at faster paces over solid fences.

'Dropping' the horse. Horse flat, on forehand.

Hands too high or unsteady, either on approach or take-off. Distracts the horse, and makes him raise his head and neck just when he should be lowering them for take-off. Makes him jump with a flat or hollow back.

Hands too high on approach. Horse hollow, above bit. These two riders are to be congratulated on their masterly portrayal of faults in the last four pictures.

Elbows lifted. Brings the hands *back* and prevents them following.

Thigh and knee. Tight grip. Makes for stiffness and 'gripping up'. Brings lower leg away from the horse's side and makes correct application of leg aids difficult.

Lack of contact — knees turned out. Insecure.

Lower leg. Toes down. If the heel comes up, so does the knee, making the position precarious, especially over drop fences, and correct application of aids impossible.

Leg swinging forward or back. Either way affects balance and leg aids, although a slightly forward lower leg may be helpful in some cross country situations. Swinging the leg back greatly weakens the rider's position.

Correcting and Strengthening Jumping Position

Bad habits creep in all too easily, and, once established, are hard to overcome and will hinder further progress. A strong, correct position enables you to develop the contact and control needed for the more challenging jumping at B level, and to improve your horse's performance.

Your instructor will point out faults and help you to identify the root causes of problems. It is then up to you to make the effort to put things right. How you go about it will depend on the fault, but the following basic exercises will allow you to concentrate on improving position:

1. Work in jumping position on the flat, changing pace, maintaining balance, contact, control. Transitions on the large circle in the open and serpentines (check bends) are good warm-up exercises for both rider and horse. Also lengthening and shortening in canter.

2. Use trotting poles or cavalletti — check that the distance is correct so that the horse can do them smoothly. Concentrate on allowing full use of his head and neck without losing contact. When you have established balance, rhythm, control, practise over simple exercises using trotting poles and small fences. (See *Manual One*, pages 85-88, and the tables on page 69 of this book.)

3. Jump a single fence several times. Use a simple spread or a placing rail (page 189), to ensure that the horse meets it in stride.

4. Jumping without reins. (See *Manual One*, pages 89-90.) Work on the lines suggested there. Excellent for all balance problems, strengthens the seat and reminds you just how much the horse likes to use head and neck. You can gradually increase the height to about 60cm, and use a series of three or four varied fences.

Good leg and head position enable this rider to adapt her
balance in a demanding exercise over a 'bounce'.

A near-perfect position resulting from the previous practice.
Note especially the straight line from elbow to bit.

Try to have someone watching throughout who knows your
problems and can comment on progress. If they could take a
photograph, or, better still, a video film, this would really show you
what is happening. As in dressage, constant checking of position is
essential for all riders. Provided the basics are correct, everything that
follows in this chapter will help to consolidate position and develop
technique.

TYPES AND CONSTRUCTION OF FENCES

Good results in schooling depend largely on safe, varied and
well-built fences, which the horse will respect, and on correct
distances for jumping exercises and combinations. False distances can
be confusing and dangerous.

Materials

Poles should be a minimum of 9cm diameter. 4m is a good length. Very heavy poles are difficult to handle and may injure the horse, flimsy ones make him careless and may also injure him by getting caught up in his legs. If your stands have cup fittings, it is essential to cut all your poles to the same length.

Stands. Various types of stands are shown in the jumping pictures.

Filling — drums, tyres, etc. (See *Manual One*, page 87.)

TYPES OF FENCE

There are two basic types of fence, upright and spread.

An upright fence is vertical. It may be solid — a wall — or see-through — poles one above the other, a gate or road closed. It involves height but not width.

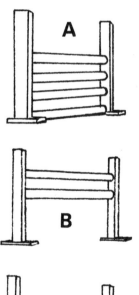

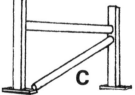

To build a good, solid-looking upright fence requires approximately one pole per 30cm of height, plus a ground line, i.e. four poles for a 90cm fence. Filling (drums, haybales, etc.) could be used in place of some of the lower poles, and would tend to make the fence easier.

A fence of 90cm with only two poles will be too 'open'. This is uninviting and difficult for horse and rider to sight. By dropping the lower pole at one end the fence becomes acceptable, although it is still rather open, and would be improved by the use of three poles, the lower one a 'dropper'.

A. A good, solid-looking upright.
B. Two poles only — bad.
C. Single pole with 'dropper'.

Spread fences involve both height and width. There are four main types: pyramid, staircase, parallels and water or ditches.

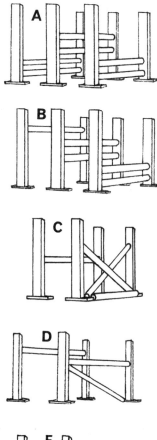

The pyramid, where the highest point is in the middle — e.g. a hog's back or hen coop. When correctly built, as shown, a hog's back is one of the easiest and most encouraging fences.

The staircase — e.g. a triple bar. Best built as shown here, with the middle element slightly higher than halfway between the other two. This helps the horse to round his back and jump in good style.

Another type of 'staircase', and a most useful schooling fence.

Uneven 'parallels', also called an 'ascending oxer', where the far rail is slightly higher than the front one, are easier than true parallels because the horse can see both elements clearly on the approach, and they allow a little more latitude if he takes off too close.

True parallels, where the top rails are the same height, are the most difficult type of fence, requiring great accuracy in the approach.

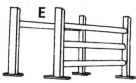

A. Pyramid
B. Staircase.
C. Another type of staircase.
D. Uneven parallels — ascending oxer.
E. True parallels.

NOTE. When building a staircase or parallel fence there should normally, for reasons of safety, be only one rail on the landing side. However, for schooling purposes, small, true parallels are sometimes required to be jumped from either side, in which case they should have sufficient poles and good ground lines on both sides.

Spreads encourage a horse to jump boldly, but should be used in conjunction with uprights, otherwise he may become rather excited and tend to flatten in his jumping.

Water and ditches, unless combined with a fence, involve only width, although the horse has to jump quite high to clear them well. Ditches are an essential part of a horse's training, but can be dangerous if not correctly constructed. If you wish to build one for schooling at home, seek advice (and assistance!).

GROUND LINES

Ground lines are extremely important in fence construction, because a horse judges his point of take-off by looking from the base of the fence up. If there is no ground line the horse, particularly if he is inexperienced, is likely to become confused and unable to sight the fence accurately.

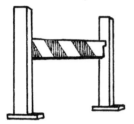

In this 'road closed' fence, the absence of a ground line makes it difficult for the horse to judge his take-off. Such fences should not be used for inexperienced horses and/or novice riders.

Road closed.

A 'true' ground line, underneath or slightly in front of an upright fence or the first element of a parallel, helps the horse to judge it correctly. If he is inclined to 'get under' his fences, bringing the ground line slightly forward will encourage him to 'stand off' further. Pyramid and staircase fences are comparatively easy for the horse, because the lower elements prevent him from taking off too close to clear the top rail.

A 'false' ground line, on the landing side, is misleading, and could make a parallel fence particularly dangerous by bringing the horse in too close to clear the first element.

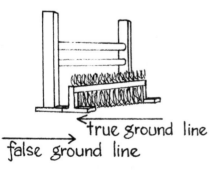

true ground line

false ground line

Jumped from right to left, the brush fence provides a well-defined, 'true' ground line for the horse to sight, and makes the jump easier than if it were placed directly underneath the rails.

Jumped from left to right, the horse would look under the rails at the false ground line formed by the brush and would be totally confused. It should not be attempted from this direction.

Other examples of a false ground line would be a gate leaning towards the horse, or a triple bar jumped back to front.

Trotting poles should be heavy, round poles — a minimum of 10cm in diameter and 2.7m in length. To prevent them rolling and to give them a little more height, they may be set on half-round blocks, bringing them up to 15-20cm.

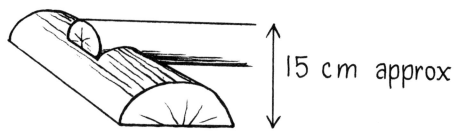

15 cm approx

Cavalletti (see *Manual One*, page 88) should also be made of heavy, round poles — *never* iron pipes, which could frighten or injure a horse. It is dangerous to pile cavalletti up to form jumps — if hit, they may roll with the horse and bring him down.

TRAINING METHODS

The basic training for all types of jumping is the same, involving the use of trotting poles and all the above kinds of fences, singly or in combination, incorporating them in various jumping and gymnastic exercises.

Uses of Trotting Poles and Cavalletti (lowest height)

For the rider, they:
1. Improve balance and rhythm.
2. Improve contact and control of pace.
3. Give practice in approaching obstacles on a correct 'track'.
4. Develop judgment and an eye for distance.

For the horse, they:
1. Improve balance, rhythm and impulsion.
2. Develop a good jumping style, lowering the head and neck, rounding the back and engaging the hocks.
3. Use and develop all the jumping muscles.
4. Develop calm obedience, co-ordination and concentration.
5. Help to adjust and regulate the stride.

Finding your horse's stride. Start with trotting poles at an average horse's distance of 1.37m apart, and ride over them at a normal working trot. The poles should be ridden in rising trot, which helps both horse and rider to maintain the rhythm. Sitting trot would tend to restrict the horse and to flatten his back.

Ask your helper on the ground to check if the horse steps evenly in the middle of each space. If not, adjust to suit. 1.1m would be a short stride, 1.5m a long one. Pony distances would naturally be shorter, depending on the size of the pony, and a slightly shorter distance may be needed for raised poles or cavalletti.

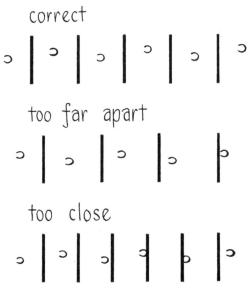

Once you know your horse's natural length of stride, the poles can be gradually readjusted to help him to lengthen or shorten it, as required. Combinations are normally set for an average horse's stride, and those with extremes of stride will have difficulty unless they learn to adjust accordingly. Trotting poles and gymnastic exercises are ideal for this.

NOTE. Hurried or excitable work over trotting poles with the horse trying to break into canter or to jump does more harm than good. If you have problems of this kind, refer to 'Rushing' on page 78.

Once they are being negotiated correctly, these poles can lead on to, and form part of, many jumping and gymnastic exercises. For example:

Opposite page: Start at trot — 1. Poles only, either way. 2. Poles, jump 1a, 2 or 3. Sometimes go through gaps between fences. Keep horse guessing — especially valuable for the impetuous. 3. On curve, 2 and 3, on either rein. 4. Make up course, including returning over poles. 5. Poles (always at trot) canter over 1a, 2 or 3. 6. Add 1b to make a double. Distances for 1 stride are shown. For 2 stride or bounce distances, see page 68.

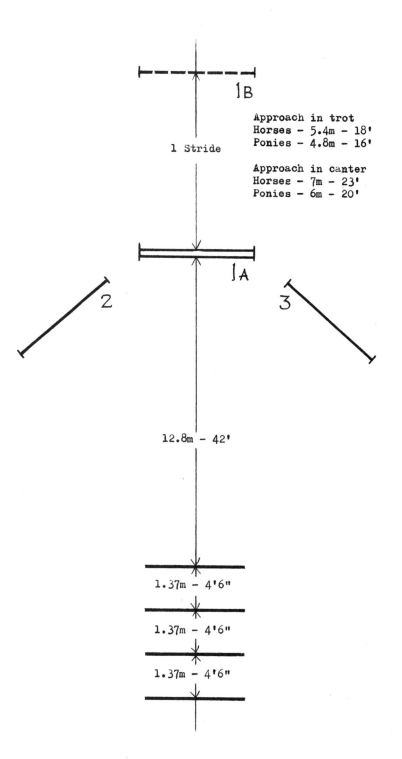

1B

Approach in trot
Horses – 5.4m – 18'
Ponies – 4.8m – 16'

Approach in canter
Horses – 7m – 23'
Ponies – 6m – 20'

1 Stride

1A

2

3

12.8m – 42'

1.37m – 4'6"

1.37m – 4'6"

1.37m – 4'6"

Jumping at Trot:

1. Assists and emphasises the rider's control and the horse's obedience and confidence.

2. Teaches the horse to jump calmly, off his hocks, and to develop spring rather than relying on speed to carry him over.

3. Gives horse and rider time to think what they are doing. It is easier to meet fences 'right' in the shorter stride of the trot.

Jumping at Canter:

1. Encourages more freedom and flow — too much jumping at trot could be restrictive.

2. This is the normal pace for jumping — distances in combinations and related fences are usually based on a horse's canter stride.

Gymnastic exercises involve lines of ground poles and small fences at measured distances. They often include bounce strides, and the initial approach is in trot.

Their objects are:

1. To increase the horse's agility and suppleness.

2. To help horse and rider to learn to adjust the stride, and to develop the rider's eye for distance and for 'seeing the horse's stride'.

3. To speed up the horse's reactions — and those of his rider!

4. To develop concentration, and the confidence of the partnership to tackle multiple obstacles.

Exercises of this type teach the horse to listen to the rider, whether to change pace, turn or circle either way or to lengthen or shorten the stride.

NOTE:

1. Distances must be measured accurately.

2. Each exercise must be established, with the horse going through calmly and easily, with correct strides, before going on to the next.

3. It is better to have each successive jump slightly higher to discourage 'diving'. Use uprights only until the horse is completely confident. Keep the fences very small (30-45cm) to begin with, building up progressively to a maximum of about 75cm.

4. If in any doubt, ask your instructor's advice regarding distances and use of these exercises for your horse.

COMBINATIONS

Combinations consist of two or more fences, each less than 12m apart. Two fences comprise a double, three a treble. The distances in between are carefully measured so that the horse, approaching in canter, will take either one or two non-jumping strides before taking off at the next fence.

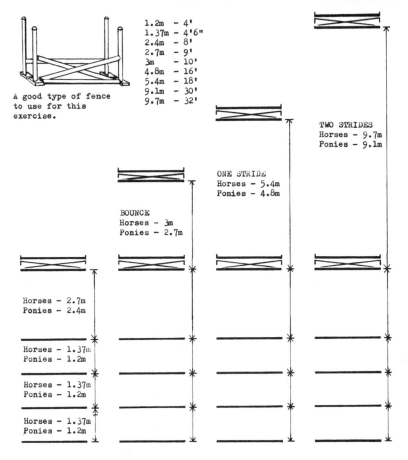

```
1.2m  - 4'
1.37m - 4'6"
2.4m  - 8'
2.7m  - 9'
3m    - 10'
4.8m  - 16'
5.4m  - 18'
9.1m  - 30'
9.7m  - 32'
```

A good type of fence
to use for this
exercise.

TWO STRIDES
Horses - 9.7m
Ponies - 9.1m

ONE STRIDE
Horses - 5.4m
Ponies - 4.8m

BOUNCE
Horses - 3m
Ponies - 2.7m

Horses - 2.7m
Ponies - 2.4m

Horses - 1.37m
Ponies - 1.2m

Horses - 1.37m
Ponies - 1.2m

Horses - 1.37m
Ponies - 1.2m

Above: Simple gymnnastic exercises. Distances are given for average horses and ponies and *must* be adjusted to suit. May need to be longer for big horses, shorter for small ponies. Fences 45cm (1'6") to 85cm (2'9") approximately, upright or type shown. Measurement between fences from inside element to inside element.

Below: Combinations. Easy distances for average horses and ponies for fences up to about 90cm.

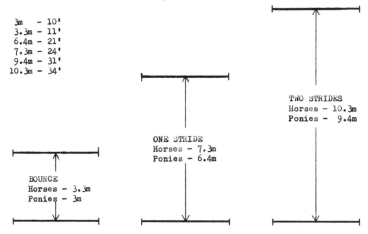

```
3m    - 10'
3.3m  - 11'
6.4m  - 21'
7.3m  - 24'
9.4m  - 31'
10.3m - 34'
```

TWO STRIDES
Horses - 10.3m
Ponies - 9.4m

ONE STRIDE
Horses - 7.3m
Ponies - 6.4m

BOUNCE
Horses - 3.3m
Ponies - 3m

These distances are longer than those given for gymnastic exercises because, with the approach in canter, the horse will take a longer stride.

Points on Combinations:

1. Begin with a two-stride distance — it allows more scope for recovery if the horse makes a mistake.

2. A simple staircase or ascending oxer for the first element helps the horse to take off correctly, while an upright is less demanding than a spread for the second element, especially if the horse tends to lose impulsion.

3. Establish confidence and ability over the foregoing gymnastic exercises and over one and two-stride doubles of all types before attempting trebles.

THE 'BOX'

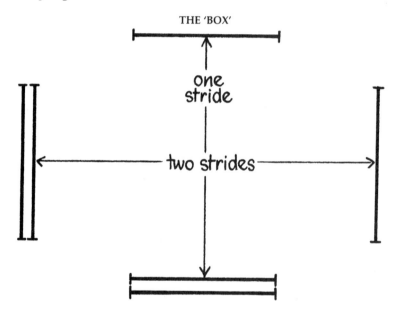

This offers at least three useful alternatives for training:

1. As a trotting exercise, with small fences, all 'jumpable' both ways. Trot round and through the box, taking single fences only — i.e. in over a fence, out through a corner, or vice versa. Two or three riders can do this together, working individually, not following one another. Develops concentration in all concerned!

2. For practice (one at a time) in jumping right-angle fences — often met with in cross country. A good exercise in co-ordination.

3. With somewhat bigger fences, for practice in combinations at canter.

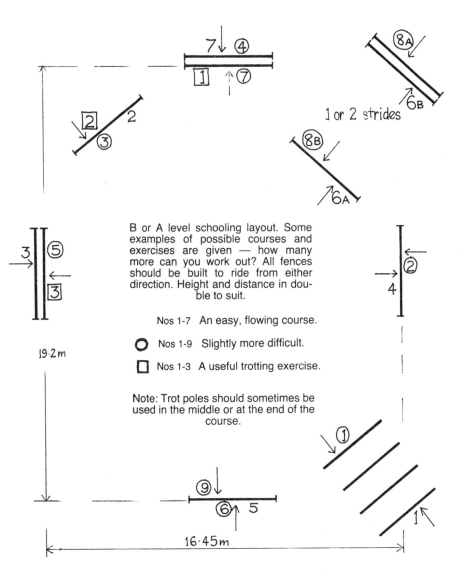

B or A level schooling layout. Some examples of possible courses and exercises are given — how many more can you work out? All fences should be built to ride from either direction. Height and distance in double to suit.

Nos 1-7 An easy, flowing course.

○ Nos 1-9 Slightly more difficult.

□ Nos 1-3 A useful trotting exercise.

Note: Trot poles should sometimes be used in the middle or at the end of the course.

1 or 2 strides

19·2m

16·45m

SHOW JUMPING

Manual One, pages 99-102, gives basic guidelines for walking and riding jumping courses. With further training and experience, you should now be taking a more knowledgeable approach.

Walking the Course

1. Work out the most economical track you can take, covering no more distance than necessary to allow sufficient straight strides on the approach to each fence. Avoid 'pulling out' to make room on turns — it breaks the horse's concentration and stride, often causing him to become disunited.

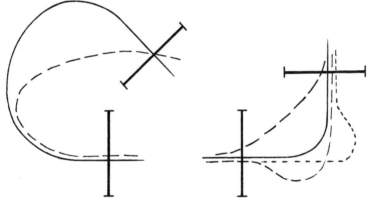

Good and bad 'tracks' between fences. The solid line shows the safest course.

2. Pace out combinations. Practise doing this with measured distances at home, so that you know how many of your paces make up an easy one- or two-stride distance for your mount. If the combination is on the long or short side for him, be prepared to ride it accordingly.

3. Jumping at an angle. Can save time in some circumstances, but the exact angle must be worked out accurately. Don't attempt it at cross bars, wide spreads or combinations, or with an inexperienced horse.

Riding the Course

1. Think ahead, look along the track you have decided to follow. If there is a 'tight' turn, begin to place the horse while still in the air — it is too late after he has landed and taken several strides. Never look down or back.

2. Make sure the horse is balanced, bent and on the correct leg for the first turn by circling in that direction before passing through the

starting flags. Maintain balance and bend by keeping contact with hand and leg and giving very clear turning aids throughout the round. The horse should be beginning to show the results of his training by changing leg himself on changes of direction if he is properly placed.

3. Aim to keep an even pace, don't let the horse get faster and flatter as he goes along, but 'round him up' on landing over each fence. Turns between fences, so long as the horse is correctly bent, will help with this rounding up, but be firm about it where there are several fences in a straight line, especially if the horse is somewhat excitable. Make sure the horse has sufficient freedom over his fences, but avoid dropping him in front of them, or last-minute kicks.

4. Combinations. If you noted any problems when you paced them, control the stride accordingly on the approach.

5. Try to train your horse to listen and obey, without losing his initiative and enjoyment.

CROSS COUNTRY

In cross country, there are certain recognised types of fences and problems which are used by course builders to test the boldness, training and fitness of horse and rider. These naturally vary according to the terrain and the standard of the competition, but they are fairly sure to include most of the following:

1. The bold, spread fence — e.g. a log, ascending oxer, hog's back, or fence with ditch in front or behind. These are the 'fun' fences, usually to be jumped on a long stride at a fair pace, which must never become a wild and uncontrolled gallop. The horse must always be steadied and 'rounded up' several strides out, to ensure that he is balanced and aware of what is coming, prior to being sent on into the fence.

Horse and rider showing good style over a natural fence.

2. 'Ups and downs' — e.g. fences on slopes, drops and fences where the take-off and landing are on different levels, though both may be on flat ground; banks and staircases; the steep slide, often with a fence at top or bottom, sometimes both.

General Rules for Ups and Downs

Pace. Fairly steady but maintaining impulsion. May be back to trot off staircase type, more freely over sloping, uncomplicated downhill fence.

Jumping downhill or over drop fences. Body fairly upright, and steady contact with hand and leg to keep the horse balanced on the approach.

Over the fence the rider's balance is vital. If too far forward or the lower leg slips back, you can easily go over the horse's head if he pecks or stumbles. If too far back, you may have to slip the reins to the buckle and it may take several strides after landing to get everything together again. Lower leg should be slightly forward.

Warning. Big drops, over about 1m, either off a bank or over a fence, put great strain on a horse's forelegs, especially if the landing is hard, rough or slippery. Such fences must not be practised excessively — not at all, if there is any suspicion of unsoundness in the horse.

Jumping up. Body well forward to keep weight off horse's back and loins. Make sure he has ample freedom of head and neck — never hesitate to hold the mane or neckstrap if necessary. A little extra pace, where feasible, can reduce the muscular effort required of the horse.

Jumping on and off a bank. Go steady, especially if the top is narrow, otherwise the horse may land too far over, making the jump down precarious, or he may even attempt to jump it all in one. It is always essential to look ahead and to keep the leg on throughout to maintain impulsion.

3. Ditches and water. Horses are naturally suspicious of holes in the ground and of water of unknown depth, so progressive training to build up confidence is essential.

Plain ditches (with no fence). Make sure the horse has seen the ditch by a steady approach but push on strongly in the last few strides. Look over, not into, the ditch, and keep forward to be sure of going with the horse.

Ditch on take-off side of fence. Equally vital to look over, not into, the ditch. If jumped boldly, the ditch acts as a ground line and helps the horse to stand back and jump in good style.

Ditch on landing side should be ridden fairly strongly, especially with a solid obstacle or hedge in front, as in this case the horse may be unaware of the ditch until the last moment. A normal jump at cross country pace is usually sufficient to carry him over the ditch without any extra effort.

Trakhener — rails over or diagonally across a ditch or water. Ride similarly to a ditch on the take-off side.

Ditches may form part of many combinations — e.g. a 'coffin', rails — ditch — rails, or on either or both sides of a bank.

Water. Plain water is ridden as for a plain ditch. Remember that even a pony covers approximately 3m in a canter stride, so there is no problem in getting the spread so long as he doesn't hesitate. It may help the horse to understand that he must 'lift' over water if you put a low rail (60cm approximately) over a practice water jump, towards the take-off side.

Water splashes. Jumps into or out of water, or set in the middle, so that both take-off and landing are in the water. These are largely a matter of confidence — first get the horse thoroughly accustomed to wading and fording creeks and streams. *Always* check that the bottom is firm but not stony, and that the water is no deeper than 30cm. Puddles after rain are often useful. Start by jumping out of water, then into it, before putting your obstacle actually in the water. Water splashes must be ridden at a steady pace but with plenty of impulsion. Sit a little more upright when jumping into water, as water can have a definite braking effect.

4. The 'clever' fences, requiring agility and obedience in the horse and judgment and accuracy in the rider. These include: narrow fences, e.g. a stile; fences with a short approach or a sharp turn on landing; some combinations, which may include any of the foregoing elements, and often have several ways in which they can be negotiated. A good example is the 'fishtail'.

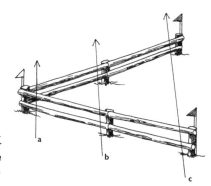

A. For the bold, across the apex. B. For the nippy, with a bounce. C. For the less experienced, with one stride — the safest route, but takes longer.

Problems of this kind require very careful walking, bearing in mind your horse's length of stride, temperament and experience.

The pace at which you jump combinations naturally depends on siting and circumstances, but remember that straightforward one- or two-stride distances are usually measured more generously than in show jumping, to allow for the longer stride across country.

To sum up, the principal differences between cross country and show jumping are:

1. The overall distance and the distances between fences. The 'wide open spaces' can cause great excitement if the horse is allowed to go too fast before he is sufficiently trained. The 'time allowed' for cross country is calculated at a faster speed than for show jumping, but this speed *must* be developed gradually if calmness and obedience are to be maintained.

2. The terrain — ups and downs, variations in going, jumping into and out of shady places.

3. The fences themselves. Banks, ditches and bounce strides are rarely met with in show jumping, and the idea that the fences are immovable may take some getting used to. In fact, the more solid the fences, the better horses usually jump them.

4. The degree of fitness needed in both horse *and rider*. It is no use getting your horse supremely fit if your own mental and physical fitness doesn't match his!

Walking Cross Country Courses

1. Attend the official course-walking, when all alternative fences and complex sections will be explained. If in doubt, ask for further clarification. This first walk only gives you a general idea of the type and layout of the course.

2. Walk it at least once more, either alone or with your instructor or team. Work out your exact track from start to finish, noting snags to be avoided, such as patches of bad going or overhanging branches. Economy of distance is even more important than in show jumping — more time faults come from going too far than from going too slowly! The aim is to maintain an even, strong canter throughout, but there are sure to be places where speed must be reduced, so note where time can be made up if necessary.

3. Decide the exact speed, place and angle at which you intend to jump each fence. Where accuracy of approach is essential, look for landmarks, which will be easy to pick up when riding, to help maintain your chosen line.

4. Walk and evaluate all alternatives, especially in combinations. Decide which route to take, but circumstances could arise (the state of the ground, the way your horse is going) which would necessitate a

76

change of tactics, so be familiar with all possible routes. Bear in mind the position of the sun at the time you will be riding, as this can affect your choice of alternatives or the angle of approach to some fences.

JUMPING PROBLEMS — HORSE

Most faults stem from one or a combination of the following causes. If your horse has or begins to develop faults in his jumping, check this list thoroughly. Ask your instructor to help you, to make sure that you have identified the root cause of the trouble.

Checklist of Common Causes:

1. **Riding faults,** e.g.

a. getting left behind and hurting the horse's back and/or loins and mouth.

b. reins too long, too short, not allowing sufficient freedom over the fence, dropping the horse and other contact faults.

c. poor presentation — not looking and thinking ahead, not getting straight or riding a good 'track'. If you intend to jump at an angle, accurate presentation is vital.

d. lack of nerve, decision or determination — soon sensed by the horse.

e. poor judgment — over-riding or over-restricting a keen horse, or sitting passively on one who is unsure or who has no intention of jumping. Over-facing.

f. lack of appreciation or understanding. Asking the horse to jump when tired or off-colour, over-jumping, or asking more of the horse when he has already done his best.

2. **Pain** from:

a. saddlery — ill-fitting or uncomfortable, especially saddle coming down on withers or spine, or too severe a bit.

b. bad riding.

c. lameness or soreness. E.g. shoes left on too long, potential or actual corns, splints, tendon trouble, muscular soreness, especially in the back.

3. **Fear,** caused by:

a. pain. Even when the cause is remedied, the residue of fear will remain for some time.

b. over-facing — fences too big or too difficult for the state of training.

c. loss of confidence due to bad riding, slippery going, badly built fences, incorrect distances in combinations and exercises, being put 'wrong' at fences.

d. hitting fences, falls.

4. **Lack of or incorrect training,** both on the flat and progressively over fences, shown in:

a. wilful disobedience.

b. stiffness and lack of balance, making obedience difficult, uncomfortable or impossible.

c. excitement, loss of mouth and manners when jumping.

d. inability and/or unwillingness to lengthen or shorten the stride when asked.

5. **Temperament.**

a. excitable or impetuous.

b. nervous, lacking in courage or confidence.

c. sluggish.

Any extremes add to the difficulties of training, and will require more time.

6. **Conformation.**

a. poor natural balance.

b. lack of scope, often due to a poor front, upright shoulder, etc.

c. an exceptionally long or short natural stride, making it difficult for the horse to adjust to normal combination distances.

7. **Poor horse management.**

a. lack of fitness.

b. unsuitable feeding — too many concentrates for the hot-headed, not enough for the sluggish or 'stuffy' type.

As a starting point, the most likely causes are given with each problem — together with suggested training methods.

Refusing (Stopping or Baulking)

Check whole list of causes — it could be any or several of them. (See *Manual One,* pages 91-93.)

Running Off

Check list 1b, c, d and e, then 4a, which may easily develop if the rider's shortcomings have allowed the horse to get away with it continually! (See *Manual One,* as above.)

Rushing

Check especially 1a, b, d and e, 2a, 3a, and b, all of 4, 5a.

Suggested Training:

1. Check your training on the flat. If the horse is disobedient there, he will usually be even more so in his jumping. Work on lengthening

and shortening the stride in the open, first on the large circle, then on the straight.

2. Work the horse among jumps and over scattered single poles on the ground at walk and trot. Then use a line of three poles at 2.7m at walk. If the horse tries to rush or jump, circle away after the first pole, come round again, halt facing the poles, pat the horse and get him calm, circle away again. When he steps quietly over one pole, take in two before circling away, and finally walk over all three, if possible on a long rein.

3. Approach the poles in walk, with light contact. Step over the first two, then ease the horse into trot over the third. Trot about halfway round to approach again, walk, repeat, trotting two poles and then all three if all is well. Finally, approach in trot, then fill the gaps to give a line of poles at 1.37, or whatever distance the horse's stride requires. Don't have them too wide.

It is well worth taking time over this pole work to establish obedience and confidence. Never hesitate to go back as many steps as necessary if things go wrong.

4. Place two poles together on the ground between stands, 2.7m from the line of trot poles. When the horse trots quietly over these in his stride, convert to cross poles about 30cm high in the centre — just enough to encourage him to hop over it. Generous praise if he does this calmly. If not, either lower the poles again or circle away without jumping after the trot poles. Finish for that lesson when success is achieved. This is an important landmark.

5. Enlarge the jump to about 45cm, then add a 'bounce' at 2.7m. Use other small, scattered jumps, each with a placing pole at 2.7m. If the horse attempts to rush at these, circle as shown below. All approaches should still be in trot.

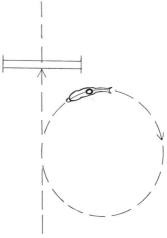

The circle (20m approx.) must be close to the fence, with one edge in line with its centre. The horse will try to 'dive' at the fence at first, but concentrate on the pace and bend and keep circling until he listens and obeys you. When calm, allow him to pop quietly over the fence, and reward him immediately.

6. Introduce canter strides in jumping exercises, back to trot on landing. Work on calm, rhythmic canter among jumps, lengthening and shortening the stride, and on frequent transitions, including 'working halts'.

7. Introduce single jumps at canter, alternating with trot poles and fences with a placing pole.

8. Continue on these lines. The 'box', and poles and fences on a circle (see page 184) are especially useful for horses that rush.

9. Check 'Judgment of Speed and Distance', page 51, for introducing the impetuous horse to faster paces.

It is essential to make constant use of trot poles, jumping and gymnastic exercises and variations of pace, in addition to regular dressage work, for all horses who tend to 'hot up'. If the habit is confirmed, systematic retraining as outlined above, is the only answer. It is useless to continue with hunting or competitive jumping, especially against the clock, until control is established.

'Putting in a Short Stride'

'Putting in a short stride', also 'propping' (almost stopping) and general hesitancy in jumping.

Check whole list of causes, especially all aspects of your riding, and the horse's soundness and fitness if this type of problem appears suddenly.

Suggested Training:

1. Dressage work, to improve balance, suppleness and the ability to lengthen and shorten on demand.

2. Trotting poles. Correctly ridden poles on a curve can help to stretch and supple the horse if he is lacking in scope. (See page 184.)

3. Progressive jumping exercises, placing rails and a timing rail. Distances must be easy for the horse, on the short side at first, but he must be kept going with plenty of impulsion and not allowed to hesitate.

4. Flowing courses of well-built fences with good ground lines, jumped at an active, rhythmic canter. A lead from another horse, or jumping with several others, follow-my-leader fashion, can encourage the unsure. If no others are available, make sure that the more difficult fences are jumped towards 'home' — i.e. the gate of the paddock. Reward and encouragement are essential. If the horse jumps two or three successive fences really well leave it at that.

5. As confidence and ability increase hunting, round the ring jumping, and some faster work on the flat, could all help the horse to go more freely.

Take great care not to over-face or over-jump, and check fitness, soundness and all likely causes of trouble before every schooling session.

Jumping in Bad Style — with a flat or hollow back.

Check especially 1b and 2a and b.

The whole object of the progressive method of training suggested here is to develop the horse's muscles, supple and balance him so that he can use himself correctly in his jumping, and to build up his self-confidence.

Experience and knowledge are necessary to diagnose the cause of any problem, skill and judgment to effect a cure. It can be extremely difficult even for the most experienced riders to analyse their own and their horses' problems — often it requires an expert instructor to watch the combination in action — something no book can do!

If you are on your own, the ideas suggested here, applied step by step, should certainly help, but if things do not begin to show signs of immediate improvement, do seek advice. If the trouble stems from unsoundness, for instance, or it is your riding that is at fault, any attempts at retraining will do more harm than good.

JUMPING PRACTICE

Re-read 'Points and Principles', *Manual One*, pages 90-91. These still apply, no matter how far you go. Consideration for the horse or pony, reward for effort and finishing on a good note are always particularly important.

By now, your jumping practice should have clearly defined objectives. These could be:

1. Maintenance and general improvement. Variety is important — use different exercises, especially those which will help to strengthen weak areas or correct faults. You could jump twice a week, as follows:

1st session: trotting poles and one or two jumping/gymnastic exercises.

2nd session: 6 to 8 bigger fences at canter, including a double; or a second period of exercises, finishing with 3 or 4 full-size fences. This applies to show jumping or cross-country. For height of schooling fences, see below.

NOTE: Most horses, when jumping at shows on a regular weekly basis, will need little if any jumping at home. One session over trotting poles and exercises, or over three or four larger fences, is usually ample.

2. Preparing for a new season. Check 'Bringing a Horse Back Into Work After A Spell', page 89. Note that work over trotting poles

should never begin before the third week, followed by 'a few easy fences' a week later. Then proceed as above, working up the degree of difficulty as fitness increases. Start small and build up gradually.

3. Building up a partnership with a new horse. Find out all you can about the new horse — his likes and dislikes, good points and problems. It takes time to get to know one another and work up a good partnership. Schooling periods as for 1.

4. Purely for enjoyment. Most riders at this level have a goal in mind — hunting, eventing, show jumping. For the non-competitive, good training is still worthwhile. Without it, neither member of the partnership will get much enjoyment. Be sure that the horse is fit enough for the work required and that the usual principles are observed.

5. Teaching a young horse to jump. (See page 187.)

As with dressage, jumping training is not an all-the-year-round affair, but will tend to go in cycles. Since a considerable physical effort is required, the number of maximum-size (for your horse) fences that can be included is limited. This is yet another reason why trotting poles and gymnastic exercises play such a big part in training.

Whatever your aims in jumping practice, always make sure that the horse is well worked in. At least 15 to 20 minutes work on the flat, including circles, transitions, lengthening and shortening and trotting poles before jumping commences.

Take the trouble to build good fences, to measure heights and distances accurately and to change the 'track' frequently, so that you and your horse have new and interesting problems to think about. Heights should not exceed 75cm for trotting fences and gymnastic exercises, and 75-90cm is generally quite big enough for canter fences, though when preparing for competition you must be sure that your horse is capable of jumping round about the height he will meet in the first round. In this case, you could work up to 1m or even 1.1m towards the end of your round of 6-8 fences. It is often better to increase the spread rather than the height when additional effort is required. Jumping bigger fences frequently at home will only make the horse stale, sour and very probably unsound before he gets to the competition.

5

PADDOCKING, FEEDING, CONDITIONING, EXERCISE (B)

PADDOCKING

Chapter 9, *Manual One*, contains all the essentials in caring for a pony in the paddock. You should now be applying this knowledge in a practical way, and taking full responsibility for the day-to-day wellbeing of your mount.

Points to be checked are:

1. **Horse:** Condition and soundness, all the usual signs of health. Swelling and/or heat in the legs. Feet and shoes. Discharge from nose or eyes. Anything unusual in his appearance or behaviour.
2. **Paddock:** Water supply, state of feed, weeds and poisonous plants, rubbish, holes. Fences and gates.

Apart from the daily routine check, you should begin to learn to assess the feed value of your pasture, and how to maintain and improve it. You should, as suggested in *Manual One*, have found out what manures or fertilisers are needed in your district to keep pastures 'in good heart'. Regular application of these, especially lime, is essential in small paddocks, or those grazed only by horses.

POISONOUS PLANTS

Some plants may cause severe colic, others are deadly. Nobody would expect you to know them all, but at least try to identify those commonly found in paddocks. If in doubt, ask your instructor or the local Ministry of Agriculture and Fisheries.

Ragwort. One of the most common and most dangerous plants toxic to horses. It is a slow poison, affecting the liver over a period of time. Not usually eaten when growing, but dangerous when dried, in hay, or after being sprayed.

Hemlock. Fortunately not very palatable, but lethal if eaten.

Castor Oil Plant. Found mainly in warmer districts, on wasteland in built-up areas, so more likely to invade town sections. The beans, in particular, are very poisonous to horses and people.

Tutu. N.Z. Not so commonly found in paddocks, but could be encountered on scrubland or the edges of bush. Watch for it when riding.

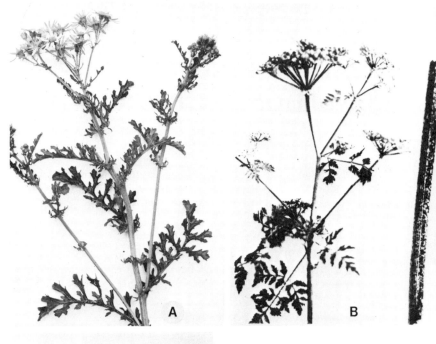

A. Ragwort: yellow, daisy-like flower. B. Hemlock: has a flat, white flower similar to hedge-parsley (which is harmless) but it is distinguished by purple blotches on the stems. C. Castor oil plant: grows to a height of 4m approximately. D. Tutu: fruit black or purple.

Tree nettle: note sharp hairs on leaves.

Mexican Devil Weed. Northern N.Z. only. A scrubby weed, with small white flowers, found in ditches and paddocks. Affects respiratory system.

If you find any of these in your paddock, grub them out and destroy them. DON'T leave them lying about.

Other weeds that can be poisonous include foxglove, bracken fern, and some types of buttercup, so they, too, should be dealt with.

C

D

CAUTION. Many plants become more attractive to animals when the plants are wilted, especially if they have been sprayed. This is because some sprays turn the starch in the plant into sugar. Some lose their toxicity on drying out; others remain just as poisonous.

Trees, Hedges, Shrubs

Many, particularly evergreens, are both palatable and poisonous to horses — some, such as privet, are poisonous only when in flower. The following have proved to be toxic:

Laburnum, oleander, yew, rhododendron, cherry laurel, ivy, box, ngaio and macrocarpa. The last two are usually out of reach; any fallen branches should be removed.

Garden plants. Apart from those listed above, many are poisonous. Never throw any away in horse paddocks, and remove them at once if anyone else does.

Potatoes. The tops are poisonous, and so are the potatoes themselves if they are green or sprouting.

Grain poisoning. Can occur if the horse raids the feed store and eats large quantities.

Whole linseed. Can be poisonous, so it must *always* be boiled.

Ryegrass and paspalum. Not, of course, poisonous in themselves. In fact, ryegrass is one of the best pasture plants, but both can develop a parasitic ergot which can cause staggers. (See *Manual One,* page 165.)

Lawn mowings. Like the above, lawn clippings are not poisonous in themselves, but if left in a heap they quickly heat up and ferment, in which state they will cause severe colic or even death.

Tree nettle. Unlikely to be eaten, but its sting is very painful and dangerous to horse and rider. Beware of this, too, in scrubland and bush.

Symptoms of poisoning vary according to what has been consumed. They can include excessive salivation, changes in respiration — breathing abnormally fast, slow or irregular — unusual excitement or lethargy, scouring, shivering, staggery gait, sweating or colic. Sometimes, as with ragwort, the effects are insidious and will not be apparent for some time. However, if you know or suspect that your horse has eaten something poisonous, or he shows any of the above symptoms, seek veterinary advice without delay.

FEEDING

Most of what you need to know about feeding at this stage is contained in Chapter 10, *Manual One*. Once you have a thorough understanding of the principles, methods and rules set out there, you should be able to apply them to any horse.

In addition, you should have more knowledge of the following:
1. Recognition of the different types of hay, chaff and grain.
2. Preparation and use of boiled feed and bran mashes.

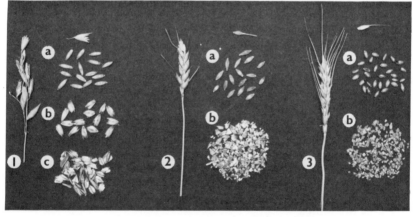

Grains   1. Oats: a) whole b) bruised c) crushed.
2. Barley: a) whole b) kibbled (coarse ground).
3. Wheat: a) whole (do not feed) b) bran.

BOILED FEED

Linseed. Whole linseed *must* be boiled so that the seeds are

86

cracked, otherwise it can be poisonous. There is an enzyme in raw linseed which can generate prussic acid. You will need about a cup of linseed per horse, and a really strong pan to prevent it burning. Pour on one to two litres of boiling water, add salt, and keep it boiling vigorously for ten minutes, stirring all the time. Then turn the heat down and leave it *just* simmering for several hours. Add to bran while still boiling, mix well, cover and steam. Feed as a bran and linseed mash. Palatable, digestible, superb for improving the coat. Linseed should not normally be fed more than twice a week.

Barley. Weigh uncooked — half to one kilogram, according to size of horse. (For method of cooking, see *Manual One,* page 131.)

Apart from its value as a winter feed for young and old horses, boiled barley may be fed up to three times weekly to the fit horse who is inclined to be light in condition.

Oats. Cooking tends to make oats more fattening and less exciting. Whole oats become more digestible and less likely to go straight through the horse.

About one hour's cooking should suffice — try to steam rather than boil, as oats absorb water readily.

Boiled barley and oats are best mixed with a little bran and/or chaff and given in the evening feed. The mixture should be crumbly, never sloppy. Pour off any excess water before mixing.

BRAN MASH

Bran mashes are palatable, easily digested and mildly laxative. They are therefore valuable for:

1. A tired horse after a hard day's work.
2. The fit horse on the night before his 'day off'.
3. A sick horse, to tempt his appetite and keep his bowels functioning properly if he is getting little or no exercise. (For method of making a bran mash, see *Manual One,* page 130.)

To make the mash more laxative, add dissolved epsom or glauber's salts instead of plain salt.

A small amount of boiled linseed and/or crushed or boiled barley or oats may be added to the basic mash.

To tempt a sick horse, or one who is off his feed, try adding molasses, glucose (excellent for a tired or sick horse) or sliced carrots.

Points to Note

1. With any of this feed, check that it is *not too hot* when given to the horse. It must feel comfortable to the back of your hand.
2. Boiled feed and mashes begin to 'go off' and ferment very quickly, so:

a. remove any not eaten within two or three hours — never mix it with fresh.

b. scrub feed containers thoroughly afterwards.

3. These feeds tend to be fattening, and may make the horse rather 'soft' for fast work such as hunting and eventing, but they can be essential to maintain condition in some horses. It all depends on the type and temperament of the horse and the work he is doing.

4. Never feed a bran mash or boiled feed the night before any fast or energetic work is required of the horse.

Commercial Vitamin and Mineral Additives

These are expensive, and should not be used without experienced advice, as they can create an imbalance if used incorrectly. However, many areas suffer from a shortage of minerals, essential to the horse's wellbeing. Consult your instructor or vet if your horse is not 'doing' well in spite of a good, well-balanced diet. They will recommend what, if anything, is necessary.

CONDITIONING

'Conditioning' a horse means bringing him into the best possible physical condition for the work he has to do.

Here are some of the terms used to describe condition:

Gross. Immensely fat, especially on the crest and over the back and loins. In great danger of 'foundering' or contracting laminitis. (See *Manual One*, page 164.) Any exertion will cause discomfort, and fast work will be likely to strain the heart and lungs. Because the legs have so much extra weight to carry, they will be liable to sprains, especially in jumping. A horse in this condition must be brought into work slowly and with the utmost care.

Big. Still somewhat overweight for most purposes. Show horses should ideally be in bigger condition than those in faster work — e.g. hunting, eventing, polo-crosse.

Good. Neither too fat nor too thin, and fit enough for the work required. Showing all the signs of good health.

Light. On the thin side, beginning to show ribs and probably 'poverty marks' — lines down the buttocks. May be 'run up ' — i.e. the line of the belly runs sharply upwards from girth to flank. If worked hard in this state the horse will lack stamina and will continue to lose condition.

Poor. Really thin and ribby, with a generally gaunt appearance. Liable to injury due to weakness, especially brushing, forging, over-reaching and sprained tendons. (Causes of poor condition are given in *Manual One*, page 162.)

Soft. The probable condition of a horse after having a spell for a month or more — quite big, but with very little muscle. Because the skin in the girth and saddle areas will have become literally softer, he will gall easily. (See *Manual One*, page 171.) When asked to work, he will blow and sweat profusely and will soon tire, though he may be lively enough at first. The sweat will be frothy and will not dry quickly.

Hard. Athletically fit, capable of sustained physical effort of whatever kind his work demands.

Bringing a Horse Back Into Work After a Spell

The first aim should be what may be called 'good working condition' — having sufficient muscle and stamina for average daily riding and Pony Club work. This will take several weeks, depending on how long he has been out and how soft or gross he has become.

1. Have the horse shod, and wormed if he is due for it. Have his teeth checked, and rasped if necessary.

2. Check fitting of saddle — the horse's shape may have altered considerably during his spell.

3. Saddle up in plenty of time before the first ride — don't tighten the girth up immediately. If the horse is very soft, use a good, thick numnah and a string girth. Lead him for a short distance before mounting. For the first day, twenty minutes at walk will be sufficient. On return, check thoroughly for roughness or raised patches of hair in girth and saddle areas. If there is the slightest suspicion, treat with dilute meths, witch hazel or saline solution.

4. First week. Keep to the walk, gradually increasing the riding time, possibly up to one hour by the end of the week. Continue to watch for galls.

5. Second week. Start with three-quarters of an hour's walking exercise, increase to one hour. Short trots may be introduced. Canter is better left until later — postponement essential if the horse was really soft.

6. Third week. One hour approximately of steady riding, more walk than trot. Could include some hill work, at walk only, short canters, 10 to 15 minutes dressage in the open, trotting poles.

7. Fourth week. Up to 1½ hours of steady riding. Could include a little hill work at trot, up to 20 minutes dressage at all paces, trotting poles, a few easy jumps on one day of the week. Must still include plenty of walking, particularly at the end of the work, so that the horse finishes up cool and calm.

This is an approximate guide only — if the horse was really fat and soft, it could take six or even eight weeks to bring him to this stage.

Feeding. Depends on the time of the year, the condition of horse and pasture, and on what feed he has been having. If he is very fat, it can help to yard him during the day for about a week before you start to ride him. He would then be given a little hay, or a small feed.

If in light condition, he should be getting some supplementary feed anyway. A maintenance ration should be adequate for these first few weeks, but the horse's condition must be carefully watched, and extra feed given if necessary. Remember to make any changes of diet gradually.

Grooming. Even with slow work, a soft horse will sweat more than usual. If dried sweat is left on the coat and skin, it increases the risk of galls and clogs the pores. Thorough daily grooming is therefore essential. Washing is no substitute.

Clipping. If the horse is to be clipped, it is best done as soon as he can be got clean enough, to avoid loss of condition by sweating and the risk of chills.

At the end of this four- to eight-week period, the horse should be in good working condition. This should describe the average well-cared-for Pony Club mount, who is ridden three to six days a week, goes regularly to rallies and to the occasional show or gymkhana. He should look and be very well, although not in hard condition.

Hard Condition — Fitness

For harder work, the horse must be fitter. To bring a horse from good working condition to hard condition will probably take about four weeks. He should be ridden six days a week, if possible. He will need a suitable programme of work and exercise, with feed adjusted accordingly.

Work for the horse requires physical effort of one sort or another, plus concentration and often considerable courage. If he is properly conditioned and trained, he should enjoy it. Training (work), dressage, jumping, etc, often require even more concentration, especially when he is learning new things.

Fast, or 'pace' work. Strong canter or gallop. Some is essential for horses whose work requires speed or endurance, to clear their wind, strengthen muscles, and, in some cases, to sharpen them up. Too much, especially if the horse is a highly strung thoroughbred type, may hot him up, run him up, put him off his feed or cause unsoundness. Once a week is ample for most horses (see 'Judgment of Pace and Distance', page 51), but if pace work is new to you, do get advice from an experienced person as to what your particular horse needs.

Exercise is sustained, steady activity, comparable to an athlete's jogging, which gradually develops muscles and lung capacity. It must be interesting and mentally relaxing to both horse and rider.

Pace — mainly a brisk walk or a steady trot.

Terrain. As varied as possible — on the road, round the farm, on hills or on the flat, on the beach, in the forest, whatever is available. Some road work helps to harden the horse's legs, but the pace must be steady and the surface smooth, not stony. If you must cross any ground that is rough, heavy or slippery, do so at the walk. Long, steady trots up a gradual incline are wonderful for building up the muscles of the loins and hindquarters and clearing the wind.

Finding the Balance Between Work and Exercise

1. Most horses need an average of 1½ hours overall riding daily to get and keep them even moderately fit.

2. Training is necessary to develop the ability of both horse and rider. The essential thing here is quality, rather than quantity — half an hour is usually enough.

3. Therefore the balance must be made up of exercise.

With too much work, the horse may become stale and edgy and go back in performance. He may even go off his feed and lose condition. If any of these signs appear, give exercise only for a few days. In any case, one day a week could well be devoted to a good, long exercise ride.

You may find it more convenient, and better for some horses, to divide your riding time, perhaps working the horse in the morning and exercising him in the afternoon.

Signs of Fitness

As the horse gets fitter, he should:

1. Lose any excess fat, but he must not be run up or show ribs or poverty marks.

2. Become more muscular, especially on the crest, shoulders, loins, hindquarters, forearm and thigh. The muscles should be strong, but rippling, not rigid.

3. Sweat less, and the sweat should become clearer and dry more quickly.

4. Feel stronger and probably livelier when ridden. You should feel that he is enjoying his work, and that it is becoming easier for him.

5. Show all the signs of good health — clear eyes, alert expression,

loose shining coat, cool fine legs with no suggestion of puffiness or heat, good appetite.

Since every rider's objectives will vary to some extent, and every horse is an individual, hard and fast rules cannot be laid down. It may, however, be said that to get and stay fit, any horse must have:

1. Regular dosing, to keep internal parasites to a minimum.

2. Unlimited fresh, clean water.

3. Feed of the right type and in the right quantity for the work he is doing. The harder the work, the more hard feed will be needed, but he must always have sufficient bulk.

4. Thorough daily grooming.

5. Rest — a day off once a week. A period of peace and quiet during each day, especially if he is being ridden twice, is most important.

6. A balanced programme of work and exercise, tailor-made for him. Ask your instructor to help you work this out.

The whole art of conditioning lies in bringing the horse to a state where he has the necessary energy and stamina for his work, while remaining sensible and manageable. Acute daily observation is the crux of the matter, so that you notice the smallest changes in condition and behaviour at once, and adjust your management accordingly.

Roughing Off

The gradual letting-down of condition before giving the horse a spell. Suddenly to stop riding or feeding a horse who has been in hard work on a concentrated diet would be just the kind of abrupt change that is to be avoided.

Cut down both work and feed gradually, confine grooming to remove mud and sweat and keeping the horse tidy. If he is to have his spell at a warm time of year, he will be better without a cover, so start by taking it off in the daytime. The process should take about two weeks from hunting or eventing fitness to turning out.

If the horse has been stabled, letting him down slowly is even more important. He should only be put out in the paddock for about an hour at first, especially if the grass is rich, so that his system can adjust to the change of diet.

It is best to have the shoes removed and the feet trimmed before turning out. This helps to ensure greater frog contact which keeps the heels open, and the feet will benefit generally from the spell without shoes. If the feet are brittle or the ground rough and hard, grass tips could be used. (See page 214.)

A horse in consistent work should have at least three or four weeks' spell yearly. During this time, if he normally lives in a small paddock, it would be an advantage if grazing on a farm could be arranged. This would provide an opportunity to clean up and manure his paddock and make a most welcome change for the horse.

6

HANDLING, GROOMING, TRIMMING, PLAITING, CLIPPING, SHOEING (B)

HANDLING

You must be aware of and observe all the safety factors in 'Handling', *Manual One*, page 141.

Holding a Horse for Veterinary Treatment, Clipping, Shoeing, etc.

As the assistant, you should:

1. Always stand on the same side of the horse as the person handling the hind legs, and keep the horse's head towards you — then his quarters will swing away if he kicks.

2. Be alert, and pay attention to what is going on. Engage the horse's attention by talking to him and/or giving him feed. If he is restless, a snaffle bridle gives more control than a halter. Holding up a foreleg can help to keep the horse still.

In some cases, it may be necessary to use a twitch (see page 208) on the horse's top lip. The vet, or other experienced person, will apply this and show you how to hold it. *Never* stand in front of a horse with a twitch on. Do not, at this stage, attempt to apply one yourself.

Holding a Horse to Show Him Off

Stand *almost* in front of the horse, facing him, and hold one rein in each hand. If he tries to nibble your wrists, raise your elbows. Keep him alert and standing still and square, to show off his conformation to the best advantage.

Running up in Hand for Lameness or Action

(See 'Leading in Hand', *Manual One*, pages 38 and 141-2.)

When testing for lameness:

1. Leave the horse's head as free as possible, with a slack rein or rope, because lameness often shows in the nodding of the head as the sound leg comes to the ground.

2. Use a hard, smooth surface, so that any unevenness can be heard as well as seen.

3. Follow the vet or examiner's directions accurately as to pace and direction. When turning, always stay on the outside of the turn, both for safety and so that the horse can be more clearly seen by the person examining.

When showing off a horse's action:

1. The reins should be slack enough to let the horse carry his head naturally.

2. The pace should be active — the horse encouraged to stride out freely and confidently, without haste.

One method is to walk the horse directly away from the person inspecting, turn correctly and trot back and past — the judge will step back to allow you to maintain a straight line. Then walk, turn again and walk back.

3. Make sure the horse is standing as described above at any time he is being inspected. (For handling horses in stables, see page 117.)

All horses should be trained to lead in hand as freely as this one.

GROOMING

The basic method of grooming is given in *Manual One*, pages 145-8. In addition to the tools shown there, you may need a hay wisp — its use is explained under 'Strapping' below.

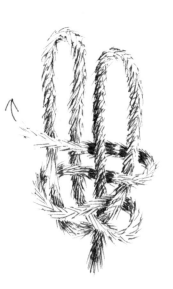
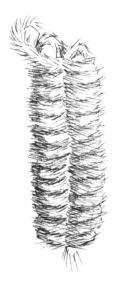

Making a hay wisp.

To make a hay wisp. Take about two 'slices' of soft hay, shake it out and damp it thoroughly. Starting in the centre of the heap, begin twisting the hay tightly to form a rope. As it gets longer, ask somebody to hold the end and keep it taut, while you continue twisting until you have a rope about 3m long. Now make two loops at one end of the rope, one slightly larger than the other. Twist each loop in turn under the spare end of the rope until it is nearly all used up. Push the end through the two loops, and finally tuck it firmly under the last twist. Trim off any loose ends with scissors, and bang it on the wall to knock it into shape. The end-product should be hard, tight and of a size to fit your hand comfortably.

Quartering

A quick 'tidy-up' for the grass-kept horse before work, for the stabled horse first thing in the morning.

Pick out the feet and check shoes, sponge eyes, nose, lips and dock. Then undo the cover, and, in cold weather, turn it back while you brush the front part of the horse and the mane, then fold it forward and brush the back part and the tail. The object is to remove all dried mud and grass or stable stains — use a damp sponge for the latter, if necessary.

Strapping (or 'Stropping')

A thorough and vigorous grooming, entailing energetic use of the body brush to remove scurf, grease and dried sweat from coat and skin. It should also include some form of massage, such as wisping.

Daily strapping will improve the appearance and condition of any horse, and is an essential part of getting a horse fit or preparing him for showing.

It is best done when the horse is warm, but of course dry, after exercise, when the pores will be open and the scurf looser.

The method is similar to that for basic grooming:

1. Collect grooming kit, tie horse up short.

2. Pick out feet, and wash them if they are muddy. It is permissible, and convenient, to pick up all feet from one side. Use a 'drop skep' (page 114) when picking out feet in a yard or stable.

3. A quick brush over with the dandy brush or rubber curry comb, to remove dried sweat and mud. Pay particular attention to the girth and saddle regions and under the belly.

Reminders. The dandy brush is used with a brisk, light, to-and-fro movement, across the lie of the hair, finishing with the lie of the coat. It may be held in either hand, as convenient. Avoid using it on the bony or ticklish parts, and on the head, mane and tail.

If your horse is clipped, or if he is exceptionally thin-skinned, it may be best to go straight on to the body brush, omitting the dandy altogether.

4. In summer and autumn, check for bot eggs, and remove them.

5. Take the body brush and curry comb, the brush in your left hand, curry comb in your right. Begin behind the poll on the left side, and work methodically over the neck, shoulder, chest, between the forelegs, down the foreleg, inside and out, over the body, girth, belly, hindquarters and hind leg. The body brush may be used with a circular action, but always finish with the lie of the coat. Stand well back with a fairly straight arm and put your weight behind it. This forces the short bristles through to the skin, removing scurf and grease. Every three or four strokes, rub the brush over the curry comb. It is safer to change the brush and curry comb over to do the hindquarters and under the belly, especially if the horse is restless.

Move to the right side, and, starting with the brush in the right hand, brush the mane, then the right side of the horse and the tail. Finally, brush the head and knock out the curry comb, into a drop skep if in a yard or stable.

6. Wisping. This is a form of massage which develops the horse's muscles (and the groom's!), produces a shine on the coat by drawing out the oil in the glands of the skin, and increases the blood supply to the skin. It is best done with a hay wisp, but failing this, a towel folded into a firm pad or a grooming mitt could be used.

Damp the wisp slightly, and begin on the neck on the left side. Stand far enough away to use a fairly straight arm, and bring the wisp down with a gentle bang on the upper half of the neck. If the horse objects, just stroke him with the wisp at first, gradually introducing very light 'bangs' as he gets used to the idea. The wisp is used on the muscular parts, especially the top half of the neck, shoulder, forearm, back muscles (but not over the loins) hindquarters and thigh. Never on bony or ticklish areas, such as the flank or belly. It is usually best to use the left hand for the left side of the horse's forehand, and change to the right for his hindquarters. Reverse this on his right side.

One of the most important effects of the 'banging' is to make the horse contract the muscle in rhythm. It is these contractions that develop and harden the muscle. Once the horse is used to it, the wisp should be used quite vigorously, but never roughly.

Begin with two or three minutes a side, working up to a good five minutes if you want to get your horse really fit. Concentrate on any muscles that need to be stronger and more developed — it is amazing what a difference correct wisping can make.

7. Sponge the eyes, nose, lips and dock.

8. Lay the mane and tail with a damp water brush.

9. Wipe the horse over with a slightly damp cloth or towel, to remove any surface dust and give a final polish.

10. Oil the feet.

If the weather is cold and/or the horse is clipped, keep him half covered, as for quartering.

Regular strapping removes much of the natural grease which insulates the horse in winter, so extra covers may be needed.

Cooling Off a Hot, Sweating Horse

If, due to very hot weather or after the finish of a cross country, it is not possible to bring a horse in cool:

1. Slacken the girth, lift the saddle to allow air to circulate underneath but leave it on for a few minutes.

2. Remove the bridle, put on halter, then remove saddle.

3. In warm weather it is permissible to hose the horse, after which he should be scraped down and led around until dry, or turned out. A sweat scraper is most useful for this.

In any other weather conditions, cover the horse immediately, then sponge his head, neck, chest, between the forelegs, saddle and girth areas, under the belly and between the hind legs. On no account allow the loins to become wet. Dry off each part after sponging, and keep the horse covered as much as possible by folding the cover forward or back. Finally, put on a sweat sheet (see page 290) or 'thatch' the horse with straw under the cover, and lead him around until he is completely dry.

Never hose a hot horse over his back and loins unless the weather is really warm. Apart from chills, it can cause serious muscular problems.

TRIMMING

The process of tidying a horse up, especially the mane, tail and heels. Properly done, it can greatly improve the appearance of any horse.

Mane

Pulling. This is done to shorten and/or thin the mane. It makes it much easier to keep clean and to plait, and encourages it to lie flat. It is best done when the horse is warm and the pores open after exercise.

Method. Brush or comb the mane thoroughly, so that it is completely free of tangles. You will need a short-toothed mane comb, or any ordinary hair comb. Begin at the withers. Take a few of the longest hairs from underneath, hold them firmly in your left thumb and forefinger while you back-comb the rest of the hair in that spot with your right hand. Using the second finger for leverage, pull the long hairs sharply straight downwards. So long as the horse is warm, it shouldn't hurt him — if he objects, you are probably trying to take too much at a time. Make sure you pull the hair from the roots and don't break it off halfway.

Work gradually up towards the head, always taking the hair from underneath and pulling everything over the required length — probably 15-20cm. Remember to pull the forelock too. It should be approximately level with the horse's eyes.

If the mane is very long and thick, don't try to do it all at once, spread the job over several days.

Never use scissors or clippers to shorten a mane.

Hogging. This means removing the mane completely with clippers. It should only be done with the heavy, cobby type of horse or pony, who has a rather coarse mane.

Advantages: 1. It can make this type of horse look smarter.

2. It saves having to look after and/or plait the mane.

Disadvantages: 1. It deprives the horse of the natural protection of his neck and crest. In cold weather, or when flies are bad in summer, the hogged horse may need a neck cover.

2. It deprives you of a handy 'lifeline' when riding. A hogged mane can be extremely painful to land on!

3. Once started, you really have to continue hogging. A mane will take about two years to grow fully.

4. If you have no clippers, it may be difficult to get it done when

needed — about every three or four weeks. (For method, see page 211.)

Tail

Pulling. The hair at the top of the tail may also be pulled. Once this is done, it will be too short to plait. A pulled tail looks neat and is easier to keep clean, but it, too, deprives the horse of some warmth and protection. He will need a cover that comes well down over the root of the tail, especially in colder districts. (For method of pulling, see page 209.)

Never use scissors or clippers on the top of the tail.

Shortening the tail — also called 'banging' the tail.

Advantages: neatness; shorter tail doesn't get so muddy.

Method. Notice how high the horse carries his tail when moving. Ask someone to put a hand under the dock and hold the tail up to this height while you measure the length and cut accordingly with a pair of large, sharp scissors. A good, practical length is just below the point of the hock when the tail is carried.

Heels

Heels that are rather hairy may be tidied up by discreet use of scissors and comb. This takes practice, but it is much better than clipping the back of the legs, because it doesn't shave them closely. The fetlock hair acts as a downpipe to prevent water from running into the heels and the backs of the pasterns. Horses with white legs are especially sensitive in these regions, and removing too much of this hair can be a major cause of cracked heels and mud fever.

Comb up, scissors down
when trimming heels.

99

PLAITING MANES AND TAILS

Requirements

A bucket of water and a water brush.

A large, blunt needle or a bodkin.

Thread or wool the colour of the hair. (Wool is less liable to break the hair.)

A comb and a pair of scissors.

A box may be needed to stand on.

Method

Mane. As mentioned above, the mane is easier to plait if it is pulled fairly short. Brush out well, then wet it along its whole length and divide into the number of parts you want to plait. These divisions may be temporarily secured with rubber bands. There is no set number for plaits, though traditionally it should be an even number, including the forelock. Skilful plaiting can make a big difference to the appearance of a horse's neck — for instance, if it is rather short and thick, more, smaller plaits can make it look longer.

A. Starting the plait. B. Secure the end, turn it under and sew. C. Turn the plait under again, sew and finish off neatly. No. 1 is a good plait. No. 2 has been turned under too far, making it lumpy. No. 3 is secured with a rubber band — permissible for most occasions, apart from turnout classes, provided the band is narrow and matches the colour of the hair.

Hairs too short to plait at the wither end may be trimmed off with scissors, and about 2cm of mane may be cut out behind the ears for the bridle headpiece, but don't let these areas extend further than is strictly necessary.

Tail. There are several methods of plaiting tails. A good one is shown below.

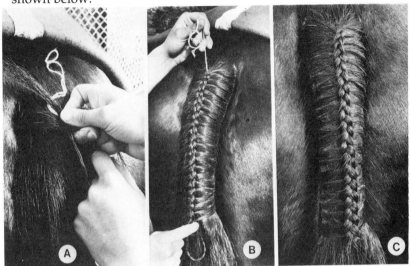

A. Lay a length of doubled string on the horse's rump, with the loop hanging down the middle of his tail. Take strands of hair from each side to start the plait. Continue, making an underhand plait, down the length of the tail. B. Tie a knot, put the plaited end through the loop of string and pull it up under the centre plait as far as it will go. Remove the string by pulling one end. C. The finished plait.

NOTE. It is quite correct for showing and other special occasions to have a plaited mane with a pulled tail. But if the tail is plaited, the mane must be plaited, too.

Never leave mane or tail plaited for any longer than necessary. The only exception is the untidy mane which refuses to lie on the side required. Plaiting it fairly loosely without turning it under and leaving it plaited for about twenty-four hours will help.

CLIPPING

Unless the horse has an exceptionally fine coat, some form of clip will almost certainly be necessary if he is in regular work during the winter. With a long, heavy coat there will be excessive sweating and a constant danger of chills, due to the difficulty of drying him off after work. Excessive sweating also causes rapid loss of condition.

It is important to choose the type of clip to suit the horse, the work required and the climatic conditions.

On no account should horses be clipped right out merely for appearance or for the owner's convenience.

Types of Clip

The belly clip. Suitable for ponies/horses who are not in particularly hard work. Especially useful for those who are ridden after school or work, and could otherwise be turned out wet at night. The hair is removed from the parts that sweat the most — under the throat, on the chest, round the girth, under the belly and between the legs. The only clip that should ever be used for an uncovered horse.

The trace clip. The best clip for most horses living out. Enables them to do harder work, such as regular schooling, occasional hunting or novice horse trials, without discomfort or loss of condition; but still leaves the full natural protection on the upper parts of the body.

(The above clips are shown in *Manual One*, pages 149 and 150.)

The blanket clip. Useful for heavier-coated horses in hard work — e.g. hunting regularly, area trials, championships, etc. In cold districts a neck cover must be provided.

Blanket clip.

The hunter clip. The hair is left on the legs, for warmth and protection, and on the saddle patch.

Hunter clip.

The full clip. The horse is clipped 'right out' — i.e. the entire coat is removed.

The last two are most suitable for stabled horses, or at least for those living in warmer areas and sheltered paddocks. In cold conditions, it is most unwise to clip a horse who lives out over his back and loins. The weight of covers needed to keep him warm will be very tiring, especially when they get wet, he will be liable to chills and will also require more feed for warmth. When riding, never keep a clipped horse standing about in the cold.

When to clip. When the winter coat has 'set' — usually late March - early April. If clipped before this, the horse will soon need clipping again. If he carries a very heavy coat and the first clip is done as early as possible, he could be given a hunter clip the first time, and thereafter be given a blanket or trace clip.

Rate of growth varies considerably, but clipping generally needs to be repeated every month to six weeks. Never clip once the horse begins to change his coat in the spring — this would spoil his summer coat.

Preparing and presenting a horse for clipping. He must be as clean as possible: it may even be wise to wash him the day before, provided the weather is suitable. A horse must be perfectly dry for clipping — the clippers won't cut if the hair is even slightly damp, and dirt and scurf in the coat will clog them up and blunt them.

Be sure to tell the person who is clipping your horse exactly what type of clip you want.

(For further details of clipping and clipping machines, see page 210.)

THE FOOT AND SHOEING

Manual One, pages 150-4, gives basic information on the horse's foot, the necessity for regular shoeing, types of shoes, and what to look for in a newly shod foot. Although you may be fortunate enough to have a qualified farrier, you should still study the subject further, so that you can do everything possible to safeguard your horse's feet.

SHOES

For types in normal use, see *Manual One*, page 153. Further points to note:

Clips should be fairly small and rounded, not sharp. Toe clips are used in front, quarter clips are preferable behind because:

1. There is more twisting action on the hind feet, and the two clips help to keep the shoe in place.

2. If a horse over-reaches, a toe clip causes far more damage.

Heels. If too long on the front shoes, the horse may tread on them and pull the shoe off; if too short or too finely pencilled, the shoe will be liable to slip in onto the 'corn place'.

The heels are sometimes turned down, or preferably doubled over on the hind shoes only, to give the horse more grip on steep country. This should be done in the form of a 'calkin and wedge'. With the carefully shaped wedge on the inside, the horse is less likely to hit himself.

Hind shoe, showing
A. calkin and B. wedge.

Disadvantages of 'heels': 1. Danger of injury to other horses and to people, if the horse kicks or treads on them.

2. If used much on the road, heels soon wear down.

Heels are not nearly so helpful for giving grip in jumping as screw-in studs.

Bearing surface. It is absolutely essential that any shoe should have a level bearing surface, against the horse's foot. To check this, hold the shoe up and look at it edgeways.

Readymade Versus Handmade Shoes

'Readymades' are available in concaves or in road shoes. They are widely used, and although adequate in many cases, they have certain disadvantages, including:

1. The concaves are all made of the same weight of steel, which is rather light for the larger sizes. They generally do not last as long as handmade shoes, which will give one or even two removes.

2. They are not usually available with quarter clips or with heels, if required, and the light steel will not take a thread for screw-in studs.

For treks and other long journeys, readymade road shoes may be perfectly satisfactory. For hunting, jumping and eventing, it is better to have the horse's shoes made for him, particularly if he has any foot or action problems.

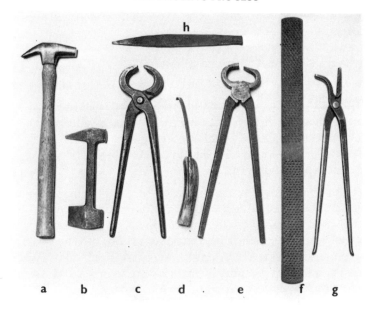

The farrier's tools. A. Shoeing hammer. B. Buffer. C. Pincers. D. Drawing knife.
E. Cutters (some have two sharp edges). F. Rasp. G. Clencher, H. Pritchel.

There are five stages in shoeing:

1. Removal

The clenches are cut with the buffer and shoeing hammer, then the shoe is eased off, starting at the heel, with the pincers. Any nails left in the foot are tapped out with the pointed end of the buffer.

Faults that may occur. Clenches not cleanly cut, so that the foot is damaged as the rough ends are pulled through.

2. Preparation

Ragged pieces of sole and frog are removed with the drawing knife. The cutters may be needed to remove excessive growth of horn, then the rasp is used to provide a level bearing surface. It is essential that the natural proportions of the foot should be maintained. A small 'v' is cut for the clip.

Faults that may occur: a. excessive use of the knife on sole, bars or frog. This weakens the foot and can lead to loss of frog pressure and contracted heels. (See page 136.)

b. too much or too little shortening of the toe or heel, or on the outside or inside of the foot. This can throw the whole leg out of balance.

c. the place for the clip badly cut, especially if it is too big or too deep. Weakens the foot, and can be a contributory cause of seedy toe. (See page 240.)

3. Fitting

The farrier selects the weight and type of shoe most suitable for the horse and the work he is doing.

Faults: Shoe too heavy — tiring for the horse, and can cause or aggravate brushing, especially in young or unfit horses.

Shoe too light — they will wear out or break before they have given a reasonable period of wear.

Hot shoeing allows a much closer fit, and is therefore to be preferred. The hot shoe is brought on a pointed instrument called a 'pritchel' and pressed briefly on the foot. The resultant singeing shows whether the shoe is in contact all round, or whether further adjustment is necessary. The length of heel is also checked. Hot shoes are easily adjusted by the farrier. When a perfect fit has been achieved, the shoe is cooled off ready for nailing.

Fault: Excessive burning may occur, which causes brittleness.

Cold shoeing. The shoe is measured against the foot, and the fitting judged as accurately as possible. While some limited adjustment can be made in the way of opening or closing the branches of the shoe, this may weaken a cold shoe if overdone.

4. Nailing On

Nails must be driven between the white line and the edge of the wall. They should come out 3-4cm up the hoof, and should be level. The nails are twisted off to form the clenches. It is important that the nails used are the right size to fill the holes completely, and that they are driven right home.

Faults: a. clenches too low, called 'fine nailing'. The shoes will be liable to come off before long, possibly taking part of the foot as well.

b. clenches too high, 'coarse nailing'. There is an obvious danger of pricks and nail binds.

c. nails, too big, may damage the foot; too small, not driven home, the shoes will probably come loose before long.

5. Finishing

The clenches are smoothed off, and a 'bed' made for them with the rasp. They are then tightened with the hammer and pincers or with a clencher. The clips are lightly tapped back, and finally the rasp is run round the lower edge of the wall.

Faults: a. 'dumping'. This sometimes happens if the horse's toe overlaps the shoe, either because the shoe is too small, or because the toe was not correctly shortened from underneath during the preparation of the foot. In order to make the foot fit the shoe, the wall is rasped straight downwards. This does great damage to the shape and balance of the foot and to the horn, which will soon become brittle and liable to crack. *Any* rasping of the wall removes the protective coating of the foot, and should be kept to a minimum on the lower third of the foot.

b. excessive tightening of the clenches: will often make the horse go sore after shoeing. Happens very easily with a clencher in unskilled hands.

c. daylight showing at any point between the foot and the shoe. This shows that one or the other does not have a level bearing surface, and the shoe was not correctly fitted. Allows grit to work in between foot and shoe.

As will be seen from the above, shoeing is a highly skilled process, not to be undertaken lightly by the uninitiated!

YOU AND YOUR FARRIER

1. First of all, try to find a qualified person, preferably a member of the Master Farriers Association. Members are tradesmen who have served an apprenticeship of 8000 hours and have a sound, practical knowledge of the anatomy of the horse's foot and the whole science of shoeing. Shoeing can have such an influence on your horse's health, happiness and performance that it is well worth any extra trouble and expense to take him to a qualified farrier.

The effects of bad shoeing can cause permanent disability.

2. If the farrier visits you, always have the horse caught up and ready, with clean feet. If you have an appointment at the forge, be punctual.

3. Tell the farrier what work the horse is doing, if he has any problems such as forging, over-reaching or brushing, and if he has been in any way lame or sore since he was last shod. It may help to run him up in hand for the farrier to observe his action.

4. Stay to hold the horse and watch the shoeing. If you show interest, the farrier may tell you a great deal about your horse's feet and why he shoes him as he does. If he has time, he may even show you how to remove a shoe. It is most useful to be able to do this in an emergency.

5. Keep a record of shoeing dates, and ring your farrier in plenty of time. If you are unable to get the horse shod within six weeks, watch for risen clenches, pressure on the 'corn place' and excessively long toes. The latter throw great strain on the back tendons, and

when the toes are cut back, the stress on tendons and ligaments will be completely altered. Even if the horse is not sore, care must be taken for the next few days, until he readjusts. You must make every effort to avoid this situation.

Good farriers are not easily found. If you have one, follow his advice carefully, make any requests tactfully and learn all you can.

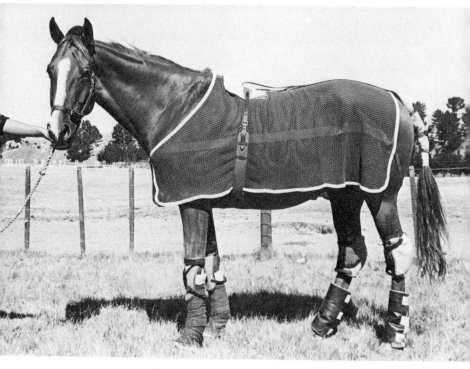

Horse fully equipped for travel.

7

TRAVELLING, CARE AWAY FROM HOME, STABLING (B)

TRAVELLING

For travelling to shows or horse trials, preparation starts a few days beforehand.

1. Check all gear, to allow time for repairs if needed.

2. Check the horse's shoes. Avoid last-minute shoeing, in case of pricks.

The day before. Clean all equipment thoroughly, pack up as much as possible. A lock-up trunk or chest is invaluable to keep everything safe and tidy when away. Stick a list of requirements inside the lid, and tick off as packed. You will need:

Saddlery (carefully checked) with spare girth, leathers, reins.

Grooming, plaiting and tack cleaning kit.

Spare covers, bandages, first-aid kit.

Possibly spare shoes and studs.

Two buckets, feed box, hay net.

Sufficient hay and hard feed for the journey, and, if feasible, for the whole time you are going to be away (to avoid change of diet).

Shovel and broom for mucking out float. **If stabling,** other tools, depending on type of bedding (see page 114).

PREPARING THE HORSE FOR TRAVEL

Requirements

1. Halter and rope.

2. Covers — depending on the float, the weather and what the horse normally wears.

3. Tail bandage or guard will be needed in most floats to protect the tail from rubbing (see page 287).

4. Protection for the legs — essential if:

a. there are no partitions between horses, or the partitions do not go down to floor level.

b. the horse is a bad or restless traveller.

c. the vehicle is cold or draughty.

d. the journey is a long one, or over rough roads, when the horse may become leg-weary and less able to maintain his balance, and therefore more likely to tread on himself.

Either bandages or boots may be used (see page 284).

In horse transporters, where the padded stalls give close support and protection all round, but horses may not be readily accessible once loaded, it is probably wiser not to use bandages or boots.

5. Knee caps (see page 288).

6. Poll guard — should always be used if headroom is inadequate or doorways low — anywhere there is a possibility of the horse hitting his poll if he throws his head up.

LOADING AND UNLOADING

(See *Manual One*, pages 142-3.)

If the horse is difficult to load, the following may help:

1. Park so that the ramp is as enclosed as possible — up against a fence, for instance, but make sure there is no chance of legs getting caught between ramp and fence. If the ramp is slippery, rubber matting or straw spread over it will help to give better footing and also deaden sound.

2. Have the front access door open, so that the horse can see through. Open the central partition wide.

3. Load another horse first, if one is available.

4. A snaffle bridle gives more control than a halter, especially if the horse tries to whip round. Put the bridle on over the halter, then it can easily be slipped off once in the float.

5. Have feed in a dipper or small bucket, and only allow the horse to have a mouthful when he moves forward.

6. Ask somebody to lift the horse's forefeet alternately and 'walk' him up the ramp.

Be quiet, but very firm. It is important that nobody, other than the person leading the horse, should get in front of his line of vision.

If none of these measures are effective, seek more experienced assistance.

Never attempt to ride a horse on to a float.

Once the horse is in, the breech strap or bar should be secured and the ramp put up as quickly as possible. Give the remainder of the feed as a reward, and tie him up short, using a quick release knot. If the horse is restless, it is best to get moving immediately.

Never travel inside the float with the horse.

Difficult horses should be loaded as often as possible at home, and fed on the float.

Care on the Journey

Check from time to time that the horse is not too hot or too cold, and adjust covers as necessary. Providing he loads easily, take him off for a leg stretch, a drink and a pick of grass every two or three hours. This will also give him an opportunity to stale (urinate).

Except when travelling to hunts or competitive events, a haynet should be available. It will help to pass the time and keep the horse happy.

NOTE. Some people disagree with the practice of feeding horses while travelling, as they fear the risk of choking.

ACCOMMODATION AWAY FROM HOME

This will be paddock, stable or yard, or possibly a combination of these. Always:

1. Make arrangements in advance. If stabling, find out what bedding will be available, so you will know what tools to take.

2. If you are going to arrive late, advise beforehand.

3. On arrival, contact the person in charge of accommodation.

4. Don't take facilities for granted. Ask where you may go with your horse, and where to park vehicles.

5. Report any damage that you cause, so it can be remedied.

6. Leave everything tidy before departure.

7. Pay your dues!

Paddock

Advantages. 1. It is what most horses are used to, so will involve the least change of lifestyle and of diet, *provided* the quality and quantity of grass is similar to that in the home paddock.

2. It may be easier to care for the horse — but see 3 and 4 below.

Disadvantages. 1. The horse may gallop about, with risk of injury and loss of condition. If he is on his own but can see or hear other horses, he may try to jump out to get to them.

2. There is a risk of injury and possible infection if he is turned out with strange horses.

3. The horse is less readily available than in a box or yard, especially if he is difficult to catch!

4. He may be wet and muddy.

5. Severe upsets may result if the grass is much richer than he is accustomed to.

If the horse is to be paddocked, make every effort to arrive in daylight. It is most unwise to put a horse out in a strange place after dark. You must check the paddock for safety and for water, and the horse should be allowed to explore it in daylight so that he is aware of boundaries and any hazards, such as trees and ditches.

If possible, exercise the horse before turning him out. Stay and watch him until he has settled down. If there are other horses and kicking matches develop, you *must* get your horse out and find somewhere else to put him. Separating mares and geldings often makes life more peaceful for everybody.

Yards

Advantages. 1. The horse is readily available.

2. His grass intake is restricted — essential in some cases.

3. You have a handy base for feeding, grooming, plaiting, etc.

Disadvantages. 1. Danger of injury from kicking, biting and infection, if in contact with neighbours. If the yard is large, people may put other horses in with yours.

2. Exposure, lack of comfort, especially in small yards with a metal surface or badly drained.

3. Change of diet. (See Note on page 116.)

4. It is often difficult to provide sufficient water.

Useful as yards are at home, their suitability for fulltime accommodation when away depends on their size, surface and safety, and on weather conditions.

Management in yards. Always check for poisonous plants and for barley grass, which may cause colic. Also check soundness of fencing and gates, and that there is nothing on which a horse could injure himself, such as projecting nails.

Keep feed and water out of reach of neighbouring horses.

Water buckets must be tied to prevent their being knocked over.

Extra covers may be needed, possibly including a neck cover, as the restricted movement leaves the horse unable to keep himself warm.

See that the horse is grazed daily, or provided with several armfuls of cut grass.

Keep yards scrupulously clean at all times.

Handling rules in stables apply (see page 117). If there are slip rails instead of a gate, make sure they are pushed right back when taking the horse in or out.

Stables

Advantages: 1. The horse is safe.

2. He is protected from the elements and has a comfortable bed.

3. He is always available, dry and relatively clean.

Disadvantages: 1. He may be unsettled if unaccustomed to confinement. May possibly go off his feed.

2. More time and skill are required in caring for him.

3. Increased risk of infection — coughs, colds, skin diseases — from previous occupants of the box, or from neighbours.

4. Change of diet — need not be a major problem provided precautions are taken.

Stabling is often the best choice, sometimes there is no alternative. The ideal, if possible, would be to have a fairly small paddock on his own or with friends at night, with a box as a daytime base, which could be used fulltime in adverse weather.

If stabling, it is again important to try to arrive in daylight. Lighting may be inadequate or non-existent, and the horse naturally unwilling to enter a dark, unknown place. Bedding down and settling him will be difficult.

STABLE MANAGEMENT

Points to check in a loose box:

Doors. Stable doors should be made in two sections, opening outwards. To ensure plenty of fresh air, especially important for the horse who normally lives out, leave the top door open *unless*:

1. The bottom door is too low — minimum height should be 1.37m.

2. The horse is very unsettled and appears likely to try to jump out.

3. You are worried about outside disturbances.

Check that the top and bottom catches on the lower door are fastened whenever the horse is left.

Floor. If there is bedding down already, check that it is clean and does not contain dangerous objects such as bits of baling twine. Floors are usually made of earth or concrete — if the latter, make especially sure that the horse has plenty of bedding.

Walls. Check the inside carefully for nails or other projections that could injure the horse, and remove them.

Manger. If you intend to use it, check for sharp edges and scrub it out. If your horse is used to eating from ground level, he will probably prefer his own feedbox or tub.

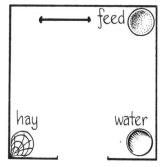

A good arrangement. Water bucket where it can be easily checked. Haynet on same side as door and water minimises disturbance to bed. Feed at back of box, either corner, away from outside influences. Always put feed container and water bucket (with the handle turned **away** from the horse) in corners.

113

BEDDING

The usual materials are straw, shavings or sawdust. Hay must never be used for bedding.

Straw

Tools required:

Two or three tine fork. The tines should be blunted.

A stiff broom.

A shovel — the square, not the rounded, type.

A 'drop skep' for picking up droppings. A plastic laundry basket or an old bucket will do quite well for this, or a split sack may be more convenient when travelling.

Split sack for removing dirty bedding when mucking out.

Use of stable tools. Ask somebody to show you how to use stable tools. As with everything else, there are right and wrong ways of using them. Be particularly careful with the fork — never point it towards the horse.

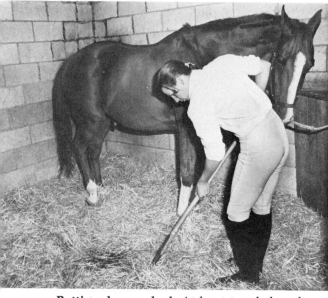

If you have to use the fork close to the horse, do it like this.

Putting down a bed. At least two bales of straw will be needed to start off a bed.

Method. Remove string from bales and put it safely away. Shake up the straw with the fork so that there are no lumps, then spread it evenly over the floor, not in clumps, a little thicker round the outside. Push up the edges to form banks, which help to keep out draughts.

114

Test for thickness with the fork — it should not strike through to the floor. If the straw is dusty, damp it slightly, especially if your horse has wind problems. (See page 235.) If he shows signs of eating it, damp with dilute disinfectant.

Mucking out. The thorough daily clean-out, usually done first thing in the morning.

Method. Tie the horse up, or remove him if practicable. Take out the water bucket, hay net and feed container; put your split sack in the doorway.

Use two sides of the box on alternate days to pile up the clean bedding — pick up any droppings from these sides first. Work from the edges into the middle, removing wet straw and droppings as you go. Sweep the floor thoroughly, sprinkle with disinfectant or lime. If the horse is out, leave the bed up to air the floor, otherwise put down enough bed to prevent his slipping. Take dirty bedding to muck heap and sweep up outside box.

Picking up droppings. Either use the fork, or get your hands either side of the droppings, with a layer of straw underneath, and flip them into the drop skep. Always pick them up immediately if the horse makes droppings when you are in the vicinity.

Bedding down. Best done after work, to encourage the horse to lie down. Pick up droppings and obvious wet patches, shake the bed up and top up with fresh straw to maintain depth. Bank up well.

Sawdust or Shavings

Tools required:
Rake — a wire or plastic leaf rake is most useful.
Shovel, drop skep, split sack — as for straw bedding.

Mucking out. Pick up all droppings, obvious wet patches and bits of hay. Use the rake for the hay and droppings, the shovel for the wet patches. Remove in split sack. Do not pile up as for straw, but leave otherwise undisturbed.

Droppings *must* be picked up frequently, as they quickly get mixed up with this type of bedding.

Bedding down. Remove droppings, rake up to prevent the bed becoming too tightly packed and lumpy. Top up as needed, banking up the sides as much as possible.

In general. Never go away leaving tools in the loose box when the horse is in it, or the door open, even if he is tied up.

Always keep the stable yard, or at least the area outside your horse's box, tidy.

A set routine is essential for a horse who is stabled regularly (see page 222). This is difficult to establish at trials or shows, where the horse may be competing at all hours, but try to have as many 'fixed points' during the day as possible. For instance, start early so that the horse can be mucked out, fed and groomed while things are quiet — the quieter it is, the more likely he will be to eat up. Keep as close as you can to his regular feeding times, bearing in mind that he must have finished his feed at least an hour before any class — two hours before cross country. The biggest feed and the bulk of the hay should be given at night. Visit him last thing at night to see that all is well. See below.

NOTE. A horse who is used to living out must be held out or turned out to graze for at least an hour daily, not necessarily all at once, or given a good supply of cut grass — otherwise there is a real risk of colic or constipation.

What to Look for First Thing in the Morning and at Night

a.m. Obvious injuries, filling and/or heat in legs. General appearance and alertness. Whether feed and hay have been cleared up, how much water has been drunk. Whether the horse has been lying down — shown by stains on coat or cover and bedding in tail. Quantity and type of droppings — loose, constipated.

p.m. State of feed, hay, water, bedding. Empty and refill water bucket and tidy bed if necessary. Check whether the horse is warm enough or too hot, or has broken out. Be very quiet and cause as little disturbance as you can during this visit.

Breaking Out

The horse breaks out in a cold sweat some time after he has been returned to his box after exercise.

Possible causes: Exhaustion, horse not properly cooled off, stuffy box or horse unaccustomed to stables. Usually occurs in highly strung horses.

To avoid this, make every effort to bring the horse in cool and calm. Being led out for half an hour's grazing may help.

If you find the horse wet, take off his cover and put on a sweat sheet or a layer of straw over his back, then throw the cover loosely over the top. This allows air to circulate underneath so that he cools off without getting chilled. Then dry his ears by 'stripping' them — gently pulling them with your hands. Rub him down with a towel over head, neck, throat, chest and shoulders. If he is still damp, and weather and circumstances permit, lead him out for a few minutes. Remove the straw or sweat sheet when dry, and put on a fresh cover.

116

Covers when stabled. Use your discretion about this. The horse is sheltered from the elements in a box, but he is unable to move around and keep himself warm. If the box is draughty, he may need his normal cover, or even an extra one. If it is stuffy because the top door has to be kept shut, he may only need a light sheet. Being too hot can contribute to breaking out.

Handling Horses in Stables

As always, be quiet but quite firm and definite, so that the horse is in no doubt as to what you want him to do. Insist on good manners, never allow the horse to push you about.

Tie the horse up short when mucking out, bedding down, grooming, saddling up, etc. Never leave him loose when saddled up.

It is useful to teach a horse to move his hindquarters over when tied up. Stand by his head, keep it slightly towards you, then push him over with your hand in the girth area, saying 'Over' as you do so. He will soon learn to step across when told, even when you are not at his head.

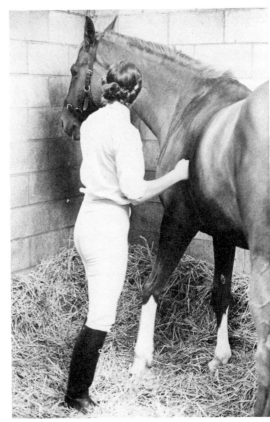

'Putting the horse over' in the stable.

Leading in and out of a loose box. Fasten both sections of the door back. If this is not possible, keep yourself between the horse and the door. The horse must be square on to the doorway. Face him to ensure that he comes through straight and doesn't bump a hip on the doorpost. This could cause serious injury, so be especially careful if the doorway is narrow. If the horse is saddled, stirrups *must* be run up.

Never mount a horse in a box, or ride him into one.

Never put more than one horse into a box.

A 'Cast' Horse

A horse gets 'cast' when he has lain down rather close to the wall and rolled over, so that he can neither roll back again nor get up. He will probably be kicking and struggling violently.

If it happens, don't panic, but get help at once. Meanwhile, talk quietly to the horse to calm him.

SMOKING

If you must smoke, NEVER, NEVER do so in or around stables or barns where hay and bedding are stored. Fires start and spread with appalling speed in these inflammable surroundings, especially in wooden buildings. This is one rule that must *never* be broken.

These notes are intended to help when travelling or when you wish to stable your horse for a short period. (For fuller information on stable construction and routine, see page 218.)

8
HEALTH (B)

Chapter 12, *Manual One*, provides ready reference for signs of health, symptoms, causes and treatment of common injuries and ailments. It is important to know this chapter thoroughly, and also to increase your practical experience so that you can avoid potentially dangerous or harmful situations, notice early symptoms and carry out different types of treatment. While minor problems can often be treated by the owner, you must know when to send for the vet, be able to give him clear information and follow instructions efficiently.

You should now have formed the habit of checking all signs of health automatically whenever you see your horse, so that you will be immediately aware if something is amiss.

There are three other important indications of a horse's state of health. These are temperature, pulse and respiration.

Temperature. A horse's normal temperature is 38°C (100-100.5°F). It is always helpful if a sick horse's temperature can be taken and any rise reported, but get an experienced person to do this. (For method of taking the temperature, see page 228.)

Pulse. Between 36 and 42 beats per minute, though ponies and young horses may be as high as 45. The pulse rate is the rate at which the heart is pumping the blood, so it is felt most easily where an artery passes over a bone. It may be felt just in front of the cheek, on the inside of the lower jaw, where the facial artery passes over the jaw bone. Apply the middle finger gently to press the artery against the inner surface of the bone.

A horse's pulse is softer and slower than most animals, and it can be hard to feel. Ask an experienced person to help you to find the exact spot. Don't forget your thumb has a pulse of its own, so you must take the horse's pulse with a finger, to avoid confusion! Use very light pressure.

Respiration — from 8 to 15 breaths per minute. Watch the flank to count respiration — count either the 'ins' or 'outs', not both. It is useful to know your own horse's normal pulse and respiration rates so that:

1. You can report any abnormalities if he is sick.
2. You can check how quickly they return to normal after exertion. The quicker the recovery rate, the fitter the horse.

Detection of Lameness

Any signs of lameness should be investigated immediately.

Identifying the lame leg. Ask somebody to run the horse up in hand (see page 93) so that you can watch and listen for any unevenness of stride. If lame in front, he will nod his head as the sound leg comes to the ground, and this beat will sound heavier.

Lameness behind is harder to detect, but he may take a shorter stride at the walk, drag the toe or swing the affected leg wider than the sound one.

Finding the trouble. Begin with the foot. Clean it out thoroughly and search carefully for anything that may have been picked up in sole or frog. Notice any offensive smell. Feel both feet with the palm of your hand, to see if one is warmer than the other. Tap gently with a light hammer on each of the clenches — if he flinches on any of them, feel again for heat around it. Look for signs of bruising or over-reach round the heel.

Then work up the leg, coronet, pastern, fetlock joint, tendons and ligaments. Constantly compare the two legs, looking for the three signs of trouble — heat, swelling and tenderness. Pick the foot up, and gently pinch each of the tendons between the knee and fetlock — you should be able to feel them as distinct and separate hard cords. If the horse flinches at any point, keep going, then come back to that spot again. Pick up the other leg and feel it in the same way. Some horses are ticklish and will flinch equally on both, but most will give a distinct snatch when you get to the sore place. Feel along the cannon bone, too, for signs of heat or soreness, which could indicate the start of a splint (see page 128).

REPORTING A SICK OR INJURED HORSE'S SYMPTOMS

If in doubt about the necessity for a visit from the vet, ring up and describe the symptoms clearly over the telephone, so that the vet may decide.

Sickness

In all cases, it will be helpful if you can tell the vet:

1. The history of the ailment, when first noticed and the cause, if known.

2. If the horse is off his feed, drinking more or less than usual.

3. Droppings — normal, loose, constipated?

4. Urinary problems, especially difficulty in staling or dark coloured urine.

5. Changes in the horse's normal pulse and respiration.
6. Stiffness or difficulty in moving. Filling in all four legs.
7. Abnormal behaviour, especially excitement, nervousness or lethargy.
8. Changes in diet or routine.
9. Any treatment already given. It is essential that the vet should know about this. In addition, for:

Coughs. When does the horse cough: constantly, when first ridden, during or after exertion? Type of cough: hard, soft, deep, causing distress, gasping or choking? Is it accompanied by cold and discharge from the nose?

Colds. Nasal discharge, clear, thick, yellow? Whether constant or intermittent. Whether the horse is coughing or sneezing. In both coughs and colds, examine the glands under the throat and report any swelling, hardness or tenderness.

Colic. Constant or intermittent? Length and frequency of spasms. Whether the horse is sweating, kicking, wanting to roll. Whether he has passed any droppings.

Wounds, Kicks and other Injuries

The exact site, especially if on a joint or bony place.
The amount of bleeding and/or swelling.
Whether the horse is lame.
In the case of wounds which have been treated and appear to be healing, be sure to report any sudden increase in swelling, soreness or lameness. Check pulse, respiration and temperature, if possible, even if they were previously normal. Check for heat, discharge, pus, smell. If a dent remains after pressure from your finger on the swelling, or if the swelling goes up the leg above the wound, these are signs of infection, requiring urgent veterinary attention.

Lameness

The site, if known.
Constant or intermittent — does it go off or get worse with exercise?
At what pace(s) the horse is lame. Worse going up or downhill?
If there is swelling, whether it goes down with exercise.
Any unusual behaviour before the lameness was noticed, such as unwillingness to canter on a particular leg or to jump.
Even in emergency, try to report the situation calmly. The more accurate the information you give the vet, the better he can help your horse, especially if he is unable to come at once.

Don't ring the vet after hours, except in case of emergency or serious doubt.

Have the horse caught up, with halter and rope handy. Where possible, he should be brushed over, and feet must be picked out and scrubbed if the vet is to examine them.

Have hot water, soap and towel on hand.

Make sure that all relevant information, as above, is available.

Have a notebook and pencil. Check with the vet, and write down full details on the following:

Medication — how much, how often.

Other treatment. If dressings or bandaging are involved, ask exactly what is required, how often and the purpose to be achieved.

Feeding and exercise.

ADMINISTERING MEDICINE

In the feed is the easiest way, if the horse will eat. If the medicine is unpalatable, mix it first with molasses, treacle, icing sugar or anything else the horse specially likes, then add this mixture to the dampened feed.

Worm pastes usually come with their own 'gun' for dosing. Follow the directions on the packet, and if you have any difficulty, get help.

TREATMENTS

Bathing and Dressing Wounds

1. Collect everything needed.
2. Tie the horse up, or have somebody to hold him.
3. Wash your hands.
4. Remove dressings very gently. It may be necessary to swab them off with wet cotton wool or a clean cloth.
5. Bathe the area with cotton wool or clean cloth — not a sponge — using saline solution or whatever the vet orders. Never use strong antiseptics, detergents, or disinfectants. Horses are extremely sensitive to these things, which will delay healing and may cause severe irritation.
6. Dress or bandage according to vet's instructions. Except with puncture wounds, it is usually better to use antibiotic powder or ointment rather than wet the wound after the initial cleansing. Wetness may soften the wound and delay healing. Depending on severity, it may be necessary for the vet to give antibiotic injection.
7. If flies are bad, the following is a useful repellent:

Add half a teaspoonful of oil of citronella to a litre of water and a few drops of detergent to emulsify the mixture. Wipe sparingly round, but not over, the wound.

8. Untie the horse.
9. Burn all used dressings.
10. Clean any bowls or buckets used with disinfectant.
11. Wash your hands.

Hosing

May be done in two ways:

1. A gentle trickle to clean up a scratch or small wound, or to relieve soreness in acute bruising. (See *Manual One,* page 161.) The fine garden type spray, providing volume but little pressure, is ideal for this.

2. For relieving pain and reducing inflammation in sprains. In this case, the hose is used with much more pressure (as much as the horse will stand). Hold the nozzle about 1.5m from the leg and play the jet up and down over the affected area, both on the inside and outside of the leg. This provides an effective form of massage. It should be kept up for at least twenty minutes, two or three times a day. An excellent first aid treatment for severe sprains — may help to control swelling until the arrival of the vet.

This type of hosing is also good for horses working (particularly jumping) on hard ground, if their legs begin to show signs of windgalls or puffiness. When hosing, it is advisable to grease the heels with vaseline to prevent cracked heels, especially in horses with white legs, or if there is a cold wind.

Poulticing

Poultices are a means of applying continuous heat to wounds or bruises for the following purposes:

1. To 'draw' a puncture wound, and thereby remove pus, thorns, or other foreign bodies.

2. To clean up an infected wound of any type.

3. To reduce pain and inflammation.

They can only be used where they can be kept in position by a bandage. Among the most usual types of poultice are:

Animalintex — a proprietary brand of poultice, consisting of gauze, impregnated with a dressing and backed with cotton wool. To use it:

1. Cut off a piece big enough to cover the injured area plus about 3cm all round and lay it in a flat dish or tray. Pour on sufficient boiling water to soak it thoroughly, then let it cool until it is comfortable on the back of your hand. Wring out the surplus water.

2. Apply the dressing with the smooth, gauze side against the skin. Cover with plastic, foil or other waterproof material, a layer of gamgee or cotton wool and bandage. The bandage should be similar to a travel bandage, covering the whole leg from knee or hock to coronet, and just firm enough to keep it in place.

Antiphlogistine or Kaolin paste. Very soothing and with good drawing power. To apply it:

1. Remove the lid of the tin and replace it loosely, otherwise the steam may blow it off as the paste heats. Put the tin in a small pan with water about halfway up the side of the tin and heat until the paste is warm.

2. Spread the paste on a piece of lint or thick brown paper. Do not apply to the horse until it has cooled to a comfortable back-of-the-hand temperature.

3. Cover and bandage as in Animalintex 2.

Bran. Used for foot injuries, such as pricks or bruised sole.

1. Take about half a small bucket of bran. Dissolve a handful of epsom salts in boiling water and mix with the bran. Allow to cool.

2. If a poultice boot is available (see page 290), this is by far the best way of applying a poultice to the foot. Put a layer of bran in the boot, put the horse's foot in, then pack more bran round it, up to coronet level, and fasten the boot round the pastern. Failing this, several layers of sacking may be used, similarly fastened round the pastern. In this case, it would be preferable to keep the horse boxed or yarded so that he will not move about too much.

Poultices should generally be changed night and morning, unless the vet orders otherwise.

Tubbing. An alternative treatment for foot injuries. Method:

1. Use a rubber, heavy plastic or wooden tub or bucket, *not* a metal one, about two-thirds full of hot water to which a handful of epsom salts has been added. You must be able to bear your hand in it comfortably.

2. Grease the horse's heel with vaseline, then put his foot in the tub and keep it there for ten to fifteen minutes, topping up as needed with hot water to maintain the temperature. Repeat as often as possible, at least two or three times a day.

You may have to be quite firm about this at first, but most horses will stand happily once they realise how much relief this treatment gives to a sore foot.

Fomentation — a method of applying heat or cold to parts which cannot be bandaged or tubbed. Particularly useful for kicks and other bruises after initial application of cold water or ice packs.

Requirements: Hot water and epsom salts, as for tubbing. A towel or other large, fairly thick, cloth. Dip the cloth in the bucket, leaving the ends out, then wring it out by the ends. Apply to the injured area, warming up again as necessary. Ten to fifteen minutes, several times daily. If a cold application is required, use iced water.

WARNING. Great care must be taken in applying heat to horses. In spite of their hair, which might be thought to give some protection, they are very easily scalded, and cannot stand such high temperature as humans. If in doubt, cool it!

Ice packs are valuable for relieving acute inflammation. Ice and water in a plastic bag tied at the top and held or lightly bandaged in place makes a useful application. Alternatively, special packs may be obtained and stored in the freezer.

INTERNAL PARASITES

All horses have some internal parasites — worms and bots. They become infected when grazing, by swallowing eggs or larvae (immature worms), which can lie dormant in the grass for very long periods. The eggs or larvae hatch out and grow in the horse's intestines and other organs.

There are three main types of worms — redworms, roundworms and pinworms. (For life cycle of worms and bots see page 230.)

Redworms, especially the large type often called bloodworms, are by far the most dangerous — in fact, they are one of the major health hazards in horses.

Roundworms, although much bigger than bloodworms, cause little damage to mature horses, unless the worms are present in large numbers, but they are very dangerous to foals.

Pinworms cause irritation in the anal area and make the horse rub his tail.

The drugs used to control bloodworms are generally effective against these other types of worms as well.

Bots can be largely controlled by removing the eggs, which are laid on the horse's coat by the female botfly during the summer months, and by dosing in the autumn, after the botflies have disappeared.

Symptoms of heavy worm and/or bot infestation are:
1. Staring coat and tight skin (hidebound).
2. Poor condition, ribby and often pot-bellied. Even if the horse is being well fed, he will not be deriving the full benefit from his food. Young horses, and those already low in condition, are even more susceptible to damage by worms.

3. Lack of vitality, tiring quickly.

4. Gums and mucous membranes of the eye pale or bluish in colour. This is a sign of anaemia, often caused by bloodworms.

5. Attacks of colic — worms are one of the major causes of colic. The horse may also suffer from indigestion and frequent bouts of diarrhoea.

6. Persistent cough.

Treatment

Where there are only a few horses in roomy paddocks with other farm stock (e.g. a farm situation), dosing three or four times annually may be sufficient. In small paddocks or where horses are grazed continuously in large numbers, as in Pony Club paddocks or other shared grazing arrangements, dosing will be necessary *every six to eight weeks* throughout the year. Every horse owner must, according to circumstances, work out a programme to control this problem.

Points to bear in mind:

1. **Good paddock management.** Pick up droppings at least twice a week in small paddocks, don't overstock with horses, alternate with other stock whenever possible, lime and topdress regularly. Don't feed hay made from horse paddocks.

2. **Work with your vet.** There are several different drugs, or combinations of drugs, which are effective against worms, but if the same one is used continually, resistance will build up and it will lose its efficacy. Your vet will advise you what to use and how much to give. Occasionally stomach tubing may be necessary. *In no circumstances* must this be attempted by anyone but a veterinary surgeon.

3. **Check the effectiveness** of your treatment by having a sample of the horse's droppings tested twice a year. This is a good indication of the number and type of worms present. Your vet will arrange this.

4. **In shared grazing,** at Pony Club or elsewhere, co-operate fully in any communal worm control programme. Don't expect or allow any new horse to join the company without prior dosing.

'TYING-UP'

An ailment, the precise cause of which is not known at present. It affects the muscles of the loins and hindquarters, usually in horses who are in training for demanding work such as eventing or hunting, even though the feed and work schedule may appear normal and reasonable. It can occur when the horse is first mounted and ridden off, or sometimes if he is allowed to stand about after a gallop or other strenuous activity.

Symptoms

1. The horse is very stiff and hunched in his back, and the stride behind is shortened to such a degree that he may appear lame.

2. The muscles over the loins are rigid and painful.

3. There may be a rise in pulse and respiration rates. In bad cases, the horse may be sweating or blowing, with dilated nostrils.

Treatment

1. Dismount, slacken the girths. In cold weather, throw a cover, coat or jersey over the horse's loins.

2. Lead him about quietly. He should loosen up as he gets moving, and he may then be ridden slowly home, or continue with steady exercise, depending on when the attack occurred and its severity.

3. Consult your vet as soon as possible. Several treatments are available to help to relieve this disorder and prevent its recurrence. On no account continue with hard and fast work without veterinary advice, otherwise permanent harm could be done.

NOTE. If the horse does not improve with gentle exercise, but becomes staggery in his gait, keep him warm and still and try to get the vet urgently, as the symptoms could then be due to a similar but much more serious ailment called 'azoturia' (see page 234).

SPRAINS (STRAINS)

Sprains of the tendons and ligaments between the knee and fetlock, and of the fetlock joints of the forelegs, are a major cause of lameness and breakdown in eventers, hunters and other hard-working horses and ponies. Some knowledge of the causes, symptoms and prevention of sprains should assist in keeping your horse sound.

Causes

1. Lack of fitness for the work demanded, particularly failing to build up condition gradually after a spell.

2. Galloping or jumping in heavy or rough going, especially when the horse is tiring.

3. Bad riding — failing to keep the horse balanced (you must be just as fit as he is to give him the maximum help); flopping about in the saddle; turning too sharply; pulling up abruptly from a gallop.

4. The horse not up to the rider's weight.

5. The horse slipping or putting his foot in a hole. Jumping too many drop fences.

6. Poor foot care — allowing the toes to get too long.

Symptoms

Heat, pain and swelling may all be present. Usually very slight warmth and puffiness at first. If the first small symptoms are missed or ignored and work continued, the condition will be aggravated and pain and lameness will soon follow, with considerable swelling.

Prevention and Treatment

1. Get to know your horse's legs, so that any unusual symptoms however small, will be noticed immediately. Run your hands down his legs every day, before and after work.

2. If you find any sign of heat, soreness or swelling, even if the horse is perfectly sound at present, give walking exercise only and hose both legs night and morning until the symptoms subside. Opinions vary as to the advisability of bandaging for exercise, but if you do, be sure to bandage both legs.

3. If your horse is obviously tiring out hunting or on a cross country, pull up. It is never worth risking injury to horse or rider from this cause.

4. The day after a big effort (hunt, event, · etc.) examine legs thoroughly and run the horse up in hand to test for lameness.

5. If in doubt at any time, consult your vet. Immediate, expert treatment may save the situation. Meanwhile, rest the horse and hose him as often as possible. Your vet may recommend a firm, not tight, supporting bandage. This should be applied from below the knee to the coronet with gamgee underneath.

6. Remember that working a horse with a doubtful 'leg' can result in months off work or even in total breakdown and a permanently incapacitated horse.

SPLINTS

A splint is a bony enlagement (see page 244) on the cannon bone, the splint bone, or between two of these bones. Splints usually form on the inside of the foreleg, more rarely on the outside or on a hind leg. They are fairly common in young horses, whose bones are still forming and hardening, seldom occurring over the age of six, except possibly as a result of a kick or blow.

Causes

1. Concussion, especially in horses of upright conformation.

2. Overwork on immature limbs — galloping and jumping on hard ground or excessive weight on the back.

3. The horse hitting himself, due to weakness, tiredness, lack of balance or poor action.

128

Symptoms

Lameness. The horse may walk sound and trot lame; lameness may be intermittent, but it will certainly get worse with continued work. After a few days, there will usually be heat and very slight swelling on the bone, rather than on the tendons. There may be pain on pressure with a finger. Later, the bony enlargement will become quite plain to sight and touch.

Once formed, splints do not normally cause trouble, unless they are close to the knee or interfering with the tendons or suspensory ligament. They often disappear of their own accord in time, but may become large and permanent if the horse is worked while they are forming.

Treatment

While the splint is forming, rest the horse completely, or give walking exercise only if the horse is sound at this pace. Hose him at least two or three times daily to reduce inflammation. If lameness and inflammation persist after a few days, consult your vet.

Prevention

1. Always use brushing boots when lunging or riding young horses.

2. Avoid jumping or fast work on hard ground.

3. Be alert for early symptoms. Once a splint has formed, be especially careful with that horse in future.

4. Check shoeing — make sure there is adequate frog pressure and that the shoes are not too heavy.

5. Check diet. Mineral imbalance can lead to poor bone formation (see page 200), but consult your vet if in doubt.

For further information on health matters, see Chapter 17.

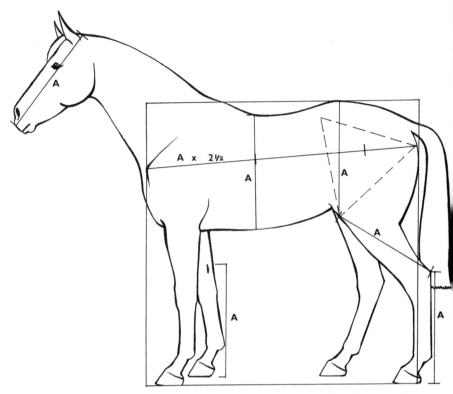

In a well-proportioned horse, the length of the head should equal the length of all the other 'A' lines. The dotted lines should also be of equal length.

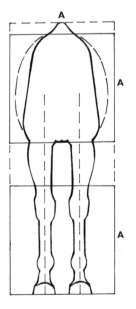

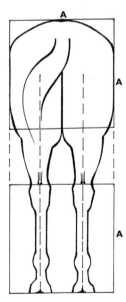

9

KNOW THE HORSE (B)

CONFORMATION AND ACTION

Conformation, or 'make and shape', concerns the structure of the horse. It affects his performance, 'ride' and soundness. A good knowledge of conformation is invaluable, helping you to understand why a horse may have certain problems in his training, and to avoid purchasing an unsuitable horse who may not be capable of performing the work required of him.

For a start, you should learn to:

1. Recognise good and bad points of conformation.
2. Know what is definitely to be avoided, so that,
3. With further experience, you will be able to form an accurate assessment of a horse's potential for different types of work.

Even if you are gifted with a natural 'eye for a horse', this assessment takes much practice.

General Impression, Balance and Proportion

1. **Outlook.** A horse should stand four square, with a bold but calm and kindly outlook, taking an alert and intelligent interest in his surroundings. He should not look nervy, aggressive or evil-tempered. *If the temperament is bad, the most perfect conformation counts for nothing.*

2. **Balance.** In a mature horse, the highest point of the wither should be higher than the croup, otherwise the horse will inevitably be on his forehand. (Young horses tend to grow in 'steps', and may at times be higher behind than in front.) He should stand with his hocks well under him, so that a line dropped from the buttock to the point of hock would continue down the back of the cannon bone to the ground.

3. **Proportion** — also affects the balance.

4. **Quality and substance.** Quality in a horse denotes elegance, fineness and speed. It comes mainly from thoroughbred blood, and shows in a small head, thin skin, fine coat, mane and tail, clean heels and fairly light, very flat 'bone'. (This refers to the cannon bone.) Taken to extremes, without substance, it can become weediness.

Substance denotes strength, sturdiness and weight-carrying capacity. It can come from common (draught horse) blood, in which case it may show in a large head, coarse coat, rounder bone, hairy heels, big feet and a generally heavier build. If this is taken to extremes, without quality, the horse will be slow and probably rather clumsy.

Consider the balance between these two — does the horse combine sufficient activity and speed for his work with sturdiness and the ability to carry the weight required, plus a reasonable degree of elegance and good looks?

Having formed a general impression, look at the horse in more detail, as follows. Common terms used to describe conformation are shown in inverted commas.

THE FOREHAND

PART	GOOD	UNDESIRABLE OR BAD
Head	Wide between the eyes. Broad across cheek, narrow at muzzle. Big nostrils.	Coarse, large and heavy. Bump on forehead — often denotes sullen or ungenerous temperament.
	General. 'Dish face' shows arab blood, 'roman nose' common blood.	
Eyes	Large, dark, prominent, alert. Confident, friendly expression.	Small, sunken, half-shut. Rolling constantly — indicates nervousness or temper.
	General. Deep hollows over the eyes are a sign of age.	
Neck	Top line longer than bottom line, more muscled above than below. Small dip in front of wither. Junction of head and neck must allow for flexion — 'Head well set on.'	Long and thin — weak. Short and thick — likely to pull; if combined with big head and low wither to be heavy and unbalanced. 'Ewe neck', top line concave, like a sheep. Likely to be above the bit.

General. Length and shape of neck combined with a good wither and shoulder are essential for 'good length of rein' — a self-explanatory term.

Head *well set on. Well laid shoulder.* Good *length of rein.*

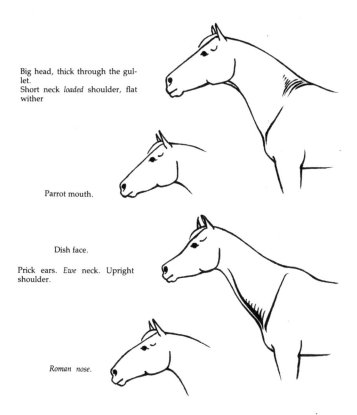

Big head, thick through the gullet.
Short neck *loaded* shoulder, flat wither

Parrot mouth.

Dish face.

Prick ears. *Ewe* neck. Upright shoulder.

Roman nose.

PART	GOOD	UNDESIRABLE OR BAD
Wither	Well-defined. Highest point behind elbow, and higher than croup.	Broad and flat — can spread saddle tree. Combined with 'loaded shoulder' (see below) gives poor balance and action. High and sharp — creates difficulties in fitting saddle.

General. Flat withers are often a problem with small ponies, 'knife' withers with thoroughbreds.

Shoulder	Lean and sloping, with well-defined point, 'well laid back'.	'Upright' or 'straight' — especially bad if combined with upright pasterns. Heavy and fleshy — 'loaded'.

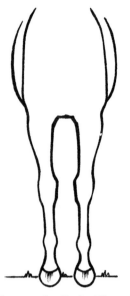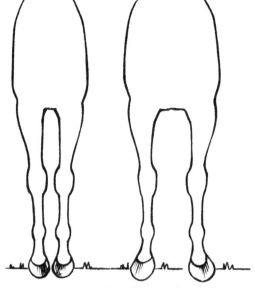

Well sprung ribs. Good width chest. Straight.

Slab sided. Narrow chest. *Calf* knees. *Pigeon* toed.

Wide chest. Splay feet.

PART	GOOD	UNDESIRABLE OR BAD
Chest from front	Moderately broad and deep.	Very narrow — poor stamina, due to lack of lung room. Very broad gives clumsy, lumbering paces.
Elbow	Free, well clear of the body and straight.	Close, fleshy — liable to gall, restricts freedom of action.
Forearm	Long, broad and muscular — 'well let down'. *General.* The forearm may appear weak, due to lack of muscle, if the horse is in poor condition.	
Knee	Broad and flat.	Small and round — 'calf knees'.
	Straight.	'Back at the knee' puts great strain on the tendons. 'Over at the knee', generally strong, but unsightly.
Cannon	Short, with flat bone. 'Clean' free from lumps and bumps, with tendons and ligaments standing	Long — excessive length of tendons makes for weakness. Round bone shows lack of quality.

PART	GOOD	UNDESIRABLE OR BAD
	out clearly. For 'good bone' circumference just below the knee should measure at least 20cm for a horse.	'Tied in below the knee'. A weakness — does not allow sufficient room for back tendons.
Fetlock joint	Clean and as flat as possible.	Round or puffy joints.

General. Windgalls or signs of brushing merit investigation.

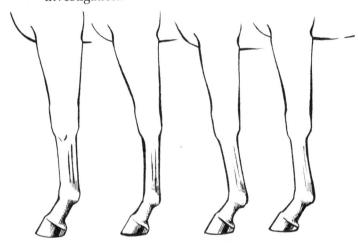

Well let down, good bone.　Back at the knee.　　Over at the knee.　Tied in below the knee.
Puffy joints.

Pastern	Medium length, and a slope of approximately 45 degrees.	Short and upright — liable to cause concussion injuries. Jarring ride. Long and sloping — comfortable ride, but liable to strain.
Feet	In proportion to size of the animal. Round, hard, smooth, preferably black. Slope approximately 50 degrees. Even in size and shape. Wide heels, large, firm but elastic frog, concave sole.	Narrow, upright — 'boxy' or 'donkey' feet. Soft or 'shelly' (brittle) often found in white feet. Uneven in any way. Turned in — 'pigeon- or pin-toed'. Turned out — 'splay-footed'. Contracted heels, small frog, flat or convex sole.

To sum up: The forehand carries three-fifths of the weight. Most problems arise from concussion. A well-proportioned head and neck, sloping shoulder and pastern, straight limbs and good feet will make for soundness, good balance and elasticity of movement.

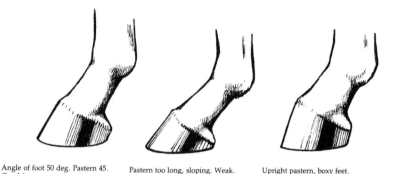

Angle of foot 50 deg. Pastern 45. Good foot.

Pastern too long, sloping. Weak.

Upright pastern, boxy feet.

Good frog and heels.

Small frog, contracted heels.

PART	GOOD	UNDESIRABLE OR BAD
	BODY	
Girth	'Deep through the heart' — i.e. good depth from wither to girth place, allowing heart and lung room.	Shallow — may lack stamina. May also appear 'on the leg' — i.e. legs too long in proportion to depth of body.
Ribs from front	'Well sprung' — i.e. rounded, to allow room for internal organs.	'Slab sided' — flat. Often goes with narrow chest.

PART	GOOD	UNDESIRABLE OR BAD
From side	'Well ribbed up' — there should just be room to insert fist between last rib and point of hip.	
Back	Should appear strong, especially over the loins. Well rounded along the spine.	Very long, weak over loins, not well ribbed up. 'Roach back', curving upward over loins. Strong but stiff. A hollow back is weak, usually a sign of age.

Good depth. Well ribbed up. Tail well set.

Roach back.

Lacking depth. Long back. *Herring gutted. Goose rump.* Tail set low.

Belly	Lower line of body should slope only slightly up towards the flank.	''Herring gutted' — excessive slope. Often goes with long, weak back. Not to be confused with 'run up' when in poor condition.

To sum up: Stamina depends on depth and well-sprung ribs. The body should give an impression of strength without being too heavy for the legs — 'heavy topped'.

HINDQUARTERS

PART	GOOD	UNDESIRABLE OR BAD
Quarters	Long, and sloping slightly from croup to dock. Many good jumpers are 'goose-rumped', with a high croup and sharply sloping quarters. Also called a 'jumping bump'.	Short, narrow and weak-looking. Cobs and sturdy ponies often have rounder quarters than horses.
Quarters from behind	Wide and well muscled. Hips absolutely level. Buttocks close and well rounded.	One hip higher than the other — probably due to injury. 'Split up behind' — wide space between buttocks.
Tail	Set high on quarters, carried proudly. Strong dock — should feel firm when lifted up.	Low, drooping tail carriage. Flabby dock.
Thigh	Hind leg long from hip to hock, 'well let down'. Thigh broad and muscular.	Short thigh, especially if combined with long cannon bone.
Hocks	Large, strong, set directly below buttocks, clean.	Small, 'curby' hocks — liable to curb — see page 245. 'Sickle hocks' — excessive bend, weak.
From behind	Must appear straight and level.	'Cow hocks' — turned in. Often seen in young horses. May cause strain in mature horses. 'Bowed hocks' — turned out. A weakness in any horse. Excessively straight hocks.
Cannon	As for foreleg, but will be longer.	Excessive length.
Fetlock Pastern	As for foreleg.	
Feet	Less round and a little more upright than forefeet.	Faults as for forefeet.

To sum up: The hindquarters supply most of the driving power in jumping and galloping. They also play a big part in braking. They must be strong enough to carry their share of the weight, not merely to push it. Most injuries occur from strain. Lack of muscle and condition must not be confused with genuine faults in conformation.

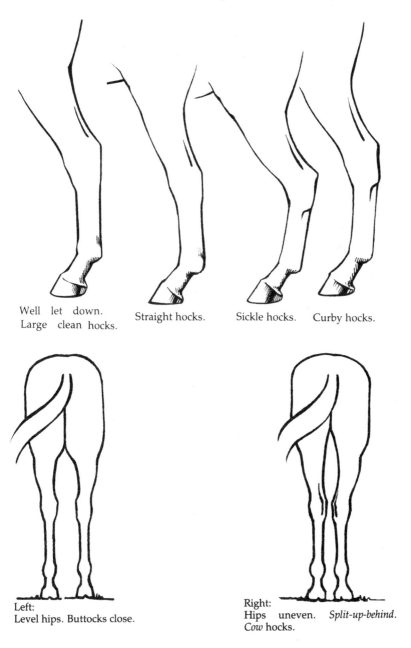

Well let down.
Large clean hocks.

Straight hocks.

Sickle hocks.

Curby hocks.

Left:
Level hips. Buttocks close.

Right:
Hips uneven. *Split-up-behind*.
Cow hocks.

PART	GOOD	UNDESIRABLE OR BAD

ACTION

GOOD	UNDESIRABLE OR BAD
Absolutely straight, light, even. Long, swinging stride, especially in walk, with good overstep. Good natural extension is a great advantage.	Any irregularity in the stride. 'Dishing' — throwing forelegs outwards. Little detriment in moderation, except for show horses, or for advanced dressage. 'Plaiting' — crossing fore or hind legs. May cause horse to strike himself. Short, choppy strides. High knee action. Brushing, stumbling.

General. Brushing and stumbling may occur due to tiredness in a young or unfit horse. Although boots may be used to protect the legs, these faults should be avoided when they are definitely due to poor action. A straight mover gives a better ride and is more likely to remain sound.

Rather than learning this table in a theoretical way, use it as a reference for practical application.

Start by analysing your own horse or one you know well. Look first at his overall proportions, then at the details. As well as good points, you are sure to find some faults — the perfect horse has yet to be foaled!

Then look at other horses in the same way. Shows, sales, Pony Club rallies all offer rich opportunities for observation and comparison. It may help to concentrate on one part at a time. Identify a good pair of hocks, then look for horses with sickle, straight, curby or cow hocks. Do the same with feet, knees, shoulders and other parts. (Be tactful with comments in the presence of the owner!) In this way, you will gradually become familiar with the various terms, and will begin to develop your 'eye for a horse'.

TEETH

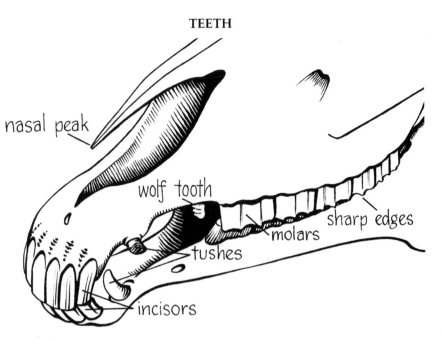

Incisors. Six in each jaw — total twelve. Pre-molars and molars. Six in each jaw on either side — twenty-four. Tushes (rarely in mares) two in each jaw — total four. Grand total — males, forty; females, thirty-six. Wolf teeth, if they occur at all, usually fall out at an early age. Otherwise, they may cause bitting problems and require veterinary attention. Note: 'sharp edges' on molars, caused by grinding action. Outside edge, upper jaw, inside edge, lower jaw.

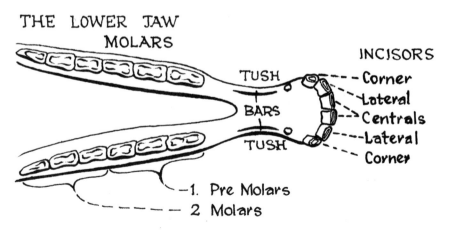

Teeth. See *Manual One*, page 163.

10
TEST SHEET: A CERTIFICATE

Minimum age: 17 years

Candidate must hold B Certificate

This is the highest award of the Pony Club. It provides a comprehensive examination in horsemanship and horse management for well-trained and experienced associate members.

Candidates must show that they can carry out in practice, in a logical sequence, all that they have learned from the New Zealand Pony Clubs Association manuals and from their instructors.

OBJECTIVES

To become an educated horseman, able to ride with confidence, style and polish on the flat and over fences.

To understand the principles of training, including young horses, as taught in the Pony Club, and be able to put these principles into practice.

To be capable of riding and jumping horses of all temperaments and stages of training, and of assessing a horse's potential and how it could be schooled to improve ride and performance. To gain wide knowledge of the care and conditioning of horses, and to be capable of taking charge of horses, either stabled or at grass, over a limited period.

To have sound knowledge of the organisation and running of the New Zealand Pony Clubs Association, including the candidate's own branch/club, and some knowledge of other societies and organisations connected with horses.

RIDING

Turnout of horse and rider.

Have a deep seat on the flat, and be able to apply aids unobtrusively and effectively.

Have a sound knowledge of training terms (e.g. impulsion, on the bit, etc.) and of the stages of training.

Show correct paces, with the horse on the bit.

Perform the following movements:

Medium trot and canter.

Demi-pirouette at walk.

Simple change of leg.

Counter canter.

Rein back.

Shoulder-in.

Leg yielding, half pass, travers and renvers are optional, but the candidate should have some knowledge of these movements and be able to discuss them.

Know the principles of handling, lunging, backing and riding young horses.

Show a strong, correct and adaptable jumping position over show jumps and cross country fences, with control of the horse's pace and stride.

Have a sound knowledge of the use of gymnastic exercises to improve a horse's jumping, and of building schooling fences and courses.

Ride and jump horses of any type, temperament or stage of training, including spoilt or awkward horses. Assess the horse's potential, present performance and how it could be improved. Ride pace work correctly.

Maximum height for A Certificate fences, 1.15m.

KNOWLEDGE OF PONY CLUB

Knowledge of New Zealand Pony Clubs Association — its formation, objects and organisation.

Knowledge of running of own branch/club, and the names of branch, club and area officials.

HORSE MANAGEMENT

This section is as detailed in the H Certificate Test Sheet, Chapter 13, except that A Certificate candidates will not be examined in practice on lunging and ride and lead, though they may be questioned on these subjects.

NOTE. The syllabus for A Certificate includes all work for previous certificates, whether or not it is specified on this Test Sheet.

11
RIDING AND TRAINING: A CERTIFICATE

Training Objectives

1. To consolidate all the basic training. As knowledge deepens and ability increases this work becomes both easier and more meaningful.

2. To be able to continue the training of your own horse on progressive lines, improving his balance and suppleness to the point where he can show some degree of collection and extension, and is capable of doing some lateral movements and other work to Elementary dressage standard.

3. To be capable of riding horses of all types, temperaments and stages of training, and of assessing their way of going and how it could be improved.

4. To be capable, with some supervision, of the initial training of young horses.

THE RIDER

The more advanced the work, the greater the importance of the rider's seat and position. As the horse progresses, he becomes more sensitive and his balance becomes more responsive to the actions, whether voluntary or involuntary, of his rider.

As you obviously cannot see yourself unless you have a mirror, and then only fleetingly, it is vital to be checked frequently by somebody else. Straightness, depth of seat, stillness in relation to the horse's movement, and absence of tension, are the things the observer should be looking for.

Being lunged on a horse is an excellent way of developing these qualities. A few lessons from an experienced instructor to get you started would be invaluable — after this, riders of a similar standard could get together to lunge and check one another, watched from time to time by the instructor.

LUNGING THE RIDER

Requirements. A calm, well-trained lunge horse. It is especially important in the early stages that the horse should have smooth, even paces.

The horse should wear brushing boots, snaffle bridle, cavesson, side-reins and, preferably, a dressage saddle with a deep, central seat. The saddle must fit both horse and rider. A sheepskin numnah helps to distribute the weight and cushion the horse's back.

An enclosure is most desirable, though, if the horse is completely reliable, a quiet corner of a paddock could be used.

For method of lunging the horse, see page 256. The person lunging must be experienced in this technique.

A lunging session. Begin by lunging the horse without side-reins or rider, to warm him up. If necessary, then fit the side-reins and lunge him for a few minutes more with them on.

Undo the side-reins while the rider is mounting and the position is being checked at the halt. When the horse is being ridden on the lunge, the bridle reins should be knotted on his neck, and the side-reins attached below the bridle reins. Riders who are not accustomed to being lunged may find it best to keep the stirrups at first — a few circuits in rising trot can help to settle both horse and rider.

Now cross the stirrups, or remove them altogether.

Begin with a few suppling exercises at walk or halt. Ask your instructor's advice as to which would benefit you most.

Then to the trot. Two important points:

1. The pace must be *steady*, if anything it should be on the slow and lazy side.

2. The circle must not be too small; 15m is the minimum, but 20m is much better. A small circle is hard on the horse, and makes it more difficult for the rider because of the greater centrifugal force.

It is essential that the rider sits straight — best checked from behind. *Right:* Good fun and excellent for balance — *provided* the horse is absolutely quiet. Rider throwing and catching a ball. Note deep, steady position and relaxed fingers.

The great advantage of riding on the lunge is that the horse is controlled by someone else, leaving the rider free to concentrate on correcting faults in position. The person lunging should not make sharp corrections, which would cause tenseness, but quietly and persistently work on one or two problems at a time, so that the rider remains relaxed and able to concentrate calmly. Although it is hard work for all concerned, it ought to appear almost casual and quite unspectacular.

The rider should rest the outside hand on the pommel at first, and, if in the least unsteady, put the inside hand on the cantle. Otherwise, the inside arm and hand may hang straight down, be carried in riding position (as when holding the reins), or perform various suppling exercises.

Initially, two or three minutes at a time at trot, interspersed with rest periods at walk, with a total of ten minutes altogether, will be ample. Be sure to work equally and to check the rider's straightness, on both reins.

Gradually increase the trot periods up to about five minutes, and begin to take the outside hand off the pommel. Both hands should then normally be in the same position — down to the sides, resting on hip or thigh, arms folded; in riding position or at shoulder height. Both arms out to the side at shoulder height is especially good for checking the rider's straightness. Circling both arms can come later, but it is generally better to keep the more acrobatic exercises to the walk. The main objective at trot is for the rider to learn to absorb and conform to the movement of the horse.

Canter on the lunge. This should only be done under the supervision of an instructor. It requires a really experienced lunge horse. Even then, there is much more centrifugal force than at trot, and this may easily cause the rider to slip to the outside and collapse the inside hip.

It would be much better to practise walk-trot transitions, aiming to maintain balance without being left behind the movement on the upward transition, or being in front of it on the downward one.

As the rider improves, the horse may be asked to trot with more impulsion. It is good practice to change horses as often as possible, to become accustomed to their varying actions.

Lunging sessions should not last more than about twenty minutes, and a horse should not be asked to do more than two of these sessions consecutively. Be sure to reward him at the end of it all!

Lunging four or five times a week would be ideal, but even once or twice a week can make a tremendous improvement in a rider. If lunging is impossible for you, it becomes even more important to spend time in every training session working without stirrups, both on suppling exercises and improvement of position, as on the lunge. Take every opportunity to be checked by a knowledgeable person.

SEAT AND WEIGHT AIDS

Some knowledge of your own anatomy may help to explain the principles of seat and weight aids.

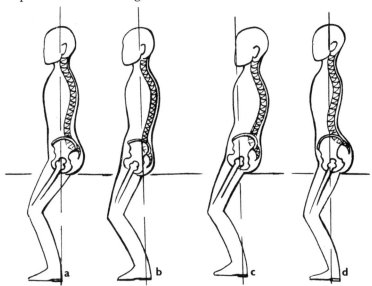

A. Normal riding position. B. The driving aid. C. Misuse of the driving aid — overdone, leaning back. D. Hollow back — impairs balance, causes stiffness and makes correct use of aids impossible.

It is the mobility of the hip joints, and the lumbar vertebrae, that makes it possible to use the back and the seat as aids. This part of the back should be soft and supple, constantly moving slightly as it conforms to the movement of the horse, so that the rider remains still in the saddle, with the weight lightly and evenly on both seat bones. This is what lunging helps to achieve. Unless you have a supple back, it is difficult to use effective seat aids.

These aids may be used in four ways:

1. By sitting deeper and closer. You should feel that the hip joints open, and that you are stretching down through the front of the thigh, the knee joint and the back of the calf, unhindered by grip or stiffness anywhere. At the same time, it is essential to lift the diaphragm and stretch upwards, to maintain the lightness of the seat. This aid is used in transitions and in the half-halt.

2. By using the aid as above, simultaneously pushing the hips and seat-bones forward, thereby tilting the angle of the pelvis slightly

147

back. This is the driving aid, used in conjunction with leg, when asking for lengthening. Sometimes, used lightly, to help to maintain impulsion in downward transitions.

3. The unilateral use of the seat, where one hip and seat bone are pushed forward in order to influence the hind leg on that side, e.g., in canter, demi-pirouette, lateral work.

4. By transferring a little more weight to one seat bone, which also helps to influence the action of the hind legs and the direction of movement. Used particularly in lateral work. Great care must be taken that the upper body remains upright, and that the seat does not slip to the outside.

It must be emphasised that these aids are very subtle, felt rather than seen. If used in a continuous or over-forceful way they will flatten the horse's back, preventing him from using his hindquarters efficiently and destroying, rather than creating, true impulsion. They must be used with the utmost discretion on young horses, and not at all in the first few months after backing.

Greater depth and steadiness in the saddle will also enable you to apply leg and hand aids with increasing finesse and accuracy. Think of the admirable precept of the French school of dressage, that the rider should be constantly 'refining his aids'.

THE HORSE

Before starting on A Certificate work, the horse should have good working paces — on the bit, with active hindquarters and a good outline. Three things must never be lost sight of:

1. Free forward movement. The horse going forward willingly but calmly in all paces.

2. The rhythm of the paces, maintained throughout his work. The 'beat' must be in the back of your mind all the time. Riding to well-chosen music can be both helpful and enjoyable.

3. The bend of the horse. Except in certain exercises, explained below, this must always be in the direction of movement.

If you have a new horse, you will have to take him through all the previous work to this level. If he is young, inexperienced or has problems in his way of going, you will have to go right back to basics. You now have one big advantage, in that you have done all the work up to this stage yourself — you know the aids and how movements should feel when correctly performed. Do not be tempted to skimp the foundations.

The Horse's Paces

Check Riding: B Certificate, page 21. Try to watch and assess other horses at work or in dressage tests, especially at Elementary or Medium level. In addition to the working paces that you have achieved, some collection is now asked for, and, instead of 'lengthened strides', medium trot and canter is expected, progressing to extended, as Medium dressage standard is approached.

A very good working trot, showing bold forward movement, combined with lightness and suppleness. Rider's lower leg a little stiff.

Collected paces. The stride is shorter and higher. The hind-quarters are engaged to the degree that they are taking a greater share of the weight, thereby increasing the lightness and mobility of the forehand. The back is well rounded, the neck raised and arched. As always, everything must originate from behind, and there must be a definite lowering of the hindquarters. Although the pace is shorter, which means it is a little slower, it should be light and lively, with the horse's back and joints soft and springy.

Medium paces are a progression from the 'few lengthened strides' already achieved. There must be a distinct and more sustained lengthening of the stride, but in trot the pace is rounder than the full extension. The horse needs to lower his head and neck a little, with an obvious increase in the drive from the hindquarters.

Extended paces. The stride is lengthened to the maximum, so that the horse covers as much ground as possible. While remaining on the bit he must be allowed to stretch his neck forward and down so that his action will not become higher, and the rhythm has to be maintained. Tremendous thrust is required from the hindquarters.

DRESSAGE

With the experience gained at B level of planning training programmes (see page 33), you should now have a good idea of what suits you and your horse and fits in with your circumstances.

Training sessions should continue to follow the same general pattern.

Work-in. A steady warm-up increases the blood supply to the muscles, enabling them to function more efficiently, reducing the risks of strains and preparing them for the more demanding work to come. The first few minutes should still be spent in walk and rising trot on a long rein, until you feel the horse loosening up and getting into the swing of his work. No horse, however advanced, should be subjected to sitting trot on a cold back.

A. With good forward movement and balance well established, the horse will easily come onto the bit. B. Forcing from the front (all hand, no seat and leg) is disastrous.

However, at this level the horse should be able to come on the bit more quickly as he warms up, and it is important to confirm the quality of the paces, their rhythm, lightness and suppleness, before attempting any movements such as shoulder-in or counter canter. In addition to circles and serpentines, the following will help with this during the second part of your work-in:

Transitions from one pace to another. These should become smoother and quicker, without being abrupt. The quality and rhythm of one pace must be maintained right up to the moment of transition, and the new pace established at once.

A useful exercise is to practise repeated transitions between trot and walk, briefly establishing the walk, then forward again to trot, working to keep the horse soft and steadily on the bit throughout. Vary this as he improves, sometimes coming down to a 'working halt' and forward to walk or trot. Work similarly on canter - trot - canter transitions — excellent on a 20m circle. When these are well established with the horse remaining on the bit, bring in more variations of pace.

You should find that the upward transitions from walk to canter and from halt to trot, improve greatly, and that you can gradually reduce the number of strides in the intermediate pace on downward transitions.

These exercises will lead up to the simple change of leg (see page 154).

Never allow the horse to anticipate any transition — if he starts to take the initiative, do something else!

Transitions within the pace. Lengthening and shortening the stride at all paces should form an integral part of every training session. It helps the horse to control his balance, and increases his elasticity and power.

The half-halt (see page 28). Increasing ability to use the back and seat aids will make this more effective. Sit erect, lift the diaphragm, use back and seat lightly, close the legs. As the horse is sent into your closed hand, you will feel the real influence of the half-halt in bringing his hocks under him, and lightening the forehand in preparation for transitions and all dressage movements. Balance and timing are everything! Too much drive will send the horse 'through' your hand; too much hand, and he will lose impulsion instead of gaining it. Remember this is a momentary aid, which may be repeated as necessary but must never be prolonged.

Strong use of half-halt on downward transition.

MEDIUM AND EXTENDED PACES

Objects

1. Improved balance, longitudinal suppleness and responsiveness.
2. To develop greater impulsion and power in the hindquarters.

'Lengthened strides', medium and extended paces are all different degrees of the same thing. In each of them:

a. the horse covers more ground at each stride. Owing to the increased length of stride the speed will be a little faster, but the tempo should remain the same.

b. the outline of the horse should lengthen, and his stride should be lower as well as longer.

c. the impulsion comes from the driving power of the hindquarters, going through the horse's supple loins and back.

d. in trot, the diagonal pairs of legs should remain parallel, never showing more lengthening in front than behind.

e. the horse must remain in balance, on the bit and light in hand.

Although a little heavy, this horse shows tremendous energy and even lengthening in medium trot.

The ease — or lack of it — with which horses lengthen their stride depends very much on their conformation and the natural brilliance of their action as well as on their state of training. Those who find it most difficult are probably the ones who need it most, but the greatest care must be taken not to discourage or overstrain any horse by being too demanding. Frequent short lengthenings, gradually progressing both in degree and distance, are preferable. Medium canter is generally not quite such hard work for the horse as is medium trot. Providing he remains in balance, more can be asked in canter. For horses who lack impulsion, or have difficulty at trot, it may be beneficial to include lengthened or medium canter quite early in the work-in to loosen them up. To assist in maintaining balance, this may be done on a large circle.

Aids. The aids are basically the same as for 'lengthened strides' (page 40) but, as the horse's power, ability and understanding develop, he will be able to respond more positively to them. The more lengthening you require from the horse, the more important is the quality of the preceding pace and the preparation. The horse must be somewhat shortened, light in hand and full of energy, ready to drive forward. Close both legs, and, as you feel the increased impulsion coming from behind, allow this impulsion to go through the horse by letting him take your hand forward a little.

In trot, you should sit during the preparation and the preliminary half-halt, but unless you are extremely steady and supple in your own back and can sit lightly as the horse lengthens, it would be better to rise.

Common faults — See 'Lengthening of Stride', also:

Fault	Possible Causes
Signs of tension — coming above the bit, ears back, tail swishing.	Poor co-ordination of aids. Asking too much, especially if the horse is unfit or has conformation problems.
Flattening the back.	Rider's driving aids, especially seat, too hard, heavy or unsteady.
Falling on the forehand.	Poor preparation: rider's hands giving too suddenly/too much. Asking too much/too long.
Going very wide behind.	Stiffness and lack of balance. Asking too much for horse's present ability.

VARIATIONS WITHIN THE PACE

Any form of lengthening of stride depends on the ability to shorten the pace. In the ultimate, the quality of extension is governed by the degree of collection.

From a good working trot or canter, with a little 'gathering together', lengthened strides may be achieved. Before medium paces are asked for, some shortening of stride with greater engagement of the hocks and lightening of the shoulders must be possible. By continued use of suppling and balancing exercises, a degree of collection will eventuate, and this is the key to extension.

SIMPLE CHANGE OF LEG

The horse is brought back from canter to walk, and, after two or three steps, is restarted in canter on the other leg. The downward transition may be progressive, but in the upward one, the canter must be obtained from the walk.

Objects
1. To confirm all the work on transitions to date.
2. To improve the horse's balance, straightness and obedience.

Introduce. When the horse will come back from canter to walk with only two or three intermediate trot strides, and the walk to canter transitions are established. This exercise may be considered the climax of the work on transitions.

Method. As with the change through the trot, this movement may be performed on a figure eight, a serpentine or on the diagonal. If the previous work was correct, it should not present great difficulty, especially if you can make use of seat and weight aids and the half-halt.

Aids. As for transitions.

Common Faults	Possible Causes
Anticipation, especially on the upward transition.	Over-emphasising preparation. Practising the whole movement too frequently.
Crookedness.	Stiffness, lack of balance or resistance, especially on the downward transitions. Anticipation. Outside leg too predominant in preparation for canter.

CIRCLES

Continue to make constant use of circles in your training. The 'Circle Exercises' on pages 35-9 are all useful, especially the variations in size and the 'Increase of Circle' — a most valuable preparation for lateral work. As the horse becomes more supple and balanced, it should be possible to reduce the size to a minimum of 8m in walk and trot and 10m in canter, without loss of rhythm.

COUNTER CANTER

The horse is required to canter on a curve or circle to the right with the left leg leading, or vice versa.

Objects

1. As a suppling exercise, particularly for the horse's shoulders.
2. To improve the horse's balance.
3. As an obedience exercise. The horse must maintain his canter lead even through changes of direction.

Introduce. When the true canter is regular, well-balanced, calm and straight. Given these essential qualities and the right approach, it is not a difficult movement to teach a horse. But without them, he is likely to change leg or become disunited and thoroughly confused.

Method. Begin with a *shallow* loop — not more than 3m — on the long side of the school. Practise this first in trot — if on the left rein, keep the horse placed to the left throughout. Make sure that the apex of the loop is opposite the half marker, and that you maintain the curve so that he is aimed towards the second quarter-marker and returns to it 'on one track', not sideways. When this is clearly understood, repeat the exercise in canter, on the same side of the school.

Counter canter. Just starting to return to track on shallow loop. Horse well balanced. Rider rather tense, drawing left leg back and up (*right* leg should be slightly back).

155

Aids. It is essential that the horse is positioned towards the leading leg throughout. To the left: the left hand maintains this placing, left leg must remain at the girth, left seat bone forward, right leg back. The right rein very delicately indicates the change of direction, without altering the placing of the head, the left leg maintains impulsion and quietly urges the horse back to the track, while the right leg controls the quarters. The rider must sit still and retain the position for canter left, while looking along the track of the movement.

When the horse holds the lead calmly and easily up to 5m deep, he may be asked to hold counter canter round the end of the school. Take the corners really wide at first, and be sure to maintain the placing and impulsion.

This exercise may also be practised on large serpentines in the open.

Common Faults	Possible Causes
Changing leg or becoming disunited.	Incorrect aids, asking too much too soon. Horse not yet ready for the movement.
Rushing, coming off the bit, stiffening, leaning.	As above. Clear, light aids and use of voice will help. Reassure and reward the horse when he is right — he may be doubtful at first.
Breaking.	Lack of impulsion, rider 'freezing'. Must act lightly with inside leg at each stride.

REIN BACK

The horse steps backwards, the legs moving almost in diagonal pairs — the forefoot of the diagonal may be raised and put down an instant before the hind foot.

Objects. This is an exercise in obedience to all the aids. The willingness and ability to rein back correctly proves that the horse is free from resistance in his mouth, and supple in the back and the joints of his hind legs.

Introduce when the horse is on the bit, has plenty of impulsion and is preferably beginning to show some degree of collection. The more supple he is, the easier it will be for him to perform this movement, which is contrary to his training to date.

Never attempt rein back with a horse who is above the bit, overbent or behind the bit, and, least of all, with one who is inclined to rear.

Aids. Obtain a good 'working halt', square and on the bit. Apply seat and leg aids as though to walk on, but at the exact instant when the horse goes to move forward, close the hands, lighten the weight on the seat bones and relax the legs to allow him to step back. The legs must remain in light contact, ready to keep the horse straight if he tries to swing his quarters to one side, and to ride him forward when he has completed the required number of steps. One or two steps will be enough initially — even with an advanced horse, it is unwise to ask for more than six. Always ride forward without any pause after a rein back.

A good rein back. Horse is 'round', light and even in his stride. Rider also light and very sympathetic with her aids.

If the horse resists, ride forward a few steps, halt and ask again. If he is really 'between your hand and leg' and you apply the aids correctly, you should not have much difficulty in obtaining a step or two of rein back. It sometimes helps him to understand what is wanted if an assistant applies light pressure on the foremost shoulder; but continued resistance shows that he is not yet ready for this movement. Wait until such exercises as lengthening and shortening stride and shoulder-in have increased his suppleness and comprehension to the point where he can do this movement without discomfort or confusion.

Common Faults	Possible Causes
Not in two-time, dragging instead of lifting the feet.	Poor initial halt, not on bit. Dragging the horse back, especially without first creating forward impulsion.
Hind legs spread.	Resistance or stiffness in the horse.
Coming off the bit — above it or overbent.	Poor balance of aids. Horse not yet ready for the movement.

| Going back crookedly. | Legs losing contact and therefore control of the hindquarters. Stiffness in the horse's back. |
| Anticipation, running back. | Hands too strong. Allowing the horse to anticipate. Never let him step back from the halt unless told to do so. Always regulate the number of steps. |

LATERAL MOVEMENTS

Movements in which the horse moves sideways as well as forwards, so that he is on two, three or four tracks. Lateral movements are:

Leg yielding, shoulder-in, half pass, travers and renvers.

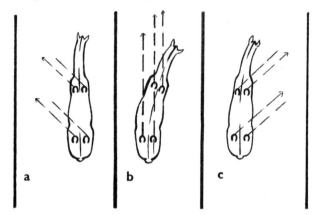

A. Leg yielding. B. Shoulder-in. C. Half pass.

Objects

1. To improve the understanding and obedience of the horse to the co-ordinating aids of the rider.

2. To supple every part of the horse.

3. To improve the balance and rhythm of the pace.

4. To increase the engagement of the hindquarters, and thereby the collection.

The rider learns to apply all the aids of seat, legs and hands in a much more subtle way. The rider must find the exact balance and timing of the aids, so that the horse is able to understand and carry out the required movement.

Seat and weight aids are extremely important in lateral work — check these aids on page 148. The seat bone, in the direction of movement, is generally pushed slightly forward with rather more weight on it, without collapsing the hip or shoulder.

In this work, the terms 'inside' and 'outside' apply to the bend of the horse, not necessarily to the inside or outside of the school.

Pace. All lateral movements should be started in walk, to enable both horse and rider to get the feel of them. Once this is achieved, trot is the better pace, because there is more impulsion. It goes without saying that all these movements are performed in sitting trot.

When working in walk, it is best to trot on in rising trot between each attempt. This re-establishes impulsion and allows the horse to relax while you assess the previous effort.

Starting lateral work. You have already laid the foundations with turn on the forehand, riding in position and the 'increase of circle' exercise. Revise these movements, to make sure that you can position the horse to either side, and that he moves freely off your leg. When this is confirmed:

1. Study the text and illustrations for the movement you intend to work on. Imagine yourself applying the aids and performing the movement over and over again, until you can really 'feel' it happening. It can help to stand the horse, correctly positioned and angled, at the point from which you will start. From there, check again where you will be looking, and the exact application of the aids. Do not, of course, go into the movement there and then, from the halt.

2. If there is any possibility of riding the movement on a trained horse, nothing could be more helpful. Then you will feel sure of the aids, and be able to recognise the movement instantly, and to praise him, when your own horse 'gets it right'.

3. Try to start each new movement with your instructor, or, failing this, with a knowledgeable friend who, manual in hand, can help to check the essential points.

4. Initially, work on one movement at a time, otherwise you and the horse could both become confused.

5. Always have the horse well worked in, supple and responsive.

6. Begin each new movement on your horse's best side. If he gives you two or three reasonably good steps, praise him with your voice while he is actually doing it, then ride him straight forward or, in the case of shoulder-in, on to a circle, giving him a good pat on the neck. It is essential that the horse should be relaxed and happy about lateral work. He has really got to apply himself to understanding what you want, and he cannot do this if he is tense.

7. Three things are necessary — placing, half-halt, timing.

a. Placing. The precise angle of the horse to the long side of the school, as explained under each movement, is vital. This angle, as well as the rhythm of the pace, must be retained without variation throughout. This calls for skill in the timing of the aids as you start the movement.

b. Half-halt. This must be applied at the exact instant the horse reaches the required angle, and followed immediately by the aids for the movement. Starting at walk makes this easier.

c. Timing. During the movement, the timing of the aid of the acting leg is another important factor. In some lateral movements, the horse crosses his hind legs. If you have sufficient 'feel' to apply your leg as he lifts the leg that must cross over, not only will you make it easier for him, but you will also emphasise the rhythm of the pace.

At first, there will probably be some loss of impulsion and uncertainty in both horse and rider, but you will have no doubt when a lateral movement begins to come right. The first sign will be a definite increase in the regularity and ease. As you continue with this work, you will notice a big improvement in the engagement of the horse's hindquarters and the freedom of his shoulders, and he should feel supple, light and springy.

The late Colonel Podhajsky, commandant of the Spanish Riding School, said, 'The horse must execute lateral work joyfully and be completely relaxed, free from any tension or constraint.' Bear these words in mind. You can play your part by sitting still and always giving your aids clearly, so that the horse learns to understand them and does not become confused or worried. Above all, try to create an encouraging atmosphere and enjoy the work with him.

LEG YIELDING

The horse moves 'on two tracks' diagonally forwards and sideways. The head is positioned slightly away from the direction of movement, but there is no bend through the body. The inside legs cross in front of the outside ones.

This is a controversial exercise, which some people use to a considerable extent, others not at all. The arguments for and against are:

For: 1. As an introduction to lateral work, it is comparatively easy for the horse because complete 'length bend' is not involved.

2. It can be performed in working trot, before the horse is ready for collection.

3. It teaches obedience to the leg, and has some suppling and stretching effect on the horse.

4. It can be a useful introduction for the rider, giving the feel of lateral movement and practice in co-ordination of the aids.

Against: 1. It may well cause confusion later on, when other lateral work is being taught, especially if the horse is asked or allowed to bend.

2. Although a recognised movement, and occasionally included in dressage tests, it is not a part of classical equitation. Movements in which the horse is bent through the whole body, such as shoulder-in and half pass, are considered of far greater value in training.

Many people find it is worth using the method recommended here just to get the feel of moving on two tracks. Once this is established, it is a matter of opinion as to the value of continuing with this or any other method.

Leg yielding is not a required movement for A Certificate, but you may be asked to express your thoughts on the subject.

Method. The recommended way is to begin by turning down the three-quarter line on the short side of the school and inclining towards the track, between the half and quarter markers. This does not entail a change in the placing of the horse, as he remains on the same rein throughout.

Leg yielding to the right. Horse's head placed away from direction of movement, otherwise straight.

Aids. Start at walk. After the turn, half-halt. Look where you want to go, sit straight, but try to push a little more with the inside seat bone. The acting leg is the inside one, used at or *very* slightly behind

161

the girth. The outside, supporting, leg is used as required to keep up impulsion or to control the hindquarters, so that the horse remains parallel with the long side. The inside hand maintains the position of the head, the outside hand indicates direction. You may find a slightly open outside rein is helpful at first, especially at the start of the movement. Be prepared to adjust your aids as necessary.

Common Faults	Possible Causes
Neck bend.	Inside hand too strong, perhaps crossing over the withers. Lack of contact and indication with outside hand.
Quarters leading.	Hands as above. Inside leg too far back.
Quarters trailing, hind legs not crossing.	Inside leg aids not clear. Horse resisting inside leg — reinforce lightly with dressage whip if necessary. Check hands.
Running away from the leg.	Inside leg too strong, lack of support with outside leg.

In all lateral work, the horse must go more forwards than sideways. To ensure this, it is sound practice to ask for only two or three steps of leg yielding, then ride straight forward before asking for more.

SHOULDER-IN

The horse moves along a straight line while bent, through his whole length around the rider's inside leg, and away from the direction of movement. He should be at an angle of not more than 30 degrees to this line, and on three tracks. (See diagram on page 158.) The hind feet remain straight in the track, the forehand is brought in. The hind legs do not cross, but, owing to the bend of the horse's body, the inside hind leg steps further under the centre of gravity (under the rider's seat). The inside foreleg crosses in front of the outside one.

Objects

1. To increase collection. The 'stepping under' with the inside hind leg while the horse is bent necessitates flexing all the joints and taking more weight on this leg, thereby lightening and freeing the forehand.

2. To supple and loosen all parts of the horse, particularly the shoulders and the inside hind leg.

3. To increase the rider's capacity to place, control and correct the horse.

Introduce when the horse is showing the beginnings of collection — on the bit, well balanced and able to shorten the stride slightly in trot, without losing impulsion. He should be responsive to the leg in the 'Increase of Circle' exercise, page 37.

A good start for shoulder-in. Horse's right hind foot has remained straight, and he shows some bend through the body. Rider is straight and sympathetic in her application of aids, but her right leg should be further back.

Method. It is helpful to begin on the long side of the school, after a 10m circle. This gives the degree of bend in the horse's body, to be maintained throughout the shoulder-in.

Start in walk, until you get the feel of the movement, and make the circle from the quarter marker. See that the horse is light and attentive and well bent round your inside leg. On completing the circle, maintain the curve as though commencing a second circle. As his quarters are level with the marker, his inside foreleg will be coming off the track, and he is in a good position to go into shoulder-in.

Aids. At this moment, half-halt and send him quietly into shoulder-in with the inside leg, to be received by the outside hand, without altering the bend. The inside hand maintains the placing. The hands must allow the horse to move along, but not off, the track. Keep your legs in the same position as for the circle, and try to use the inside leg with a pulsating action as the horse lifts his inside hind leg. The outside leg controls the quarters. Your hips should remain square with the horse's hips, and it is necessary to turn your shoulders slightly inwards to be square with his. Looking along the track helps

163

your direction, but if this brings your outside shoulder back, it would be best to look between the horse's ears.

After a few steps of shoulder-in, ride forward on to a circle, to which the horse should return quite naturally if the bend has been properly maintained. Alternatively, ride across the diagonal at a stronger (lengthened) pace. Only ask a slight angle for the first attempts.

Common Faults	Possible Causes
Neck bend only, fore-legs remaining in track.	Lack of preparation, forehand not brought off track at start. Inside hand too strong or crossing over withers. Lack of indication with outside hand.
Quarters 'escaping' to the outside.	Stiffness in the horse's back. Inside leg too far back. Lack of support with outside leg.
Horse coming out of track.	Rider not straight, not quick enough to adjust aids to maintain direction.
Uneven rhythm, variation in the angle of the horse	Unsureness in horse or rider. Asking too much too soon.
Losing impulsion, coming off the bit.	Poor balance or co-ordination of aids. 'Dead' aid with inside leg.

Where neither horse nor rider has experience of this movement, any or all of these faults may occur. There may be quite different types and degrees of evasion on the two sides. You will probably need help to analyse the situation in the early stages.

For the rider, shoulder-in is a real achievement — a new level of understanding of aids and feel. For the horse, it is probably the most valuable of all lateral movements as a suppling exercise and an aid to collection.

HALF PASS

The horse moves diagonally forward and sideways on two tracks, positioned in the direction of movement and slightly bent round the rider's inside leg. The horse's outside legs cross in front of the inside ones. He should be almost parallel with the long side, the shoulders very slightly in advance.

Objects. Half pass promotes all the objectives of lateral work, listed on page 158. It is particularly valuable at this stage to increase the horse's collection, co-ordination and responsiveness, and the rapport which should now be developing between horse and rider.

Introduce when the horse is performing fairly well in shoulder-in and showing some degree of collection.

Method. A good way to start is by making a half circle to the centre line, followed by a few steps of half pass towards the quarter marker without changing direction — left half circle, left half pass. Later, it may be carried out from quarter marker to centre line, or from a turn down the centre.

Half pass to the right, showing freedom and light-ness. 'Bend' a little lacking, but a happy partnership on the right lines.

Aids. On reaching the centre line, the outside hand, supported by the inside leg, checks the circular movement in a half-halt. Both hands then indicate the direction of the half pass, while the outside leg behind the girth asks the horse to step sideways. The inside leg at the girth helps to maintain impulsion and keep the horse moving forward, the outside hand controls the bend. Stretch down as you use the inside leg and keep rather more weight on the inside seat bone. Hips and shoulders square with the horse's, look where you want to go. After a few steps, ride straight forward.

Half pass may be performed in canter, but definitely not until it is well established in walk and trot.

Common Faults	Possible Causes
Wrong bend	Outside hand too strong, maybe crossing over the neck. Rider collapsing to the outside — perhaps trying too hard.
Quarters trailing or leading.	Poor co-ordination of aids, especially incorrect or insufficient leg aids.
Loss of impulsion.	Inside leg not maintaining forward movement. Hands too heavy, poor co-ordination.

Half pass is an optional movement for A Certificate. It is recommended for the interest and variety it adds to the training, and because it is one of the most enjoyable movements to perform. It gives the true feeling of forward and sideways action which is the essence of lateral work, and a great sensation of freedom, lightness and rhythm when it is successfully achieved.

TRAVERS AND RENVERS

In travers (head to the wall or quarters in) and renvers (tail to the wall or quarters out) the horse moves on two tracks on a straight line — usually on the long side of the school or the centre line. He should be at an angle of about 30 degrees, slightly bent round the rider's inside leg, and looking in the direction of movement.

They are considered useful but not essential suppling exercises, and are not generally included in the Pony Club curriculum.

For further information on these movements, see 'Recommended Reading', page 301.

Demi-pirouette. Forward movement well maintained, balance and confidence good.

DEMI-PIROUETTE

(See pages 48 to 49.) During, and as a result of, the foregoing training, horse and rider should perform this movement with increasing ease and confidence.

The turn should gradually become 'tighter', without loss of rhythm or impulsion, and it should not be necessary to use the corner to help in placing the horse. A trot to walk transition one or two steps before the demi-pirouette, and an upward transition to trot or canter immediately afterwards, are useful variations which maintain impulsion and add interest. These transitions should be varied, to avoid anticipation.

PACE WORK

This is a consolidation of the B Certificate work on 'Judgment of Speed and Distance', page 51. This judgment should now be well developed.

You should be able to ride a horse at the gallop, showing a strong, forward position and keeping him firmly between hand and leg, so that he remains balanced and under control throughout.

TRAINING THE YOUNG HORSE

The following notes give an outline of the principles and recommended procedure of training, which apply throughout the education of a horse, from foalhood to maturity.

Principles

1. Horses, like other animals, learn by association of ideas, by immediate reward and correction. A nice balance of confidence in, and respect for, their trainer must be established right from the start, as a basis for further progress.

2. The horse is a creature of flight and instinct, rather than of reason. It is natural for him to be nervous of humans when he is unacquainted with them, or if he has had unfortunate experiences. Until he gains confidence, he cannot apply himself to understanding what is required. Progress can only be made slowly, each step being consolidated before going on to the next. There may be times when the horse knows quite well what he should do, but doesn't want to do it. On these occasions the trainer must be strong and determined enough to insist on obedience, always using the minimum of force and rewarding the horse instantly when he complies. This is how confidence and respect are built up.

3. Horses are also creatures of habit. It is the trainer's job to ensure that he makes his demands clear and places the horse in the best position to comply with them. He must always ask in exactly the same way when a certain reaction is required, to avoid confusion and establish the most important habit of all — the habit of obedience.

4. The herd instinct, and the homing instinct, are two of the most powerful in the horse's makeup. They can be used by the intelligent trainer, especially with young horses who are nervous or uncertain. Examples — giving a youngster a 'lead' past something that frightens him, or in jumping. Cantering or jumping towards 'home' (i.e. the gate of the paddock), or towards other horses for the sluggish or unsure, and in the opposite direction for those who are too free. Naturally, these are only temporary expedients — eventually the horse must learn to go equally freely towards or away from home or other horses.

5. The trainer must be a person of mature judgment, sufficiently skilled in lunging and riding to be able to give clear and consistent aids: to recognise from the horse's behaviour whether he is frightened, uncertain, defiant or playful, and to react accordingly. A trainer needs courage, clearheadedness, quick reaction, sympathy and self-control. Most of these qualities only come from experience, which is the reason why all the classical schools of riding follow the principle that inexperienced riders learn on trained horses, until the riders acquire the necessary skill and knowledge to train young horses, or retrain spoilt ones.

6. The safety of all concerned must always be among the trainer's strongest considerations.

THE EDUCATION OF A YOUNG HORSE — AN OUTLINE

The Foal Should Learn:

to be caught, and wear a 'foal slip' or small halter.

to be handled all over.

to be brushed over, and have feet picked up and trimmed, as necessary.

to be led from either side, and obey the basic commands, 'Walk on', 'Halt' or 'Whoa',

and possibly to be tied up — opinions differ as to the advisability of this.

Provided the mare is quiet and friendly, these basic requirements should be achieved quite easily during daily visits. The aim is to instil the qualities of confidence and respect from the very beginning.

Never allow a foal, however endearing, to become cheeky and demanding. Titbits should *only* be given as a reward for good behaviour.

Between 6 and 18 Months the Young Horse Should

be weaned.

be gelded, if a colt.

be handled sufficiently to retain all he learnt as a foal, but MUST NOT be ridden.

Between 18 Months and 3 Years the Young Horse Should

be handled regularly, as above.

lead well in hand from either side, at walk and trot.

be led about and accustomed to strange sights and sounds — e.g. traffic, seen over the fence or from a wide grass verge, stepping over poles on the ground, walking through puddles.

After Second Birthday the Young Horse MAY

be taught to lunge at walk and trot (it is not advisable to use side reins at this age).

be taught to lead from another horse.

If the horse is well-grown and a lightweight rider is available, he may be backed and ridden for not more than twenty minutes at a time. Sole objectives are to establish the basic paces of walk and trot in straightforward riding. He should be ridden in a rather forward position on the lightest possible contact. No sitting trot. Work in a school is not recommended.

MUST NOT jump, gallop or work on hard ground.

At 3 to 4 years Should

if previously unhandled, learn to accept handling, leading, tying up.

be taught to lunge, and side-reins introduced.

unless very underdeveloped, be backed and establish basic paces.

revise above, if done as a two-year-old.

be taken 'out and about', alone or in company (always in company on the road until quiet in traffic).

gradually become accustomed to undulating ground, variations in going, fording streams, etc.; go to Pony Club, initially for 'young horse' activities only.

do more work on transitions and large circles in the open.

be introduced to the school. Work may include, progressively, 20m circles at walk and trot, change of rein across the diagonal, turns down the centre or across the school, gradual deepening of corners, turn on forehand, when halts are established, a few steps of leg yielding at walk, if desired. Canter on 20m circles and round school towards end of this period.

be introduced to ground poles at walk and trot and very small jumps. Pace for jumping, mainly trot, *maximum* height for three-year-old, 45cm. All types of jumps in miniature. NO jumping on hard ground.

A Three-year-old Should Not

as a general rule, be ridden for more than one hour daily.

compete in shows, except possibly maiden and novice classes on the flat.

Must Not

be ridden on very steep country.

be used for C Certificate test — 60cm is beyond his height limit.

compete in horse trials, jumping classes, endurance rides or go hunting.

At 4 to 5 Years Should

revise previous work.

work in dressage, Preliminary to Novice level — coming on the bit, with good balance and outline, working paces, some lengthening of stride in trot and canter, start most B Certificate work and exercises.

jump all types of fences at trot and canter. Average height for four-year-old, 60-75cm, occasional maximum, 90cm.

be introduced to his 'life work' — e.g. a few quiet days' hunting, show classes. Preliminary to Novice dressage tests, quiet games, stick and ball for polo or polo-crosse, 'kindergarten' jumping and novice Pony Club or training level horse trials.

A Four-year-old Should Not

be used for B Certificate test.

Must Not

compete in more advanced jumping or horse trials, however great his potential.

jump or do fast work on hard ground, or compete in endurance rides.

At 5 to 6 Years Should

be ready for the second/intermediate stages of whatever work is required, e.g.;

dressage approaching Elementary level, including rein back and shoulder-in, depending on the trainer's capabilities; jumping up to 1.1m.

perform well out hunting.

perform well in games, steady chukkas, polo-crosse or polo.

perform calmly and creditably in novice horse trials or show jumping.

endurance rides not exceeding 80km.

A Five-year-old Should Not

be used for A Certificate test.

compete in three day events (except possibly novice, autumn trials) or longer endurance rides.

At 6 to 7 Years Should

be strong and sound and confident of his own ability.

have excellent manners and be a pleasure to ride anywhere.

If time and trouble are taken in his education, the young horse should develop physically and mentally from year to year, without strain or stress. Most horses will reach their peak between seven and nine years, and, given equal care throughout their lives, should continue in top form into their teens, many going on into their twenties.

RECOMMENDED TRAINING METHODS

Teaching to lead. Begin in a yard or other confined space. A cavesson with a lead-rope about 3m long on the front ring gives more control than a halter. Wear gloves, and have a dressage whip or long switch. Stand the horse with a fence on his right side, and place yourself level with his left shoulder. Hold the lead-rope about 30cm from the cavesson in your right hand, the free end of rope and the whip, pointing backwards, in your left. Push, rather than pull, forward on the rope, at the same time giving the command, 'Walk on'. If nothing happens, or he tries to run back, repeat the command more firmly, if necessary backing it up with a light touch of the whip. If he plunges forward, steady him with a light jerk on the cavesson, get him back into position, reassure him, and try again. The moment he walks forward quietly, say 'Good boy' in an encouraging way and keep praising him while he is walking. To stop him, stand still yourself, saying 'Halt' or 'Whoa' and increasing the pressure on the cavesson as necessary. Praise him when he obeys. Be completely consistent with the commands, because they are what you will use later for lunging. Teach him to lead freely from either side before taking him out of the enclosure. Have another person there the first time you take him out. If you have the slightest doubt about controlling the horse it is much wiser to have two people to lead him, with lead-reins attached to the side rings of the cavesson. It is essential, for obvious reasons, that he doesn't learn that he can get away at this early stage of training!

Tying up should not cause much difficulty if it is taught progressively during initial handling in the yard. Use a 3m lead-rope, slipped round the top rail of the fence and back to your hand. If the horse pulls back, he cannot get away, and he is quietly brought back to the rail, until he understands that he is to stand there. Next, tie a loop of baling twine to the top rail, and tie the horse to the loop, keeping the end of the rope in your hand and staying with him at first. Use a quick-release knot. When this is confidently accepted, gradually move further away, though it will be best to keep him in sight to start with. At this stage, the normal length of lead-rope will be preferable.

LUNGING

Pony Club considers that lunging is an essential part of the training of the young horse for the following reasons:

1. To teach obedience to the aids of the voice, rein and whip.

2. To accustom him to saddle and bridle, and to light contact on his mouth through the side-reins.

3. To develop his muscles and improve his balance before he is asked to carry the weight of a rider.

4. To enable him, when first backed, to be controlled from the ground while learning to understand and obey the rider's aids.

Starting lunging. The horse must first lead freely in hand on either side, and obey the commands to 'Walk on' and 'Halt'.

It is preferable that he should also be taught to lead in hand at trot.

The Trainer MUST

be capable of lunging trained horses. (See page 256.)

have the correct equipment, and be thoroughly familiar with its uses.

have a suitable enclosure, and, unless very experienced with young horses, an assistant.

For the first few lessons, only brushing boots, cavesson and lunge rein will be required on the horse. The trainer will need gloves and lunging whip. Always check that the gate is shut. The following are the stages of training:

1. **Lunging with an assistant.** Start with the horse on the perimeter of the lunging circle, with the assistant at his head. Until the horse

understands what is required of him, he is led round on the circle. This should be done on both reins. The assistant may be on the inside or the outside of the circle.

Next, practise 'Halt' and 'Walk on'. The assistant walks beside the horse, ready to stop him and lead him on if he doesn't obey the trainer's commands. He ensures that the horse remains out on the circle, without turning in, at the halt.

2. **Dispensing with the assistant.** When this is going well, the assistant gradually moves away. At first, it may be best for the trainer to have the horse on a shorter rein (3m approximately). The trainer will then be further behind the horse than usual, following him round on a smaller circle, and must move forward towards his shoulder when halting, and back again to send the horse forward. If the horse does not stop easily, use the fence to steady him or call back the assistant.

3. **Introducing the trot.** It is obviously helpful if the horse knows the command to trot on. Failing this, urge him on quietly with the voice. Show the whip behind him if necessary, but don't hit him with it. After one or two rounds bring him back to walk. Don't allow him to halt from the trot, always establish walk first, to preserve impulsion.

Ten minutes at a time is ample for these early lessons, preferably twice a day. Horses vary in their responsiveness, but provided they have been well handled and are calm, most should be working quietly at walk and trot after three or four days.

If the horse has missed out on 'leading about to accustom him to strange sights and sounds', this should be introduced at this stage, usually for a few minutes after the second lunging session of the day. The lunging cavesson and 3m lead-rope will give the most control.

4. **Introducing the surcingle.** This is a good way of accustoming a young horse to the feel of a girth. It should be introduced when the above stage has been reached, after the second lunging session, which could be a little longer than usual to ensure that the horse is settled. Do this either in the lunging pen or the yard.

The surcingle should have a folded blanket underneath to protect the horse's back, and it is advisable to use a breastplate. The horse should always be allowed to examine and sniff anything new, so show him the items you are going to use. Rub him over with the blanket, lay it on his back and take it off again, until he ignores it.

The trainer, holding the horse on his left side, then puts on the breast girth and lays the surcingle, point end down, over the blanket on his back. The assistant, on the right, takes the buckle end, passes it through the breast girth, and hands it carefully under the horse to the trainer, who secures it just tightly enough to keep the surcingle in place. The horse is rewarded with feed and patting. The assistant then leaves the yard. When the horse is relaxed, the surcingle may be taken up another hole, and, if he is still calm, he may be led forward a few steps. If he is tense postpone this until the next day — don't be in a hurry. Next day, put the surcingle on for a few minutes after the first lunging session and, if all is well, lunge the horse in it for the second period.

When the horse lunges quietly at walk and trot in the surcingle, probably after another two or three days, the saddle, without stirrups, may be introduced in the same way.

5. **Introducing the bridle.** This may be done a day or two after the surcingle. The bit should be a half-moon or thick jointed snaffle, and *must* be the correct size for the horse. Remove the reins and noseband. Hold the bridle up by the horse's head, to gauge the fitting. Use either of the methods given in *Manual One* for putting on the bridle. If the horse is unwilling to open his mouth, a titbit, held in the left hand with the bit, may help. Put the bridle on for the first time after lunging, and leave the horse with it on in the yard for five minutes, no longer.

The horse may now be lunged with the bridle under the cavesson and with a saddle, and the lunging sessions gradually extended to twenty minutes — not more than ten minutes without a rest. Work equally on both reins. The main aims at this stage are calm, free forward movement and obedience to the voice. It is important that the horse is worked at the full extent of the rein, so that he is on a circle of approximately 20m.

6. **Introducing side-reins.** For details of types and fitting, see page 255. Most trainers prefer some elastic in the side-reins used on young horses. Initially, the side-reins should be adjusted to allow completely free movement of the head and neck at walk. After a day or two, they may be taken up gradually until there is very light contact at trot when the horse is working well, with impulsion. Contact must not be forced on the horse — he should never be upset or become overbent as a result of the side-reins. If he is driven quietly but steadily forward he will begin to seek the contact of his own accord. As his hocks come further under and his outline becomes a little shorter and rounder, the side-reins will slacken and may then be shortened again until light contact is re-established.

Always work the horse without side-reins for a few minutes at the start of the lesson. The side-reins should both be the same length. Once contact is established at trot, they will restrict the horse in walk and very little work should be done at this pace with them on. Some trainers consider it advisable to undo them when turning the horse round to change the rein.

Correct use of side-reins will result in a big improvement in the horse's outline, balance, rhythm, and bend on the circle. Lunging should continue throughout the backing process and early riding — firstly, to settle the horse down before being ridden, and secondly, to maintain this improvement in his way of going.

Remember that side-reins must *only* be used when the horse is being worked actively on the lunge. NEVER leave the horse standing in the yard or lead him with side-reins attached to the bit.

7. **Canter on the lunge.** This must not be started until the horse is well balanced, calm and obedient in trot. Begin towards the end of a lesson, on his best side. Urge him on with a clear command, 'Can-ter', if necessary showing the whip behind him. Only ask for a few strides at first.

If the horse strikes off on the wrong leg or goes disunited, don't stop him instantly, or he may think he was wrong to canter at all. He is more likely to strike off correctly if he is asked when he is on the far side of the circle from the gate — making use of the homing instinct. It takes time for a horse to find his balance and pace in canter; some may find it easier if the side-reins are removed initially. Be prepared to shorten the lunge rein if necessary for control, and to move with the horse, so that he can remain on at least a 20m circle.

It is advisable to do some canter work on the lunge before the horse is ridden at the trot, in case something startles him and causes him to break. Never canter young horses on the lunge if the going is heavy or slippery.

8. **Backing.** Preliminaries for backing may start in about the second week of the lunging programme, when the horse is thoroughly accustomed to being handled and is obeying the voice. They may begin with the assistant jumping up and down beside the horse's shoulder, first on one then the other side, while he is held and reassured by the trainer. When this movement is ignored, the assistant is legged up to lie across the horse's back, again from either side. A second assistant is useful to do the legging up. The 'backer' gradually moves about more as the horse accepts his weight — making much of the horse on the far side, eventually propping himself up on his arms so that the horse sees him at his full height. Some trainers like to lead the horse forward with the person lying on his stomach across the horse's back, but the value of this is debatable, and it is extremely uncomfortable.

All these activities should take place after the second lunging session of the day, preferably in the yard. They may be done either on the blanket and surcingle — usually the best to begin with, bareback or on a saddle. Although the horse will not actually be ridden, the backer should wear a hard hat.

Before the actual backing, the horse should have been lunged with the stirrups on the saddle, first run up and secured, then left hanging down, to accustom him to movement against his sides. Whether stirrups are used for the first time or two that the horse is 'sat on' is a matter of opinion — some people feel that they can get in the way and may startle the horse. If used, they must fit the rider, who must wear suitable boots.

After a good lunging session, the side-reins are removed completely and the bridle reins attached to the bit and tied in a knot on the horse's neck. A neckstrap is essential, and the rider must wear a hard hat at this stage. A second assistant is almost indispensable. Check the girth, and make sure, if stirrups are used, that they are the correct length for the rider.

After some preliminary lying-across exercises, the assistant legs the rider well up so that he can easily put his leg across, without any risk of catching it on the cantle or on the horse's rump. It is usually best for the rider to dismount again almost immediately, and to repeat this process several times from either side, before remaining for any appreciable time on the horse's back. The trainer and the assistant should then slip the irons on to the rider's feet — it is the rider groping for them that may disturb the horse. The rider should move about on the horse's back, patting him on the neck and shoulders and behind the saddle, leaning forward and to each side, talking quietly to him, so that he gets used to the voice coming from above.

When there are no signs of tension, possibly after a day or two, the horse may be led forward a step at a time. Although the rider holds the knotted reins in one hand and the neckstrap in the other, he does not use the reins at this stage. Control remains in the hands of the person on the ground, who gradually lets out more rein until the horse is on the lunging circle. Practise 'Halt' and 'Walk on', the rider beginning to give the commands and the trainer backing up as needed, and then the rider backing up with very light, delicate use of rein and leg aids. Give much praise when these are obeyed.

Start trot on the lunge in the same way, at first sitting slightly forward with very little weight on the seat bones, as soon as possible in a quiet rising trot. It is advisable, while the horse is still controlled on the lunge rein, for the rider to begin to carry a short schooling whip, and to use it, very lightly at first, to reinforce the leg aids when necessary.

9. **Control by the rider.** When the horse is obeying the rider's aids on the lunge, he may be ridden loose in the pen, on the lunging circle

at walk and trot. Turns and changes of direction may now be introduced. Use a wide open rein with no backward tension, and tactful legs and voice to maintain forward movement. After this, the horse should be led or lunged with the rider in the open paddock, before being ridden off the rein there.

These early riding periods usually take place after the afternoon lunging. At first, twenty minutes lunging and five to ten minutes riding is sufficient. Trotting on the lunging circle with a rider is particularly hard work for a young horse, and the time must be extended only gradually to avoid causing discomfort and resistance.

The trainer must decide, according to circumstances, whether to undertake the initial backing himself, or whether this should be done by the assistant. If the latter is a good rider, but inexperienced in handling and lunging young horses the second course would be best.

10. **Riding in the open.** At first, it is advisable to ride the horse on a circle, to which he is accustomed, but as soon as he is settled, expand the circle gradually until he is being ridden round the paddock. Long, straight lines with a minimum of turns will be less tiring and enable him to find his balance more easily.

11. **Going out on the road.** It is most unwise to take a young horse out on the road for the first time by himself. Wait until at least one quiet, older horse is available to shelter him from the traffic.

12. **Mounting from the stirrup.** This is best introduced when the horse has been ridden for a while — during or after a ride, when he is settled. The following points are important:

a. have an assistant to hold the horse and ensure that he stands still.

b. use a mounting block at first. When mounting from the ground, the assistant should pull down on the opposite stirrup leather (not iron) to keep the saddle straight.

c. when mounting from the left, check that you:

push the left toe well down in the stirrup,

have whip in the left hand, take reins up firmly enough for control, right one slightly shorter, throw the spare end of the reins over,

put the right hand on the pommel,

spring up as quickly and lightly as possible; do not pause before putting the leg over when mounting a young horse. Let yourself down lightly into the saddle.

d. *always* insist that the horse stands still for mounting or dismounting, and practise from both sides.

13. **Introducing canter.** Wait until the horse is balanced and completely obedient in walk and trot. The first ridden canters should

177

be on straight lines, with the rider adopting a slightly forward position. Only ask a few strides to start with, and it is usually best to be going away from home.

Time. It is impossible to lay down an exact schedule for this initial training, as young horses vary so greatly in physique and temperament. Most will reach the stage of quiet riding out in about six weeks. The important thing, especially if you are inexperienced, is to be sure that each stage is established before moving on to the next.

The period of quiet, straightforward riding should last for at least two or three months before serious schooling is commenced. During this time, the horse should be allowed to find his balance under saddle with the lightest possible contact consistent with control. The objectives are:

1. The physical development of the horse, and the gradual strengthening of muscles to enable him to carry weight without strain or discomfort. Riding time must be increased by degrees from the initial five minutes up to twenty minutes for a two-year-old, three-quarters to one hour for a three- or four-year-old. The latter may be introduced progressively to the activities mentioned in the 'Outline'.

2. The establishment of free, calm, willing forward movement, and the regularity and rhythm of the paces under saddle.

3. To develop confidence and obedience, acceptance of the bit and of all the aids.

Work on the lunge could continue regularly to improve the horse's activity, rhythm and lateral suppleness.

RIDING YOUNG HORSES

1. The rider must have a firm seat and sufficient knowledge and ability to apply clear, consistent aids.

2. A comfortable general purpose saddle, rather than a dressage saddle, is recommended. It must fit both horse and rider. A breastplate must be used if there is any tendency for the saddle to slip back.

3. It is always advisable to use a neckstrap, and essential when jumping young horses.

4. Ride on the short side, and use a slightly forward position in the early stages to lighten the weight on the horse's back. Use diagonals correctly. Sitting trot will be brought in gradually as the horse gets stronger — at first, use it only for a few strides on transitions. In turning, use an open rein without any backward tension until the horse understands what is wanted. Always use correct leg aids.

5. The rider must be alert but without tension. Young horses move

like lightning if they are startled, and one must always be prepared, but any apprehension will quickly be communicated to the horse. Remember that if a youngster has been well trained on the lunge he will obey voice aids. The command 'Halt' can be extremely useful in moments of stress!

6. For at least the first week after backing, the horse should be lunged and ridden in the pen before being taken outside, and must be ridden every day. Once really settled, he should have his weekly 'day off', but if he has a longer spell, lunge before riding.

ALTERNATIVE TRAINING METHODS

There are many other possible approaches to the initial training of young horses. Some of these cannot be justified on any logical or humane grounds, while others may have their uses in certain circumstances, if applied by experienced trainers.

It is appreciated that many thoroughbreds are backed during their second winter and raced as two-year-olds. Opinions differ on this practice, but at least these horses are hard fed from foalhood, tend to mature at an early age and are, or should be, only asked to carry very light weights. They are not asked to jump. Many of them have finished ridden work and gone to stud by the age of four or five.

The majority of Pony Club mounts are reared rather differently, and it is hoped that they will continue their work, which takes several years of training, for at least a further ten years. Most are not fully mature under the age of six or even seven years, and at two or three years old are liable to concussion injuries — splints, sore shins, ringbone and sidebone — and to sprains of tendons and ligaments. Training, once started, must be light but regular and progressive, and few are sufficiently developed, either physically or mentally, to begin this training under the age of three.

If left until four years or over, most horses, especially if previously unhandled, tend to be too strong, and difficult for any but the most experienced trainers.

If you have any problems with a young horse you are training, refer to 'Recommended Reading', page 301, or seek experienced advice at Pony Club.

Horse and rider well balanced.

Be sure your riding muscles are in good trim before attempting this.

12
JUMPING: A CERTIFICATE

Training Objectives

1. To have a well-established and effective position over all types of fences.

2. To be able to adapt the position on the approach and between fences to suit the situation — e.g. the type of fence, the track, the terrain and the horse you are riding.

3. To be capable of maintaining impulsion and contact with hand and leg on the approach to the fence, so that the horse can 'make his own arrangements', or of 'seeing the horse's stride' and adjusting it smoothly, so that he meets his fences 'right'.

The overall impression should be of quiet authority, fluency and style.

POSITION

The normal 'shoulder, knee and toe in line' position provides a sound basis for all jumping, but, by now, you should be able to adapt it according to circumstances. Stirrups should be shortened by at least three to four holes from the dressage length. Frequent checking of position is still essential. Rider faults affect the horse, and are much easier to correct if picked up quickly.

In show jumping there may be times when you find it best to maintain a slightly more upright position between fences, particularly when riding a strong, sticky or unbalanced horse. NOTE. Misuse of this position can lead to the horse jumping with a flat or hollow back.

In cross country some top international riders shorten their stirrups by six holes or even more. Shorter stirrups make it easier to maintain a strong, steady, forward position throughout the round, with the weight over the horse's shoulders and off the back of the saddle. They also help in controlling a pulling horse.

On a balanced, free-going horse over a bold, open type of fence, remain forward on the approach, but be ready to sit up if:

a. jumping a drop fence or into water. Over these, the body should remain upright during 'flight', to help balance the horse in landing, and the lower leg should go forward a little. (See jumping picture on page 182.) Resume the forward position as soon as possible on landing.

b. approaching a 'tricky' fence or combination, where the horse must be rounded up and maximum impulsion retained.

c. the horse is impetuous, on his forehand or trying to stop or run off.

Continue to make every effort to strengthen and improve your jumping position, especially for cross country.

Contact.   Points to check:

1. The correct length of rein and height of hands. The straight line from elbow to bit is a most useful guide.

2. That you are not relying on the reins or the horse's neck to maintain balance.

3. That the hands maintain contact and control throughout, while allowing the horse to use himself freely over the fence.

The strength of the contact varies with the pace, the horse and the type of fence, but it should always be sympathetic and never stronger than necessary to control and balance the horse.

Adapting to suit. Jumping down into water, rider looking ahead, body upright, lower leg slightly forward, fingers allow full stretch while keeping contact.   Uphill, well balanced, with the weight off the horse's loins. Contact good, despite loss of 'line'. Leg slipped a little, but heel still good.

This should now be studied in greater detail:

The take-off zone. This is the area from which a horse should take off in order to jump a fence in good style and with the minimum of effort.

For an upright fence, this zone lies *between* the height of the fence from its base (1.1m if it is 1.1m high) and 1½ times the height, 1.65m. Ideally it should be about one and a third times the height of the fence — 1.45m in this case. For bigger fences, the zone reduces in size — between the height of the fence and the height plus 45cm down to 30cm, so greater accuracy is required.

For a spread fence, especially of the staircase type, the take-off point should be as close as possible to, but not less than, the height of the first element.

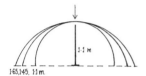 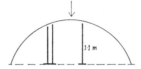 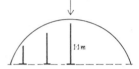

If the rider can adjust the horse's stride to bring him within the take-off zone, this will make for accurate jumping, but:

a. if you adjust the stride when you happen to see it, and at other times leave the horse to work it out for himself, or, worse still, put him 'wrong', he will soon lose all confidence.

b. it must be done smoothly and consistently, a little per stride and never later than three strides out — last-stride or drastic alterations cause confusion and loss of balance and rhythm.

c. the horse must be sufficiently balanced and responsive to lengthen or shorten his stride smoothly without losing impulsion.

The ability to see the horse's stride comes naturally to some riders, others may develop it with practice and experience, some never do. Lack of it need not affect the horse's ability to cope with all normal jumping activities up to about 1.2m, so long as the rider:

a. creates and maintains impulsion by keeping the legs on the horse, so that he is sent up to the hand, and

b. maintains this contact in front of the fence — dropping the horse in the last strides is a serious fault (see page 59).

c. on landing, rounds the horse up immediately.

d. makes sufficient use of gymnastic exercises, combinations and placing rails, which help the horse to learn to adjust the stride himself, as well as developing the rider's eye.

The following exercise will also help:

Build a good upright fence at, say, 1.1m and mark out the take-off zone as shown above. (Scratch guidelines on the ground, or use small markers.) Jump the fence three times in succession, trying to bring the horse as close as possible to the same spot within the take-off zone. You will need an observer on the ground to check. It is not a question of telling the horse where to take off, but of adjusting not less than three strides out, and then maintaining impulsion and rhythm, so that he arrives automatically in the right place. If unsuccessful, use a placing rail, about 45cm high, three strides away — 14m or 45ft. Practice for some time with this rail, counting the strides in between, then try again without it.

TRAINING

The principles and methods of training and correcting faults explained in 'Jumping: B Certificate' (Chapter 4) must now be clearly understood, so that you can apply them to all types of horses.

Jumping and gymnastic exercises learned to date should be practised, with increased height/spread of fence where appropriate.

More advanced exercises include:

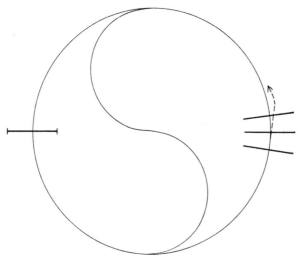

Trotting poles and jump on a circle (30m approximately). 1. Trot poles on curve, 1.37m apart in centre. Start with 3 poles, maximum 5. Curve must be maintained — dotted line is incorrect. Excellent for improving the horse's balance and suppleness. When he is doing the poles correctly, include the jump. 2. Trot poles on circle to fence. 3. Trot poles, change through circle to fence. 4. Trot poles, canter on circle to fence, back to trot for poles. 5. Trot poles, change through circle, canter fence, change or not to poles. Note: This exercise is more difficult than it looks — a real test of training!

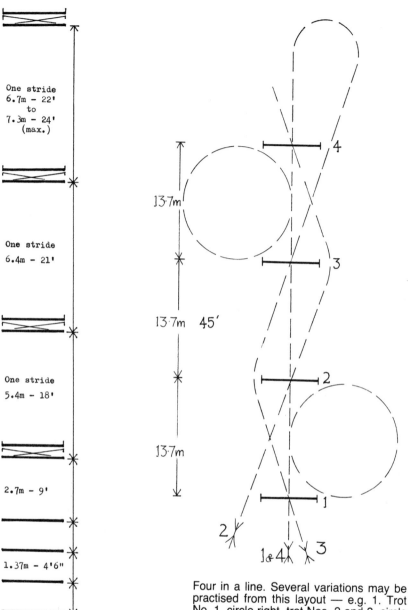

One stride
6.7m – 22'
to
7.3m – 24'
(max.)

One stride
6.4m – 21'

One stride
5.4m – 18'

2.7m – 9'

1.37m – 4'6"

13.7m

13.7m 45'

13.7m

13.7m

4

3

2

2

1 & 4

3

1

Gymnastic exercise. As each fence is added, the distance is increased to allow for the lengthening canter stride. Two stride or bounce distances may be used — the latter should always be at the start, except for very experienced horses.

Four in a line. Several variations may be practised from this layout — e.g. 1. Trot No. 1, circle right, trot Nos. 2 and 3, circle left, trot No. 4. Possibly canter back straight through, 4, 3, 2, 1. 2. Canter straight through. A good regularity and 'rounding up' exercise. The horse should take three steady, even strides between each fence. 3. Trot or canter No. 1 at an angle to pass No. 2, angle over No. 3, pass No. 4. Return jumping the alternative fences. Note: Use uprights to start with. Height 75-90cm, for experienced horses.

For fences up to 1.15m (3'9") with spreads in proportion, basic distances of 7.3m (24') for one stride and 10.3m (34') for two strides will generally be correct for most horses if the double consists of two identical fences. However, they will probably be too long if jumping from upright to spread, especially a staircase, where the horse should take off close to the first rail, so reduce the distance by 15-30cm (6-12") per stride. Going from spread to upright, a longer distance will be required, because the horse will land further out over the spread, and needs room to stand off from the upright. Increase the distance by 30cm per stride. All distances should be reduced by 30cm or more per stride for ponies, depending on their size.

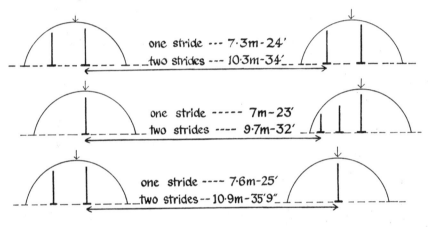

one stride --- 7·3m - 24'
two strides --- 10·3m - 34'

one stride ----- 7m - 23'
two strides ---- 9·7m - 32'

one stride ---- 7·6m - 25'
two strides -- 10·9m - 35'9"

For more advanced jumping over larger fences, these distances may require adjustment.

Generally, the best fences to use in combinations are uprights, ascending oxer or staircase types. Pyramids, although easy on their own, can be confusing. True parallels, especially in succession, should only be used for experienced horses.

Trebles should be built at true distances for the types of fence involved, never after a sharp turn or from a confined approach. An ascending oxer or upright makes a good, inviting first element.

Related Fences

Fences between three and six strides apart. True distances for fences of about 1.15m would be:

3 strides	14m	4 strides	17m
5 strides	20m	6 strides	23m

It is not necessary to alter distances, as for combinations, according to the type of fences.

Work over related fences on similar lines to combinations, always counting the strides in between and keeping them even.

Factors which Affect the Horse's Stride

Faster pace, wide, open spaces and going downhill all lengthen the stride, so the distance should be increased. Rising ground, heavy going or a restricted approach will shorten the stride. Cross country combinations are usually longer than in show jumping, except where plain ditches or banks are involved and the distance is slightly shortened.

During this more advanced training:

1. Check constantly *how* the horse jumps. Good style is shown by a confident but controlled approach and a good 'bascule' over the fence, using his head and neck fully and rounding his back, so that the wither is the highest point at the top of the arc, or parabola.

2. Measure distances carefully. If too long, they tend to make the horse jump flat, so keep them just short enough to encourage him to stay 'round'.

3. Intersperse exercises with straightforward single fences. Too much precision work can make the horse bored and take away his enjoyment and initiative.

Remember that the bigger the fences the greater the effort required from the horse. Always be sure that he is fit and well, make training progressive and NEVER over-face or over-jump.

At this stage, ride and jump as many different horses as you can — schooling, competing, hunting. However sound your knowledge, there is no substitute for practical experience.

TRAINING THE YOUNG HORSE TO JUMP

This should not be started until the horse is at least three years old — see 'Education of a Young Horse', page 168.

A good way to begin is during the initial 'leading about' periods (page 169) by stepping over poles on the ground. Progress to small jumps, crossed rails, logs, banks, ditches — anything you can hop over yourself. Wear gloves and solid boots, and never get directly in front of the horse. He should wear lunging cavesson and 3m lead-rope, brushing boots, *never* side-reins.

It is possible to continue jumping training either on the lunge or by loose schooling, if you have the skill and the facilities, but for most people it will probably be better to continue mounted.

Mounted Jumping Training

Depending on condition and behaviour, most horses should be ready to begin work over ground poles about four to six weeks after they were first ridden independently off the lunge. The horse should:

1. Be under control at all paces, going freely forward.

2. Be finding his balance under the rider, and developing some muscle.

Use fairly short stirrups and a forward position throughout when jumping young horses. Always have a neckstrap and brushing boots on the horse. Carry a short schooling whip, never use spurs or a dressage whip.

Method

A sequence similar to that recommended for the beginner rider, in *Manual One*, 'Jumping: C Certificate', page 81, may be used, i.e.:

1. Single pole on the ground, 'approachable' from either side. Walk and trot on both reins.

2. Several single poles, laid out to make a flowing 'course'. This accustoms the horse to being guided smoothly from one obstacle to another. Be sure to ride a good track and get straight at each pole. Give the horse every encouragement to put his head down and look at it, and unlimited praise when he steps over quietly in his stride.

3. Two poles on the ground together, between stands. Putting them against a fence line makes it easier to keep a young horse straight. Convert to cross poles, approximately 30cm in the centre. Trot over this on both reins — if the horse canters on landing, bring him back to trot within the next couple of strides. Gradually vary and enlarge the fence a little. Use a horizontal pole with a ground line on each side or a simple staircase (see page 63), maximum height 40-45cm. The latter can only be jumped on one rein when it is on the fence line.

4. Introduce a line of trotting poles, as in *Manual One*, page 82. This may be done, for variety, concurrently with the previous stage.

5. When the horse jumps confidently and is easily kept straight on the fence line, small, varied jumps, of types he already knows, may be placed in the open. All approaches should still be in trot. Use a similar layout to the poles in stage 2 — the 'Three in a line', *Manual One*, page 82, is another useful arrangement.

6. Return to the simple staircase on the fence line. Add an upright — one pole with dropper — 9m away. Approached in trot, this should give two easy, non-jumping strides in between. Be sure to have good leg contact and urge the horse on quietly as he lands over the first, then back to trot after the second. Then increase the distance by about 1m, and allow or encourage him to canter the last few strides

into the first jump. This use of a double will help the horse to meet his first canter jumps on a good stride, and also to keep him calm.

7. Introduce a one-stride double in the same way. For distances, see table on page 68. It is better that distances should be on the short side for the horse rather than too long, which would encourage flat jumping, diving at the second fence, undue haste and excitement. When all these doubles are taken confidently on the fence line, they may be added to the single fences in the open.

8. Placing poles. Most young horses find placing poles rather confusing if they are introduced right at the start, but they can be useful once the horse is beginning to jump a little, particularly if he tends to take off too close or too far away. Slight variations in the normal distances of 2.7m for trot and 5.4m for canter will help to adjust his stride. Jumps may also be placed at similar distances after a line of trotting poles.

9. All possible variety should now be sought — look for small logs, banks, ditches, making sure they are clear-cut, with a good approach and landing. Also small obstacles on gentle slopes. When introducing 'filling', such as drums or tyres, leave a gap in the middle initially, to allow the horse to become accustomed to them without alarm.

Since a young horse must build up his confidence and ability in an activity that is not natural to him, little and often is recommended for this early jumping. Up to six obstacles three or four times a week is better than one long session. Never jump a young horse if:

a. the going is hard, heavy, rough or slippery;

b. there is the slightest suspicion of heat, filling or soreness in a leg; or

c. he appears tired or out of sorts, or is not going well, for his state of training, on the flat.

Refusals. It should never occur to the horse to stop if the training is progressive, and he is consistently well ridden and correctly presented. Should it ever happen, lower and/or simplify the fence, and build up again gradually as confidence returns.

Showing the horse the fence is not recommended (see *Manual One*, page 90), but jumping towards home or a lead from another horse can be helpful with anything new or slightly bigger.

Running off. Although primarily due to bad riding, this can occur if speed is allowed to build up in the early stages, with consequent excitement. Always jump everything new at trot until the horse is sure of it, and then ask him to canter the last few strides.

Size of fences. The reason for using such small fences for a three-year-old is to keep the physical effort required and the jar on

189

landing to a minimum. The bones are not fully developed at this age, and the horse is extremely liable to concussion, injuries and sprains.

When he is going well at this height, only jump him occasionally or stop altogether until he is four. Do not be tempted to make the jumps bigger because he shows potential.

The Four-Year-Old

As the horse becomes stronger and his work on the flat improves, the exercises in Chapter 4 may be introduced one at a time, alternating with inviting single fences and short courses. Gradually increase the height to an average of 60-75cm. As he progresses, the *occasional* fence up to about 90cm may be brought in towards the end of the course, just to show him what he can do.

Slightly bigger cross-country fences may also be jumped, water introduced (see page 75), but very few drop fences, to avoid jar on the horse's legs.

Jump once or twice a week. The aims are to give the horse confidence and to teach him to handle himself. Be sure that all fences are well built, and give plenty of encouragement and praise throughout.

'Bringing the horse out.' His first outings should be to Pony Club rallies, to take part in activities suited to his state of training and to learn to socialise. This is where his first jumping in public should be done, over fences well within his capacity.

Jumping competitions. Try to take him to one or two shows without competing, or to enter only in flat classes (even if he's not a show horse) to let him get used to the atmosphere, before asking him to jump strange fences in the ring.

Be patient. More horses are spoilt by being over-faced in their first season than in any other way. He *must* have jumped slightly above the height he will meet in his first classes. 'Kindergarten' and practice jumping days are by far the best way of starting. Be sure that the fences are well built and the track suitable — sharp turns and trebles are out. If you think it's too difficult for your horse, don't start.

Should he have a clear round first time out, as he well may if you have trained him properly, think twice before starting in the jump-off. Whatever you do, *don't* go for speed. A couple of rounds is enough — try to finish on a good note and let him feel he has done well.

Eventing. In the cross country, be sure that you know exactly where you are going and ride at a steady, even canter. Speed must be built up progressively as he gains experience, otherwise, all your work could be undone in one outing.

Limit the number of shows or events — competitions at this stage are part of the training — winning comes later.

Hunting. Try to ride to your first meets, and let your youngster look from a safe distance — keep his heels well away from hounds or horses. He will probably become rather excited, and must be taught manners right from the start. A few short days over carefully chosen country taking a lead from a reliable hunter, where necessary, should get your young horse going on the right lines.

From these strong foundations, progress should continue steadily through the horse's fifth and sixth years. It takes at least three years to produce a good eventer or show jumper — five if you aspire to international competition!

Not everyone has the temperament or affinity with young horses to school them successfully, but to those who have, there is nothing more rewarding than bringing out a well-trained youngster.

13
TEST SHEET: H CERTIFICATE

Minimum age: 17 years
Candidates must hold B Certificate

This test is intended to afford keen associate members, holders of B Certificate, a worthwhile certificate for efficiency in horse management, without the necessity of acquiring the high standard of riding expected of an A Certificate candidate.

OBJECTIVES

To gain wide knowledge of the care and conditioning of horses, and to be capable of taking charge of horses, either stabled or at grass, over a limited period.

To be able to tack up and lunge a horse efficiently, and to exercise two horses together (ride and lead).

Paddocking

Management of a number of horses at grass — water, feed, fences, etc. Assess the quality of pasture in a paddock.

Pasture management — some knowledge of the use of fertilisers, harrowing, topping, etc.

Feeding, Watering, Conditioning

Elementary knowledge of the horse's digestive system.

Feed requirements — carbohydrates, protein, fats, fibre, minerals, vitamins.

Hay and grain feeds — types, qualities, purchasing, methods of feeding.

Feeding and conditioning programmes for different types of horses for specified work — e.g. one-day horse trials, hunting, treks, etc.

Handling

Handling horses in stables.
Handling difficult horses.
Use of a twitch.

Grooming, Trimming, Clipping

Washing a horse's sheath.
Pulling a tail.
Hogging a mane.
How to clip, including care of the clipping machine before, during and after use.

The Foot and Shoeing

Some knowledge of the anatomy of the horse's foot.
Changes in the foot that may be caused by neglect, poor shoeing or disease.
Some knowledge of remedial shoeing — e.g. feather-edged shoes, grass tips and soles.
Use of screw-in studs.
Be able to remove a shoe.

Stabling

Elementary knowledge of stable construction — dimensions, materials, ventilation, drainage.
Fire precautions in stables.
Stable routine for horses in work.
Be able to deal with a cast horse, with assistance.
Construction and use of yards.
Storage of bedding, hay and hard feed.
Siting and building a muck heap.
Vices and bad habits of stabled horses.

Travelling

Routine preparation for travelling horses by road, air or sea (inter-island).

Loading and unloading, including difficult horses.
Inspection of float.

Health, Ailments, Injuries

Be able to take a temperature.
Sick nursing.
Administering medication.
Internal parasites.
Symptoms of dehydration.
Azoturia. Tetanus.
Strangles, cough epidemics, etc.
Respiratory ailments.
Detection of lameness.
Foot ailments.
Seats of lameness — bony and bursal enlargements.
Sprains, sore shins, interfering.

Know the Horse

Basic knowledge of the horse's structure and anatomy.
How poor conformation and bad action can affect a horse's soundness and usefulness.
Ageing a horse by the teeth.
Buying a horse.

Saddlery and Equipment

Different types of saddles.
Recognise a broken tree.
Knowledge of the principles of bitting and the uses of different bits.
Care, maintenance and fitting of all types of saddlery and equipment in common use.
Uses of various covers, rugs and sheets.
Protective clothing — bandages, boots, kneecaps, hock boots, tail and poll guards.
Organisation of a tack room.

Lunging, Ride and Lead

Tack up a horse for lunging and lunge the horse as a form of exercise, in accordance with the method given in *Manual Two*.
Tack up two horses and ride and lead, with the led horse on either side.
Know the Road Code as it is applicable to horses.
Assist a person to mount, hold the horse's head; balance the weight of the rider mounting. Give a leg up.

NOTE. A Certificate candidates may be questioned on the subjects in this section, but time does not allow for practical examination as in H Certificate.

The syllabus for H Certificate includes all work for the 'Care of the Pony' sections of D and C certificates, and the 'Horse Management' section of B Certificate, whether or not it is specified on this Test Sheet.

14

PADDOCKING, FEEDING, CONDITIONING (A, H)

Management of a Number of Horses and Ponies at Grass

The number of horses that can safely and adequately be grazed per hectare depends on:

1. The quality of the grazing.
2. The time of year.
3. The weather and the state of the ground.
4. What other stock is carried.
5. Supplementary feeding.
6. The fences.

The higher the concentration of horses, the greater the risk of parasitic infection. In the best of circumstances, it is rarely possible to average more than two to three horses per hectare over a long period.

Rotation is essential for proper management, so that paddocks can be cleaned up, topdressed if necessary and allowed to grow between grazings. *The value of following horses with other stock, especially cattle, cannot be over-emphasised.* Horses should not be kept continually in one paddock. The usual rotation period is two weeks, more or less, depending on circumstances.

Fences. (See *Manual One*, page 123.) Although fencing is expensive, subdivision of large paddocks is recommended, to facilitate rotation of grazing.

Electric fences are sometimes used for subdivision, but they can be dangerous where large numbers of horses or large areas are involved. They can be effective in keeping horses off a fence line.

Electric fences require careful insulation, especially in gateways. Where they are used, horses should be under close supervision.

Division of horses. Known kickers and bullies must be outlawed from communal grazing, for the sake of the other horses and their owners.

It is often best to separate mares and geldings, especially at camps or on other occasions where large numbers of strange horses have to be turned out together.

Mares close to foaling or with new foals at foot should not be grazed with other mares, or with geldings.

Stallions nearly always have to be grazed apart from other horses. Very safe, strong and high fences are needed for them.

Introducing new horses to a group must be undertaken carefully. The ideal is to put the new horse in the next paddock for a few days.

It may be best to separate the better 'doers', who put on too much condition, so that the other horses can be given the best grazing.

Feeding out. (See *Manual One*, pages 132-133.)

Worming. All horses should be wormed at the same time, six-weekly, if only horses are grazed. (See 'Internal Parasites, page 125.) New horses should not be turned out with the group until they have been wormed. A twice-yearly worm count is strongly recommended.

Isolation. A small isolation paddock, out of all contact with others, is almost essential where numbers of horses are concerned.

Indications for Isolation

Coughs, colds, ringworm, lice.

Suspected illness — loss of appetite, moping alone, rise in temperature, staring coat, swollen throat glands.

Severe lameness or injury — to prevent galloping about with others.

Acute observation and prompt isolation will usually prevent the spread of infection.

Epidemics, e.g. strangles, equine influenza, where horses are affected or have been exposed to infection.

NO horse, even if apparently healthy, must be taken off the property to mix with others, until ALL are given a clean bill of health by the vet.

No outside horse should be brought in.

Everybody handling the horses must observe strict isolation procedures (see *Manual One*, page 168).

Healthy horses must not be put in an infected paddock until the water trough has been thoroughly cleaned out and disinfected.

PADDOCK MAINTENANCE

Topdressing and Use of Fertilisers

Objects

1. To keep the grass growing for as much of the year as possible. Young, actively growing pasture is more nutritious and more palatable than the same plants when they are old and stalky.

2. To encourage the growth of good grasses and clover, rather than weeds. A predominance of clover makes the pasture too rich for horses, and even more so for ponies, but some clover helps to maintain the level of nitrogen in the soil.

3. To supply the nutrients needed for good pasture growth, and for the health of the stock in the paddock.

Signs that a Paddock needs Fertilisers

1. Where there is a predominance of weeds, especially such things as docks, pennyroyal, thistles, blackberry, ragwort, daisies, buttercups and rushes. All these are unpalatable to horses, even if not actually poisonous, and of little food value. The last two indicate that drainage is probably needed as well as topdressing. Because weeds can grow on poorer soil than grasses, they may soon take over completely in neglected paddocks.

2. When the growth of grass is much poorer than in similar paddocks nearby, and the growth is thin and stalky, with little 'bottom' to it. The grass may be yellowish in colour.

Keep a constant watch for any of these signs developing. If they are already obvious, the paddock is in a bad state.

Why Fertilisers are Necessary

Four major elements are needed for plant and animal health. They are lime, phosphate, potash and nitrogen. Continuous grazing depletes the soil of these elements, and in very light sandy or pumice soils, especially where there is a heavy rainfall, they are often washed or 'leached' out.

Trace elements, or microelements, are also essential, though, as their name implies, in minute amounts. They are frequently lacking in Australia and New Zealand, especially magnesium, cobalt and selenium, but can be supplied as additives to the basic fertiliser.

Application of Fertilisers

If the paddock is too small for a contractor to apply the fertiliser by truck, it will have to be scattered by hand. Grass and/or clover seed may be applied at the same time.

In most districts, the pasture will benefit greatly from topdressing in spring or autumn, or fertiliser may be applied six to eight weeks before maximum growth will be required. It is best, if possible, to apply fertiliser just before rain. In any case, horses must be kept out of the paddock until there has been a good fall to wash it off the surface into the soil, otherwise they could be poisoned.

What fertilisers are needed will vary according to the composition of the soil in your area — this is why advice should be sought locally. The Ministry of Agriculture and Fisheries will always assist with advice and a soil analysis, if needed. The basis will be lime and superphosphate, but the proportions, and any additives, will have to be determined.

Harrowing. A controversial subject — it spreads droppings — and if done in humid weather, there is a danger of spreading parasites as well and encouraging their breeding. Its chief benefit is in clearing matted vegetation from grass roots, thereby allowing greater penetration of fertilisers and promoting fresh growth.

In paddocks too big for picking up droppings by wheelbarrow, they are better spread out than left lying in heaps. In these circumstances, harrowing can be useful, but try to do it in dry, hot or cold weather, when exposed larvae will be less likely to survive. The 'foot harrows' — kicking the droppings to spread them — are also useful in these conditions!

Topping or mowing. Almost essential if grass 'runs away' in late spring or early summer and becomes stalky and thin at the bottom. It produces a great thickening of the sward, encourages the growth of grass and clover and discourages weeds. Many weeds, such as thistles and blackberry, can be completely eliminated by repeated topping.

Tidiness is the hallmark of the good horsemaster and the well-run establishment. Fences and gates in need of repair, rubbish lying around (wire, string, paper or plastic bags, broken jumping gear or machinery), proclaim an uncaring attitude and a lack of responsibility for the safety and welfare of the animals in your charge.

FEEDING

The Digestive System (see diagram, front endpaper)

Some knowledge of the horse's digestive system will help to explain the reasons for basic rules of feeding and management.

1. **The mouth and throat**
a. the lips — select food, reject foreign bodies.
b. the incisors — crop the grass in grazing.

c. the tongue — controls the food in the mouth — passes it to:

d. the molars, which grind and masticate. During this process, the back of the tongue mixes the food with saliva, then passes it on to:

e. the pharynx, or top of the throat.

If: **the incisors** are badly worn, as with an old horse, or the horse is parrot-mouthed or has other dental irregularities, his grazing efficiency will be impaired.

the molars have sharp edges, the horse will have difficulty in chewing and the food will not be sufficiently ground up.

fibre — e.g. chaff — is lacking in a hard feed, the horse may bolt it, giving too little time for proper mastication.

water is not available in unlimited quantities, he will be unable to produce the 27 litres of saliva needed daily, especially if stabled and receiving mainly dry food. And saliva is only the first of the digestive juices!

2. **The oesophagus.** A long, narrow tube connecting the pharynx with the stomach. Balls of food can clearly be seen going down the left side of the gullet, or oesophagus.

If **chunks** of hard food — e.g. carrot — are given, it is obvious how choking can occur.

3. **The stomach.** Comparatively small in the horse — capacity about 14 litres. Food only remains here for one to one-and-a-half hours; long enough to be thoroughly churned up and mixed with digestive juices.

The size of the stomach limits the amount of food the horse can eat at one time — hence, 'Feed little and often'. If the horse is worked on a full stomach:

a. the close proximity of the lungs to the distended stomach interferes with their proper functioning. The lungs will be unable to expand sufficiently if strenuous activity is demanded, and this can be a major cause of emphysema, or broken wind. (See page 237.)

b. the vigorous muscular action of the stomach requires a blood supply, which is curtailed by the needs of the lungs and the muscles of locomotion.

4. **The small intestine,** another narrow tube, but about 20 metres in length, where proteins and carbohydrates are broken down by enzyme action so that they can be absorbed into the bloodstream. The roughage passes through to

5. **The caecum,** a large, sack-like organ, capacity about 55 litres. The more fibrous parts of the food remain here for up to 36 hours, being constantly churned and kneaded and mixed with the caecal

juices and with bacteria, which are able to break them down so that they, too, can be absorbed. The remainder passes on to

6. **The large colon,** where it is subjected to further bacterial action. Finally, the indigestible portions of food with most of the moisture removed, go on to

7. **The small colon,** where it is formed into balls or 'boluses', and

8. **The rectum,** whence it passes out as manure. The whole process takes one to two days.

Through the entire digestive tract, there is a continual churning and mixing of the food with the various secretions. It is a muscular process, and if it is to act efficiently, the muscles must have sufficient bulk on which to work.

Nutritional Requirements of Horses

To be sure that the horse is receiving the correct food for his needs, growth, maintenance, work, warmth, it is important to know what parts individual feeds play. Basically, they are divided into:

Carbohydrates, or energy equivalents.   These:

Principal sources (in order):
Oats, barley, maize.
Linseed, skim milk powder.
Molasses, bran.
Lucerne, clover hay, chaff.
Good pasture.

1. Supply energy.
2. Are essential for good muscle performance.
3. Provide warmth.
4. Surplus to requirements are stored and in excess form fat.

Protein

Principal sources:
Peas, beans.
Skim milk powder.
Linseed.
Lucerne, red clover, bran.
Barley, oats, maize.
Good pasture.

1. Are essential for growth and for day-to-day repair of all body cells.
2. If surplus, protein is not stored, but undergoes changes during digestion and may assist in providing warmth/energy.

Fats

Principal sources:
Linseed, linseed oil.
Other vegetable oils
— e.g. sunflower, safflower, soya bean oils.
Small traces in most energy foods.

1. Are needed only in very small quantities.
2. Excess fat is not well digested and can inhibit digestion of other foods.

Fibre

Principal sources:
Hay — all types.
Chaff — all types.
Pasture.

1. This allows access for digestive juices in all phases of digestion by preventing formation of solid masses of food, helps to maintain churning action and ensure all food is fully utilised.
2. Is essential for good health, especially if diet includes high proportion of concentrates.

In addition to the above, horses need:

Minerals to build and maintain the bony skeleton and to provide a proper mineral balance in the bloodstream. Among the most important minerals are:

Salt — essential for all living animals. Sweating causes heavy loss of salt and other elements, and this can lead to dehydration and exhaustion, especially in hot weather. Rock salt, or a mineral lick to suit the locality, should always be available.

Calcium and phosphorus. Both are needed for skeletal development and maintenance. Growing horses and brood mares must have more calcium than phosphorus. The latter should never predominate in any horse's diet.
Sources:

Calcium	**Phosphorous**
Lucerne	Bran (extremely high)
Red clover, clover mixture, hay	Linseed
Skim milk powder	Grains
Good pasture	Hay and pasture
Grains	

Minerals and vitamins (which are necessary for proper utilisation of food) are usually present in a normal good diet. Provided the horse has access to good quality pasture and/or hay, with concentrates as required, the risk of imbalance is minimal. It is where the pasture is poor or lacking in trace elements (see page 196), or where large quantities of concentrates are being fed, that problems may arise. (Mineral and vitamin additivies — see page 88.)

Electrolytes are chemical salts, which are naturally present in food and water, and are absorbed into the bloodstream along with the other products of digestion. They help to maintain the fluid balance of the body.

Some of these salts are acid, others alkaline. Normally, the body is able to hold a balance between the two.

However, with hard work, especially in hot or humid climatic conditions, electrolytes are lost heavily in sweat and other body fluids; and there may be a greater loss of either acid or alkaline salts, according to the type of work, the degree of stress and the weather conditions. The object of electrolyte mixtures is to restore both the total electrolytes in the body and the balance between them.

Signs of electrolyte deficiency or imbalance are mild dehydration, lethargy, tying-up or azoturia, diarrhoea, thick-windedness and unaccountable variations in performance.

Good grass, with normal supplementary feeding when needed, should provide sufficient electrolytes for most Pony Club mounts, but where strenuous work in warm conditions is being undertaken, especially if any of the above signs are present, extra electrolytes will almost certainly be indicated.

There are several proprietary brands on the market, but you should consult your vet as to whether your horse requires any and which ones to use. Incorrect use can do more harm than good. Whichever ones are used, it is absolutely essential that horses on electrolytes should have unlimited water, and that they should drink.

There is still considerable research being carried out in this area.

PROPERTIES OF SOME COMMONLY USED FOODSTUFFS

Oats. Energy high, protein low, calcium low, phosphorus fairly high. Although not the highest energy-producing grain, oats are the safest and most digestible. Owing to their husk, there is little danger of their compacting in the stomach. They make some horses, and most ponies, excitable. If work is reduced, oats must be cut.

Uses: For fitness and stamina — eventing, hunting, endurance riding, polo, show jumping, dressage, showing. For the last three, barley may be better — especially if the horse 'hots up' on oats.

Best fed lightly bruised — if crushed flat oats quickly 'go off' and lose food value; fed whole, they are less digestible and may go straight through the horse. Even bruised oats begin to lose value after about two weeks. Boiled oats are more fattening, less inclined to hot horses up. Better steamed with a minimum of water — if sloppy, they can make horses soft in condition.

Barley. Energy high, protein low, calcium low, phosphorus fairly high. Rather more fattening and definitely less exciting than oats. Often cheaper. Boiled barley is an excellent winter feed for old or young horses, or those in poor condition. May be given two or three times weekly to horses in hard work who tend to 'run up'.

Uses: For fitness and stamina — see 'Oats' above.

For putting on and retaining condition.

For warmth. (Boiled.)

Best fed crushed fairly coarsely or boiled whole. Raw whole barley is too hard to chew and very indigestible; ground barley or barley meal can compact. If used at all, it must be mixed with plenty of chaff.

Maize. Energy high, protein low, calcium low, phosphorus high. Fattening and heating, but not very digestible. It is generally accepted that maize should not comprise more than 30% of the grain ration. This would be excessive for horses in fast work.

Uses: For variation in the diet of difficult feeders, especially if the horse tends to 'run up'. Not for the overweight.

Best fed coarsely crushed, as for barley, not ground. Whole maize is normally too hard, although some horses enjoy chewing on a whole corn cob occasionally. Maize is not fed boiled.

Wheat. Extremely indigestible and can be dangerous. Not recommended when other, safer grains are available.

Bran. Energy low, protein low, calcium low, phosphorus extremely high, fibre high. Palatable, provides bulk, easily digested and assists in the digestion of other foods, especially in older horses. Fattening. Owing to its high phosphorus content, should not be fed in excess to young horses — half a kilogram daily would be ample.

Bran does not keep well. Feed containers must be well scrubbed out after it is used, otherwise the residue turns sour and will put the horse off his feed.

Uses: As a mash, either alone or mixed with boiled linseed, barley or oats, for tired or sick horses, or on the night before a day off.

As a mild laxative, fed wet; or as a binding agent, fed dry. To replace part of the grain ration, if it has to be cut.

Linseed. Energy high, protein fairly high, calcium low, phosphorous high. Supplies the most easily digested form of fat for horses. Fattening.

Uses: Boiled, in a mash. Tempting and easily digested after a hard day's work.

For putting on condition and putting a 'bloom' on the coat.

Best fed boiled (for method see page 86) or as linseed meal. The latter is easier to feed but does not keep well, and is less beneficial than a mash for a tired horse.

NOTE: Whole linseed *must* be boiled, soaking is not sufficient.

Raw linseed oil, about an eggcupful, may be mixed with the feed — often very beneficial for horses in the early stages of broken wind (see page 237).

Skim milk powder (not whole milk). High in protein and calcium, fattening.

Uses: Excellent for raising the calcium:phosphorus ratio for growing horses and brood mares.

Can help to tempt delicate feeders, but should not be used excessively for horses in hard work.

Feed: A cupful once or twice daily.

Molasses. Energy fairly high, palatable, easily digested, fattening.

Uses: For variety, especially with difficult feeders.

Feed: Either in liquid or powder form. A cupful a day is usually sufficient.

Pellets and other composite horse feeds contain some or all of the above ingredients, and possibly others, such as peas and beans. These feeds are excellent as a maintenance ration. Where maximum fitness is required, it is important to know the exact amount of each food being given, and this is not always easy with made-up feeds. They may prove too fattening for some horses, though for most they can still form part of the daily diet.

Carrots. Cooling, easily digested, rich in vitamins. Most valuable in winter, when grass is short. Good for horses with coughs, or respiratory diseases, and for variety.

Feed: Whole or sliced lengthways. Up to one and a half kilograms daily, according to circumstances. They must be clean and sound.

Other roots — swedes, turnips, parsnips, beets — while of slightly lower feed value than carrots, are much enjoyed by some horses, and can also be useful for difficult feeders.

Feed: Whole or sliced lengthways, well washed.

Bulk Feeds

Pasture. Really good pasture is economical, palatable, easily digested and supplies all essential nutrients in the correct proportions for normal maintenance. Growing horses may need extra protein and calcium, horses in work will require more carbohydrates and protein, but all horses benefit from the inclusion of grass as some part of their diet. Ponies do not require such rich grazing as horses — it may cause laminitis.

Hay. Grass or pasture plants such as lucerne or clover, from which a large proportion of the moisture has been removed, and therefore a more concentrated form of nourishment than growing pasture. The natural substitute when grass is deficient either in quantity or quality. A proportion of hay, rather than all grass to supply bulk, is less fattening and better for horses in hard condition.

The nutritional value of hay depends on type.

Lucerne. Very high in protein and calcium, high energy.

Red clover. Also high in protein, calcium and energy.

Both are excellent for growing horses and brood mares. Should not form more than half the hay ration for horses in hard work, or more than one third for ponies.

Meadow hay depends on the plants of which it is composed and the land on which it was grown. About one third clover with the remainder mainly ryegrass or timothy makes an excellent hay for horses in hard work. Hard hay with crisp stalks encourages thorough mastication and makes for harder condition in the horse than soft hay, which is usually cheaper and less nutritious. However, sick or older horses may find a softer hay easier to eat and more digestible, and it may be quite adequate for smaller ponies in light work.

Some good grasses: Rye
Cocksfoot
Timothy

Chaff — chopped lucerne, hay or oat straw.

Lucerne makes excellent chaff — probably the best way of feeding lucerne to horses in hard work.

Hay chaff naturally depends on the hay from which it is made. To ensure consistent quality, it is much better to cut your own with a chaffcutter, rather than buying readymade chaff.

Oaten chaff. Oat straw is less nutritious than hay, and it is always difficult to estimate the oat content of readymade oaten chaff.

Uses: To prevent compaction of grain feeds and pellets, and to keep the texture 'open'.

To discourage bolting the feed. Chaff makes the horse eat more slowly and chew more thoroughly.

Feed: A good double handful of chaff in every feed, except bran mashes.

Quantity. By now, you will be well aware of the difficulties of laying down exact quantities of feed. As a rough guide, it is generally accepted that a horse's daily dietary requirement is 2½ to 3 percent of his bodyweight. Thus, a 160cm horse, weighing about 450kgs, would need 12 to 15kg total ration, but the ratio of bulk to concentrates would vary according to work and other conditions.

The skill in feeding different horses lies in evaluating their requirements from day to day, both as to type and quantity of food. As mentioned on page 92, constant, acute, observation is the best guide, so that you are immediately aware of the slightest changes in the horse's condition, performance or state of fitness, and can adjust feed and exercise accordingly, or take any other necessary action.

BUYING FORAGE

The value of all feed depends on its quality. Good quality means that the feed has been:

a. well grown, on good land with correct manures.

b. well harvested.

c. well stored.

These conditions ensure the maximum food value and the minimum of wastage.

All feed should:

a. look clean and bright.

b. smell and taste sweet.

Dusty, musty or mouldy forage is unpalatable, bad for the horse's digestion and a contributary cause of broken wind (see page 237).

Hay

a. refer *Manual One,* page 129.

b. should be of a suitable type for the horse and the work he is doing (see page 204).

c. very new hay can cause indigestion and scouring, old hay becomes dusty. Ideally, between six and twelve months old — do not feed under three.

d. hay made from horse paddocks is not recommended — risk of redworm infection.

Oats should:

a. be plump, hard and heavy.

b. rattle when dropped on to a hard surface.

c. not be fed when the oats are under three or over eighteen months old.

There is little or no difference in feed value between black and white oats.

Barley should also be plump and heavy, rounder and much harder than oats.

The value of a grain crusher for those with horses on high concentrate diets can hardly be overstated. It is extremely difficult to judge the quality of ready-crushed grain, which quickly loses food value and should not be kept longer than three to four weeks. With your own machine, it can be bruised or crushed to the exact degree required, and fed immediately.

Hay, whole oats and barley keep well. Best and cheapest bought in bulk if storage is available.

Bran should:

a. have large flakes — the bigger the better.

b. be floury.

c. have a particularly sweet smell. Never buy bran that smells sour or has lumps in it.

Pellets should:

a. look shiny, break cleanly — they go dull and crumbly with age.

b. as all composite foods should, have the formula printed on the bag, or available in pamphlet form.

Linseed should:

a. be dark brown and very shiny.

b. if crushed, smell and feel oily.

A 'cobwebby' look indicates the presence of weevils.

Bran, composite feeds and linseed do not keep well, and are therefore best bought in smaller quantities as required.

The usual source of supply for forage is the Stock and Station agent, though hay, and possibly oats and barley, can quite often be bought from local farmers. Prices vary from year to year and from district to district. It is well worth shopping around to find exactly what you want and to compare prices, but bear in mind:

a. it pays to buy quality. Horses will not look or perform well on inferior forage, which may cause permanent damage.

b. buying in bulk, where possible and appropriate, is the best way of saving money and ensuring a regular and consistent supply.

CONDITIONING

You should now have a thorough understanding of the principles of conditioning (see page 88). The next step is to learn to apply them to all types of horses for different activities — showing, hunting, eventing, etc.

If you are able to lunge, this could be useful when bringing a horse into work after a spell, or if at any time you cannot ride him during training (see page 254).

Conditioning is a challenging aspect of horse management. It takes careful planning, a good eye for detail, experience, and a definite flair to bring a horse out in the peak of condition at the right moment.

Interval Training

This is an extremely scientific method of training, used mainly to produce the very high degree of fitness required for three-day eventers, and possibly for a sustained season of one- or two-day events. It is rarely suitable for other purposes, and can be dangerous if it is misunderstood or misapplied.

It involves repeated short periods of faster work separated by short rest periods.

At speeds over 500 mpm (30 kph) the exercise is anaerobic — i.e. the oxygen supply cannot keep up with the demands of the muscles and lactic acid is produced. The pulse and respiration increase, sometimes greatly, according to the horse's degree of fitness.

At slow speeds the exercise is aerobic, and lactic acid, pulse and respiration rates should all drop. But before *complete* recovery has taken place, the horse is asked for another effort. Strength and stamina are built up by gradually increasing the speed and/or distance of the demands and reducing the rest periods. The heart, lungs and muscular systems are progressively developed without ever being subjected to maximum stress.

To be suitable for interval training the horse *must* be sound and mature, and have done at least six to eight weeks of basic conditioning work. The rider must have good judgment of pace and be capable (or have an assistant who is capable) of accurately measuring the horse's pulse and respiration. The former is far more easily done with a stethoscope. Count for fifteen seconds and multiply by four.

It is essential to know your horse's normal pulse and respiration rates. The important thing in training is how quickly these rates return to normal after the periods of faster work. (Called the 'recovery rate'.) Careful records must be kept of the speed, distance and number of intervals, the recovery rate, and the weather and state of the going and terrain.

Points to note:

1. Interval training must *never* be carried out more than once or twice a week.

2. There must be at least thirty minutes warming up at walk and trot before faster work commences.

3. Cooling down afterwards is equally important to allow the horse's system to remove waste products accumulated during fast work. Up to an hour's quiet walking may be needed.

If you wish to use this method, seek advice from someone with proven knowledge and experience of it. An individual programme must be worked out for every horse.

15

HANDLING, GROOMING, TRIMMING, CLIPPING, THE FOOT AND SHOEING, TRAVELLING AND LOADING (A,H)

HANDLING

Twitch. A means of restraint when the horse does not respond to coaxing, holding up a foot or other measures at such times as clipping, rasping teeth or other treatment.

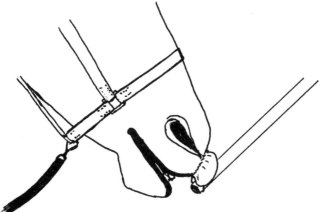

A twitch.

Method. Put the loop over your wrist, take hold of the horse's upper lip and slip the loop down over your hand. Keeping a firm hold of the lip, twist the handle until the cord is just tight enough to keep it securely in place. Be sure that the handle is clear of gums and nostrils.

Do not stand in front of the horse at any stage, as he may plunge forward or strike out with a forefoot.

Remove the twitch after a maximum of ten minutes, rub lip to restore circulation.

Never put a twitch on the ear, it is extremely painful and will make the horse headshy.

Don't use it for loading a difficult horse — its whole object is to make the horse stand still.

If the twitch is ineffective, as it may be with some horses, or restraint is needed over a longer period, the only alternative may be to tranquilise the horse. This must *only* be done under veterinary supervision.

GROOMING

This subject is fully covered in Chapter 6, page 94. A and H Certificate candidates must have a thorough knowledge of the importance of grooming in the conditioning of horses, and be able to apply this knowledge efficiently. In addition:

Washing the sheath. Sometimes necessary with geldings, due to an accumulation of wax and dirt, seen when the penis is fully extended. There may be an offensive smell, noticed when grooming, and a rumbling sound, which appears to come from the stomach, when starting work.

Requirements: Two buckets of warm water, two sponges or cloths. Soap.

Rubber or plastic gloves.

Method. Tie the horse up. Have an assistant, who may need to hold up a foreleg. Wet a sponge, add a little soap and wash inside the sheath thoroughly. Allow a few minutes for the wax to loosen, then wash again. With the second sponge and clean water, rinse carefully, then wring out the sponge for the final wipe. When dry, a little vaseline or liquid paraffin may be rubbed gently into the part.

TRIMMING

Pulling a tail. The pros and cons of pulling the tail have already been discussed (see page 99). It is best done when the horse is warm after work.

Method. Some horses object to this at first, so don't stand directly behind. The safest way is to have an assistant hold the horse backed up to a solid half-door or gate, with the tail over the top of it.

Start at the top, and with finger and thumb pull a few hairs at a time from underneath, working gradually down for about 20-25cm. Then do the same on the other side. Spread the pulling evenly, don't take too much from one spot. Check that both sides look even. With some tails this will be enough, but very thick ones will require further thinning.

Start again at the top, and pluck two or three hairs at a time, working from side to side and downwards. Haste or impatience may easily result in bare patches, which will take a long time to grow. It is best to spread the process over several days, so that the tail does not get sore and you can check progress. After each session bandage the tail. This helps to shape it and makes it easier to see if and where further pulling is needed.

CLIPPING

(Clipping, types of clip, and reasons for clipping, see page 102.)

Requirements

Clipping machine. The usual type is electric, with the motor in the head.

Power point.

Isolating transformer. Essential even with modern machines in case of damage to the cord, which could have fatal results.

Oil. A fine machine type such as sewing machine oil.

Kerosene in a plastic container.

A soft brush to use on the blades, and to keep the air-filter on the machine clear.

A spare set of sharp blades.

A sheltered yard or well lit box.

A cover to throw over the horse as clipping progresses.

A haynet to keep the horse happily occupied.

A twitch, in case the haynet is ineffective at times!

An assistant, who can help to calm the horse, if necessary, and can pull a foreleg forward to straighten out the wrinkles when you are clipping round the elbow.

The horse must be completely dry and as clean as possible.

Method. Mark out the clip with a piece of chalk or damp soap. For a hunter clip, put on the saddle and draw round it, for a trace or blanket clip, take a line just below the saddle flaps.

Check that the two sides are level.

See that the blades are correctly assembled, oil all marked holes in the head.

Run the machine for a few moments to warm it up and to accustom the horse to the sound. Start with fairly firm tension and immediately begin to slacken it off gradually until it sounds as though it is running freely and smoothly. If the tension is too tight the blades will wear quickly and may become overheated, if too loose they will not cut and will become clogged. If this happens, rinse in kerosene with the motor running, switch off and oil them before tightening them a little. Slack or blunt blades will pull the hair and make the horse restive.

Blades need frequent cleaning while in use, either by dipping in kerosene as above, or by brushing, followed by oiling. If they become hot, check the tension. If this appears correct, they may need sharpening and would be best changed. If too hot, they will soon upset the horse.

Always:

a. keep the air-filter clear or the motor may overheat and burn out.

b. treat the blades with the utmost care. They are very brittle and easily broken. A chipped tooth makes them completely useless.

When clipping, start on the shoulder, clip against the hair with long sweeps, keeping the blades flat and even so that they don't dig in or leave 'tram lines'. Don't force the clippers through the coat — the weight of the head of the machine provides sufficient pressure.

Do all the straightforward parts first, and try to complete them as quickly as possible, so that the horse does not become bored and restless. Finish with the ticklish areas — inside the thighs, the flanks and lastly the head. It is possible that you may have to use a twitch for these parts, and that the horse may be inclined to sweat — two good reasons for leaving them until last.

Special Areas

Head. If you wish to leave the front of the face in a blanket, hunter or full clip, follow the line of the bridle headpiece.

Remove only the width of the bridle headpiece behind the poll — it is very easy to take too much and spoil the mane. It is really safer to do this with scissors.

Ears. Never remove the hair from inside the ears — it is there to keep out insects and other foreign bodies. Close the edges of the ear together with one hand, then clip towards the tip to remove surplus hair.

Whiskers. Leave the whiskers round the muzzle. They are sensitive feelers, especially important to horses who live out.

Mane. Be very careful not to cut into the mane. Any trimming at the withers is best done lightly with scissors — clipping removes essential protection against cover rubs.

Hogging the mane. (For details, see page 98.)

Method. The assistant should stand to the front of the horse, holding his ears and coaxing his head down to stretch the wrinkles in the crest. If the horse has a full coat on the neck, it may be easier to hold the hair back with one hand and clip upwards from each side to avoid cutting into the coat. Work from withers to poll. For the forelock, use the clippers upwards, away from the eye and ear on that side. Do not cut too close over the withers — you risk cover rub.

Tail. Clip upwards, evenly on either side, to form an inverted V over the top of the tail. *Never* clip the tail.

Legs. It is unwise to clip the backs of the legs closely — it looks ugly and allows water to drain into the heels. Use coarse leg blades, if available, or trim the heels with scissors and comb. (See page 99.)

After clipping, remove the blades and clean them and the machine head thoroughly. Then wrap the blades in an oily cloth and store all the equipment in a dry place.

It is a good idea to exercise the horse, possibly on the lunge, to warm him up, and to follow this with a good strapping.

THE FOOT AND SHOEING

**Structure of the Foot — Changes due to Neglect, Disease, Poor Shoeing — ** Exterior

1. **The coronary band** — the junction between hair and horn, from which the wall of the foot grows downwards. Injuries to the coronet may lead to defects in the wall, such as sandcrack.

2. **The wall,** which carries the weight of the horse, is made of horn, averaging about 1cm thick. It takes approximately a year for a complete new wall to grow down from top to bottom.

The outer, varnish-like layer of horn is called the periople. It protects the wall and prevents undue evaporation. Rasping the wall removes this protective covering and leads to brittle feet.

The wall should be quite smooth. Rings around it may be due to prolonged neglect, but are more likely to be caused by severe laminitis or other disease.

3. **The sole** is made of horn similar to the wall, but is softer and is not constructed to carry weight, except at its junction with the wall. It consists of two layers:

a. the outer, insensitive sole, and

b. the inner, sensitive sole, situated between the outer sole and the pedal bone. The inner sole is very liable to bruising, especially where there has been excessive paring of the outer sole, or the foot is flat instead of concave.

If the sole is convex, or even completely flat, chronic laminitis, which causes the entire internal structure of the foot to drop, should be suspected.

4. **The white line** — a narrow ring of lighter, softer horn forming

the junction between wall and sole, and between the sensitive and insensitive parts of the foot.

Seedy toe is a separation of these parts, which may penetrate a considerable distance up the wall, and also spread sideways from the toe.

5. **The bars.** A continuation of the wall, where it turns inwards at the heels, merging into the sole about halfway to the point of frog. They act as a reinforcement to the wall.

The heels should be wide and open. Narrow, 'boxy' feet and contracted heels may be due to the horse's natural conformation, or to disease, but these conditions may well be exacerbated by interference with the bars during shoeing.

6. **The frog** is a tough, elastic cushion, also made of horn. Its functions can only be fulfilled if it is well developed and the horse's shoeing allows it to come into contact with the ground, at least when on grass. The best of frogs will shrivel away if not used!

Its main functions are:

a. as a shock absorber. It bulges outward as it comes to the ground, spreading the heels and dispersing the impact. Lack of frog pressure therefore leads to contracted heels.

b. to give the horse more grip and help prevent slipping.

c. to help support the bones of the foot, especially the navicular bone.

d. to act as a pump, assisting in the circulation of the blood back up the veins of the lower leg.

Structure of the Foot — Interior parts liable to disease or injury

1. **Bones.** These comprise:

a. the pedal or coffin bone — a light, porous bone which fits the shape of the hoof. Provides protection for nerves and blood vessels, and attachments for tendons, ligaments and the sensitive laminae (see below).

splint bone
cannon bone
{sesamoid bones
{long pastern bone
{short pastern bone
pedal bone
navicular bone

Bones of the foot and lower leg.

b. the navicular bone — a small, shuttle-shaped bone which fits at the back of the joint of the pedal bone and the short pastern bone.

Navicular disease (see page 241) affects this bone and the deep flexor tendon which passes under it.

c. the short pastern bone, which is half in and half out of the foot and articulates with the pedal and navicular bones.

Low ringbone (see page 242) affects this bone, but does not usually produce any visible changes in the foot.

2. **Tendons and ligaments.** The tendons below the knee and hock and the suspensory ligament pass over the fetlock joint and are attached to the bones of the foot.

3. **The laminae** — meaning 'leaves'. These are of two kinds:

a. the insensitive, horny laminae — thin leaves of horn on the inner surface of the wall, and

b. the sensitive, fleshy laminae which cover the pedal bone and the lateral cartilages.

They interlock to form a secure union.

4. **The lateral cartilages** — two flat pieces of cartilage attached to each side of the pedal bone. They act as shock absorbers and give elasticity to the foot.

In sidebone (see page 243) these cartilages become ossified (turned into bone) which naturally affects their function. The hardness can easily be felt, just above the coronet, when compared with a healthy foot.

SPECIAL AND/OR REMEDIAL SHOEING

Grass tips. Half shoes covering the toe only. Useful for horses turned out on hard or rough ground, or those with brittle feet. Protect the toe while allowing full frog contact.

Feather-edged shoes. Used to prevent injury from brushing (see page 246). The inner branch of the shoe is 'feathered' (bevelled) and set under the wall of the foot. There is usually only one nail hole in the inner branch.

Soles. Leather, plastic or aluminium is sometimes used to cover the horse's sole and give protection in cases of flat feet or stone bruises. If left on too long dirt may work in and cause further foot trouble.

Regular shoeing or attention by a qualified farrier is essential for any foot problems. In some cases it may be necessary to have the vet and farrier together, to decide on the correct course of action and the type of shoe to be used.

A feather-edged shoe. (Hind feet only.)   A grass tip. (Forefeet only.)

SCREW-IN STUDS

While the use of these studs involves extra work, they are invaluable for providing better grip for jumping, and, in some conditions, for dressage and showing as well.

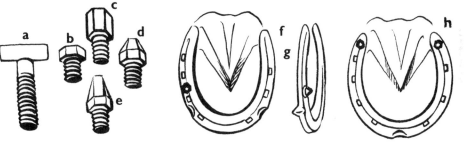

A. Tap, for clearing out hole. B.'Sleeper', to protect thread when stud not in use. C. D. E. Types of studs. F. G. Recommended placing, in outside quarter. H. Alternative placing, in the heels.

Points to Note

1. Threaded holes must be made in the shoes, either at the heels or at the quarters, preferably while the shoe is hot.

2. The holes must either be stuffed with cotton wool or a flat 'sleeper' inserted to prevent burring of the thread when the studs are not in use.

3. Use 'tap' to ensure thread is clear before inserting stud, which must be tightened up with a spanner.

4. Studs must only be used during the competition or schooling session, and removed immediately afterwards. They can cause great damage to the horse himself and to others in the float if left in while travelling.

5. Beware of sharp-pointed studs, especially on the inside of the foot. Large studs should only be used on heavy going, and on the outside. On hard ground, they could cause sprained tendons.   -

6. Keep the studs in an oily rag or an airtight tin when not in use, to prevent rusting.

TRAVELLING AND LOADING

Points to check if you are in charge of horses travelling.

Beforehand:
1. All feed and gear required for each horse for the trip.
2. Towing vehicle. Driver should check: licence, warrant of fitness, fuel, oil, water, battery, tyres, lights and correct size of towing ball for float.
3. Float: licence, warrant of fitness, tyres, lights, structural soundness, especially ramp and floor, breech bar or chain and safety chain.

Before loading, check that:
1. Horse(s) are correctly prepared for travel.
2. The float is securely hitched on, safety chain in place, lights and brakes (if any) properly connected.
3. The ramp is steady, access door open and all gear safely stowed away from the horses' feet.
4. All concerned are familiar with correct loading procedure. (See *Manual One*, page 143.)
5. Once loaded, check that the ramp is secured and horses tied up correctly.

Unloading — be sure that everybody knows the procedure. (*Manual One*, page 143.) If a horse rushes out, on no account should the leader try to hang on to him. He will only throw his head up and probably hit it — leading to endless problems.

Difficult loaders. Easy loading depends on confidence and training. Most problems stem from ignorance, fear or stubbornness, or a combination of these. Once a horse is really scared, or has 'tried it on' and got away with it, he may always be unreliable. You must decide what is the dominant cause of his reluctance, and adapt your method accordingly.

Pay particular attention to the siting of the float — the more the ramp can be safely enclosed, the easier it will be. Simple measures are suggested on page 110. In addition, experienced people could try:
1. Linking hands with another person behind the horse. The leader entices him with feed, and *must* keep the horse's head straight, without pulling. Particularly effective with ponies. Do not use this method with kickers.

2. Fix lunge reins or ropes about halfway up on either side of the float. Two assistants, with gloves, hold the reins; the horse is led to the foot of the ramp, the assistants cross over with their respective reins, which must be kept above the hocks. With encouragement, not pulling, from in front, a firm pull on the opposite rein if the horse tries to swing either way, and intermittent light flicks with both reins, most horses soon realise that the easiest way is forward.

3. Provided the horse is used to it, a breech rope may be effective.

4. With a stiff broom, bristles up, gently prod the horse across the buttocks as he comes to the ramp.

5. Blindfold the horse.

While every encouragement should be given, careful arrangements and a firm, but not rough, approach are most likely to succeed.

Loading/unloading without an assistant. Lead the horse up the ramp and partway in if a double float. Encourage him to continue alone, lay the rope over his neck, fasten the breech bar and go alongside or round to the front to tie him up. Failing this, lead him on as usual, but have a long rope or lunge rein attached. Thread this through the tie-up ring and keep hold of it while going to the rear to fasten the breech bar. A little 'feel' will remind the horse of what is expected, but if he does rush out, do not attempt to stop him.

Unloading. Untie the horse, leave rope through ring, lower ramp, undo breech bar and either catch the horse as he emerges or go in and back him out.

Unloading. The person on the right is saving her back by bending her knees while lowering the ramp. Horse untied, being held until breech bar is undone.

16

STABLE CONSTRUCTION AND MANAGEMENT (A, H)

The Stable Yard

Some form of stable yard is a valuable asset for any horse owner, especially for those who compete or hunt regularly. It could consist of:

Loose box or boxes, sited to face away from the prevailing wind.

Tack room, feed room, sometimes combined, which saves space but creates problems with dust and vermin.

One or more yards.

A hosing area.

A hay barn, which should be apart from the stables because of fire risk.

Muck heap, adjacent but not too close to the stables — attracts flies. Preferably with three sides to keep it tidy. Must have easy vehicle access.

Site Requirements

a. good drainage.
b. good water supply.
c. permit from local council.

Stable Construction

Boxes may be built either:

Opening directly on to the yard —

Advantages: more fresh air and less risk of infection than in an enclosed building.

> horses enjoy a direct view of the outside world.
>
> less claustrophobic for those used to living outside.

Disadvantage: cold and wet for all concerned if built without a covered runway in front of the boxes.

Or inside a larger building, usually with a central passage.

Advantage: convenience — tack and feed rooms are usually under the same roof.

Disadvantages: risk of infection.

> great care is needed with ventilation, otherwise the boxes may be cold, draughty or stuffy.
>
> greater fire risk, depending on construction.

Indoor boxes. Big doors at each end allow controlled ventilation. Hosepipe conveniently placed for filling water buckets and cleaning out, but could be inaccessible in case of fire. Clipping bay, with power point, on right. Doors a little low, otherwise good.

Dimensions (boxes) 3 x 3.6m for ponies, 3.6 x 4.3m for horses, are good minimum sizes. Very big boxes increase labour and require more bedding.

Walls. Minimum height, 3.6m for safety and ventilation.

Materials. Concrete block — good, fireproof, fairly cheap, but rather cold.

Brick — very good, but expensive.

Treated timber — warm, but not so durable, greater fire risk.

Corrugated iron — cheap, but must be insulated and strongly lined to a minimum height of 1.3m.

Roof. Corrugated iron — cheapest. Must be lined for insulation and to prevent condensation. Corrugated plastic may be inserted for extra light. Roof should have good slope for ventilation. With outside boxes roof should extend approximately 1.5m to provide runway and shelter.

Floor. Concrete. Practical. Must be roughened to provide non-slip surface. Good depth of bedding essential. The floor may slope very slightly towards an exit hole to an outside drain.

A well-compacted earth or clay floor is quite satisfactory for occasional use, but difficult to keep clean where horses live in continually.

Doors. Minimum size of doorway, height 2.4m, width 1.2m. For outside boxes doors should be built in two sections, the lower one at least 1.3m high. Strong construction is essential, the inside must be smooth, the top capped with metal to discourage chewing. There must be two bolts, the lower one preferably foot-operated. This lower catch prevents the door from 'springing' if the horse kicks at it. A top grille can be useful — the horse has fresh air and can see out, but cannot jump out.

All stable doors must open outwards, to allow for the bedding and for ready access if the horse is cast.

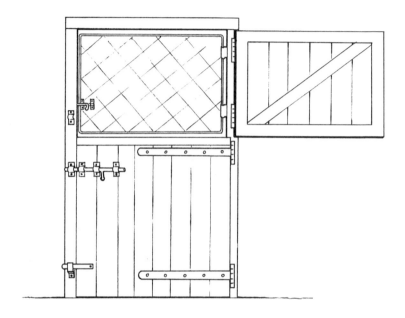

A good stable door.

Fittings. Tying rings. One close to the manger, if fitted, another about eye level, for tying up the haynet. A ring may be provided for suspending the water bucket, in a corner away from the manger and within sight of the door.

Manger. Not essential — a feed bowl could be used. Approximately 1m high, with a removable food container for ease of cleaning. There should be no sharp edges or corners and the front should be filled in to floor level.

Automatic water bowls are convenient and labour-saving, but it is impossible to tell how much the horse is drinking. They must be cleaned daily — even so, they sometimes become blocked and overflow.

Electricity. Almost essential if horses are to be stabled through the winter. The light must be high up and protected by a grid. Switches should be outside the box, waterproof, and out of reach of the horse.

Tack room. Requirements: light, dry, airy and as vermin- and burglar-proof as possible. A good stout door with a secure lock, bars on the window, and curtains which can be drawn when you are away will help to discourage intruders.

Fittings. Saddle racks, bridle brackets, storage space for spare covers, boots, bandages, clippers, etc. Saddle horse and bridle hook for tack cleaning. A closed-type heater or radiator is useful in cold or humid weather — tack is soon damaged by damp conditions.

Feed room. Should also be dry and airy. In the barn-type building, it may be necessary to enclose the sides as high as the roof with fine wire netting, to keep out birds and vermin.

Fittings. Feed containers — metal is preferable to wood. Old freezer units can be useful, and galvanised dustbins for smaller quantities. Whatever is used must have a tight-fitting lid and should be raised off the floor.

Scales; scoop for measuring feed; hook and spring balance for weighing haynets.

Cupboard or shelf for storage of salt, milk powder, feed additives, etc.

Wall chart showing each horse's diet sheet.

A chaff cutter and a grain crusher are invaluable assets.

Broom.

Hosing area. Useful but not essential. A rough concrete base sloping towards a drain, preferably enclosed on three sides.

Hay barn. Probably the most essential building, enabling hay to be bought in bulk when it is cheapest and stored through the winter. With an earth floor, slats or old tyres should be used to keep the bottom layer of hay off the ground where it would be spoilt by moisture. Good vehicle access is a must.

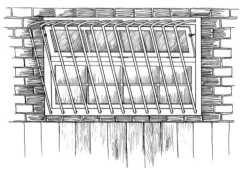

Stable windows must be well protected on the inside, should be set as high as possible, and open inwards at the top.

221

Advantages of Stabling

1. Immediate availability.

2. Smartness and cleanliness, especially for competition horses and hunters. As there is protection from the weather, the horse may be clipped out and groomed thoroughly at all times of the year.

3. Rest — so essential for maximum fitness. Once they get used to being stabled, horses really enjoy the comfort of lying down on a good thick bed.

4. Safety — fit horses quite frequently injure themselves and each other when playing about in the paddock.

5. Diet can be accurately controlled. Less feed is required for warmth.

6. Acclimatisation at home for horses travelling to shows or trials, where it is generally preferable and sometimes necessary to stable them.

7. In some cases of sickness or injury, stabling can provide total rest and/or immobilisation if necessary.

Disadvantages

1. It is a tie. The horse must be exercised and attended to at regular times every day.

2. Boredom — horses stabled for long periods, especially if they are without company or access to a paddock, are liable to become bored or difficult and tense.

In New Zealand, it is rarely necessary to stable horses full-time unless they are being got fit for top events, or prepared for show or travelling.

The Combined System

Under this system, the horse is boxed at night and turned out for part of the day, to suit his fitness/dietary requirements and his owner's programme. This arrangement has been proved to work well. In very hot weather, where there is no shade available in the paddock, the system may be reversed — out at night, stabled by day.

Stable Routine

Horses are creatures of habit, and a set routine, especially in regard to feeding times, is even more important to the stabled horse than to the horse at grass.

Every horse owner must plan a timetable to suit their circumstances. The following is a specimen timetable, based on two horses during the eventing season:

6.30 a.m. Check horses, tie up, feed, muck out, put down day bed, quarter horses, untie and leave with small net of hay (2kg), if not working early. Wash out and fill water buckets.

8.30 a.m. Work horses individually, then exercise together, ride and lead alternate days. On return, strap horses, give small haynet if not given earlier.

12 noon Check water buckets, feed.

1.30 p.m. Turn horses out.

4.00 p.m. Bed down, empty and refill water buckets, bring horses in, quarter, change covers, feed and hay. Clean tack, tidy yard.

8.00 p.m. Check horses, final feed.

This plan would obviously be impossible for anyone at school or working (except with horses!). The following alternative suggestions, for one horse in hard work, hunting or competing, could be adjusted according to working hours and available assistance:

Early morning — Check horse, change covers as required, turn out with feed and hay. Muck out, leave bed up.

Midday — Bed down, bring horse in, feed.

Late afternoon — Work, exercise and strap horse. Feed and hay. Wipe tack over — clean it thoroughly once a week.

Late evening — Check horse, last feed.

Exercise and work could be divided between morning and afternoon. The horse could be left out all day, but must have midday feed. It is better that he should be brought in, so that he does not eat too much grass and is not worked on a full stomach.

For early morning and evening checks, mucking out, bedding down and handling horses in stables, see 'Stable management', page 116.

Whatever the system, cleanliness and tidiness are the hallmarks of good stable management. A neat yard, stable tools correctly hung up, constant attention to the picking up of droppings and well-cared-for tack, all reflect credit on the person in charge.

BEDDING

Bedding is necessary to:

prevent injury, provide a soft standing surface and encourage the horse to lie down.

provide warmth and keep out draughts.

encourage the horse to stale, provide absorption and act as a deodorant.

assist in keeping the horse clean.

The choice of bedding depends on:
availability.
cost.
type of floor.
storage space.

Straw: Advantages: warm and comfortable, generally dust-free. Looks good, drains well. Manure much sought after for gardening.

Disadvantages: often expensive and difficult to obtain. Inflammable and edible. Needs a fairly large storage area.

Types. Wheat/barley. Good wheat straw looks and drains well, is light to handle and durable, and is not very palatable. Barley straw has beards, or 'awns', which may irritate the skin, and it can cause colic if eaten. However, with modern methods of harvesting and the latest hybrid strains of wheat, many of which have awns similar to barley, there is often little difference between the two.

Oat straw is less durable, though it makes a soft and comfortable bed. Its chief disadvantage is that most horses will eat it in quantity.

Wood Shavings: Advantages: usually free for collection. Deodorant. Durable and fairly soft, inedible.

Disadvantages: somewhat less pleasing appearance and not quite as warm as straw. May be dusty.

Sawdust: Similar to shavings — not so soft and is usually dusty.

Mixture: With clay or earth floors, a layer of sawdust with shavings on top makes a good bed.

Interior drains must be sealed, otherwise they will become blocked by either shavings or sawdust. These materials, being absorbent, make excellent bedding where there is little or no drainage.

NOTE. Never use shavings or sawdust from treated timber. Always check for bits of wood or sharp objects.

Mucking out — shavings. Excessive movement of shavings soon breaks them down and they become dusty and dirty. They should not be piled up daily as for straw. Extra care is needed to pick up droppings as soon as possible. Apart from this, remove obvious wet patches daily, rake the surface lightly and top up as required with fresh shavings. The box will probably need to be cleaned out completely every three to four months, depending on use.

Sawdust may be handled in a similar way.

This deep litter system is labour-saving and works well. Make sure that the horse's feet are picked out regularly, especially with sawdust.

Fire Precautions in Stables

1. Total ban on smoking in or around stables or haybarn.
2. One or more fire extinguishers on exterior walls — contents must be kept up to date!
3. Hosepipe(s) which will reach to all buildings.
4. Water or sand buckets always in readiness.

In the event of fire, the first thing to do is to get the horses out. Although terrified, they may be unwilling to leave the stable and may even try to return to it unless prevented.

Keep calm, put a halter or bridle on the horse, cover his head with anything available — a sack, coat, etc. — and lead him outside. Secure him well away from the stable, or turn him out into a paddock.

If smoke has been inhaled, call the vet as soon as possible.

YARDS

Failing stables, yards are extremely valuable.

Uses

1. For grooming, saddling up, feeding — away from others — clipping, shoeing, or veterinary treatment, and to hold the horse where he will be readily available for farrier or vet.
2. To keep a horse off the grass before work.
3. To shut up a fat horse if it is necessary to restrict his diet.
4. To restrict movement in case of injury.
5. To accustom a horse to confinement if he is going to a show or other event where he will be stabled or yarded.
6. To handle a young horse safely. A strong enclosure is ESSENTIAL for this.

Construction

Size. 4.3 square minimum (approx).

Height. 1.5 minimum.

Materials. Treated posts and rails, the top rail round or half-round and wired down, make the best fencing, strong and safe.

Galvanised piping may be used, but is less suitable for young horses.

Wire and lightweight timber are unsuitable for yards.

Gate. The usual farm type, 1.5m wide, is ideal. Slip rails could be used, or possibly a chain with a spring hook. (Not really safe if the horse is to be left alone, or with young horses.)

Floor. A base of heavy metal or pumice, compacted, topped with shavings or sawdust, makes a good floor when the yard is in constant use.

Shelter. Trees provide welcome shade. They may cause draughts and must be protected from ring-barking. A solid wall on the side of the prevailing wind is most useful.

Management in Yards

The biggest problem is exposure — the horse can suffer greatly in extremes of heat or cold, wind or rain. Unless it is essential to confine him for veterinary reasons, avoid yarding a horse overnight or for long daytime periods in the above conditions.

If a horse is yarded for any length of time he *must* have water, and not even the fattest horse should be left for more than about four hours without a kilogram or so of hay to nibble.

Use your drop skep as meticulously as you would in a stable.

Handling rules for stables apply. See that slip rails are pushed right back when taking the horse in and out.

STABLE VICES AND BAD HABITS

When horses are confined in stables or yards for long periods, especially without company, boredom often causes vices and bad habits to develop. Once formed, they are hard to break, and the horse may persist in them even when out in the paddock.

Vices

Crib biting. The horse grasps the top of the door, rail or any available edge in his teeth, arches his neck and swallows air with an audible gulp.

Wind sucking. Similar to crib biting, but without holding anything.
Causes:
1. Boredom and/or loneliness.
2. Lack of bulk food.
3. Imitating another horse.
4. Possibly stomach irritation, bots or dental problems.
5. Horse seeking minerals by licking or chewing wood.
Effects:
1. Flatulence, indigestion, possibly colic.
2. Extreme difficulty in putting on or maintaining condition.
3. In crib biting, wear on the incisors.
Prevention: Tops of doors should be capped with metal. Rails and gates should be treated with creosote. In the box, protect all exposed

edges that the horse could hold. Use fine wire netting. Fit a special strap round the throat. Use the combined system of stabling, provide plenty of bulk and rock salt or a mineral lick.

Weaving. The horse stands with forelegs apart and rocks from one to the other.

Causes: Of nervous origin. Causes 1, 2 and 3 above.

Effects: Considerable strain on the tendons and joints of the forelegs — the horse may go lame. Loss of condition, due to lack of rest.

Prevention: Very difficult. Keep the horse occupied, use the combined system or exercise twice daily, provide ample bulk and good bed.

Horses with any of these three vices cannot be guaranteed sound, and there is no certain cure. Affected horses should be kept away from others in stable, yard or paddock.

Bad Habits

Biting and kicking. As horses become fitter they often become more ticklish and sensitive, especially if thin-skinned and/or clipped. Care should be taken in the choice and use of grooming tools, and in the handling of the horse. Be firm, but sympathetic. Tie the horse up when grooming.

If allowed to go unchecked, these habits may grow into dangerous vices. A sharp slap with the flat of the hand can work wonders if administered at the right moment.

Excessive use of titbits can easily lead to nipping and biting, particularly with ponies and young horses. A titbit should be a reward, not a handout.

17

HEALTH (A, H)

NURSING AND TREATMENT

TAKING THE TEMPERATURE

Normal temperature is 38°C. Any rise is abnormal, and over 40°C could be serious. Call your veterinary surgeon.

Temperature should be taken in the following circumstances:

a. horse off colour — shivery, staring coat, tucked-up, unhappy appearance, patchy sweating.

b. coughs and colds.

c. suspected infection in wounds.

d. prolonged colic.

e. in serious illness, e.g. strangles, temperature should be taken night and morning.

f. during epidemics, when temperatures of *all* horses on the property should be taken daily.

Method. Use a veterinary thermometer, which is short and thick. Check that the mercury is shaken down below 32°C. Grease with vaseline, or moisten with cold water.

Tie the horse up, or have somebody to hold him. Lift the tail, and insert the thermometer for about three-quarters of its length into the rectum, using a twisting motion. Leave for at least the time stated on the thermometer, holding the tail to one side. Withdraw and read. Do not hold by the bulb.

Wash the thermometer in cold water and disinfect after use.

SICK NURSING

Very sick horses must be kept quiet and warm, and are usually best on their own, even if the disease is not infectious. They should be cared for mainly by one person, whom they know and trust. Good nursing by a caring person can often stimulate the will to live.

Accommodation. Discuss this with your vet. A small, sheltered paddock, alone or with one quiet companion, may be quite suitable, but in adverse weather or where complete rest or immobilisation is required, stabling may be essential.

Feeding. Damp all feed, including hay. Feed soft hay, not lucerne. Chaff may be easier to swallow than long hay or if stabled, cut grass may be preferred. Consult your vet regarding diet; usually horse and pony pellets, bran, boiled barley or linseed may be fed, but not raw grain.

A bran mash every evening, with epsom or glauber's salts if needed, is soothing and palatable and helps to keep the bowels open.

Offer very small feeds four or five times a day. Make each different by adding sliced carrots or apples, glucose, molasses, skim milk powder or any tasty extras that the horse likes. Hand-feeding may persuade him to eat.

Any leftover feed should be removed and thrown away. Do not offer it to any other animal, or mix it with fresh for the sick horse.

Scrupulous cleanliness of all water buckets and feed containers is vital.

In the stable, feed from the ground. In good weather and with the vet's permission, lead the horse out for a pick of grass several times daily. Failing this, cut grass for him.

Fresh water must be constantly available and easily accessible. Avoid giving medicines in the water, as they may put the horse off drinking.

Grooming should be kept to a minimum with a very sick horse. Sponging the eyes, nose and dock is refreshing for him, and in the stable, feet must be picked out twice daily. Possibly quarter him lightly with a body brush or stable rubber, taking care that he does not get chilled. If the legs fill, as they may with standing, hand massage or rub briskly with a rough towel. Stable bandages may help.

Bedding. A deep bed is essential to encourage the horse to lie down.

In general. Try to keep the temperature in the stable as even as possible. Feel the horse's ears from time to time. Adjust covers as necessary; they should be light and loose. A sweat sheet underneath is often useful to ensure circulation of air and prevent chills.

Note and report to the vet any changes in the horse's temperature, pulse or respiration or in his attitude — increased lethargy, excitement, etc., — particularly if such changes occur suddenly.

TREATMENTS

The following treatments must *only* be given by a veterinary surgeon:

Stomach tubing.

Inoculations and other injections.

Administration of drugs such as tranquilisers, stimulants, cortisone, phenylbutazone, etc. The last two are valuable anti-inflammatory drugs, but, wrongly used, can delay healing, suppress antibody production, affect the circulation and have other side-effects.

Rectal examination and enemas.

Blistering.

Antibiotics can only be obtained through a vet, and should always be used under veterinary supervision.

INTERNAL PARASITES

(For basic information on worm control, refer to Chapter 8, page 125.)

The worms which mainly affect horses — bloodworms, redworms, roundworms and pinworms — come under the general heading of nematodes.

The following details of the life cycles of the various types will help to explain the damage that they do, and emphasise the importance of worm treatment and control.

BLOODWORMS AND REDWORMS — LARGE AND SMALL STRONGYLES

Life Cycle

1. Horse eats larvae from infected pasture or hay.

2. On being swallowed, all strongyle larvae burrow into the wall of the small intestine.

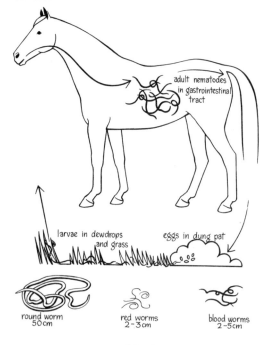

adult nematodes in gastrointestinal tract

larvae in dewdrops and grass

eggs in dung pat

round worm 50 cm

red worms 2–3 cm

blood worms 2–5 cm

3. Bloodworms enter the walls of the arteries, weakening them and sometimes causing aneurysms — balloon-like swellings which may burst and cause a fatal haemorrhage. Arteries may be completely blocked, either by blood clots or by solid masses of actual worms. Particularly affected are the arteries which supply blood to the digestive system and the vital organs, and those which supply the hind legs, but worm damage can occur anywhere in the arterial system. After migrating round the body for up to eleven months, the worms enter the caecum, competing for the horse's food and developing to the egg-laying stage.

4. Redworms remain in the intestinal tract, passing on from the small intestine to the caecum after about three months. They do much damage to the gut wall, and to the general health of the horse if they are present in large numbers, but are not quite such a serious problem as bloodworms.

5. Both eggs and adult worms are passed out in the droppings. The eggs hatch into infective larvae in three to seven days, depending on weather conditions.

The whole cycle takes approximately six to twelve months.

Effects

Massive damage to the arterial system and the vital organs by bloodworms, and to the digestive system by all strongyles. All horses are affected, young or old, and horses already in poor condition are even more susceptible.

Maximum fitness can never be attained with a heavy strongyle burden. The worms prevent full utilisation of the horse's food, and their presence in the arteries makes correct muscle function impossible.

Problems in controlling strongyles are:

a. most anthelmintics (worm killers) affect only the worms that are actually in the intestines at the time of dosing.

b. the prolific nature of strongyles — it has been estimated that a horse with only an average infestation can contaminate the pasture with *four million* eggs a day.

c. their ability to build up resistance to individual chemicals. To counteract this, the chemical base — not just the brand — of the anthelmintic must be changed at every third or fourth dosing.

ROUNDWORMS — ASCARIDS

Life Cycle

1. Eggs passed by horse in droppings. In favourable conditions (warm and humid) eggs hatch into larvae within hours.

2. The larvae are eaten by the horse in grazing. Eggs may also be swallowed.

3. These eggs hatch, and with other larvae are swallowed and penetrate the wall of the small intestine, entering veins and being carried in the bloodstream to the liver, heart and, finally, the lungs.

4. After about five days in the lungs, the larvae break through the blood vessels and migrate up the trachea, whence they are coughed up and re-swallowed.

5. The larvae return to the small intestine, where they now mature into adult worms. Each female lays thousands of eggs daily, which are passed out in the droppings to start the process over again.

The whole cycle takes about two months.

Effects

Very heavy infestations of ascarids can cause intestinal obstruction in mature horses, but most develop considerable immunity from previous infections. Foals and yearlings, however, are extremely susceptible, and may suffer permanent lung damage, severe enteritis or total blockage, causing death. It is essential that brood mares and young stock, from the age of eight weeks onwards, should be dosed regularly and kept in clean paddocks, preferably apart from other horses.

PINWORMS — OXYURIS

Life Cycle

1. Horse swallows eggs from contaminated pasture.

2. Development takes place in the intestinal tract, these worms do not migrate as the others do.

3. Female worms move into the anus, where they lay eggs under the horse's tail. The eggs drop off to re-infect the pasture.

The whole cycle takes about five months.

Effects

Much less drastic than with other worms, but pinworms do cause intense irritation which makes the horse rub his tail and buttocks on anything available. Apart from spoiling his appearance, this may well lead to wounds which will be very liable to infection. Pinworms are generally controlled by the drugs administered for other worms, and by thorough cleaning of the dock and anal area at the daily grooming.

BOTS — GASTROPHILUS

Life Cycle

1. Botflies hatch from pupae during the summer months. The

females lay eggs on the horse's coat, causing much irritation in the process, although botflies do not bite or sting.

2. The horse licks or rubs the eggs off the coat.

3. The eggs hatch into larvae, which burrow into the tissues of the lips, mouth and tongue, remaining there for several weeks before emerging at the back of the throat and being swallowed.

4. The bot grubs attach themselves to the wall of the stomach, where they stay for some months before passing through the digestive system and out in the droppings.

5. The grubs pupate (hatch from pupae) in the ground.

The whole cycle takes about a year.

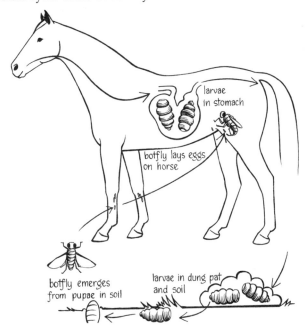

Effects

Bots are generally less harmful than worms, but their numbers must be controlled. Regular removal of bot eggs, plus two dosings in late autumn, about a month apart, should achieve this.

ANTHELMINTICS

The chemicals mainly used are the benzimidazol (B-Z) group, pyrimidines (e.g. morantel), piperazines and organophosphates. These last are used for controlling bots. They can be lethal to birds (including domestic poultry) if they eat grain or grubs from the horse's droppings after dosing, and should not be given to mares in late pregnancy.

The term 'broad spectrum' means that the anthelmintic is effective against most worms — bots are often mentioned separately.

New preparations are constantly being developed. One of the latest broad spectrum products is ivermectin, which is proving effective against all types of worms and bots, at all stages of development.

DEHYDRATION

Loss of fluid in the body tissues.

Results from excessive sweating, and sometimes from stress when travelling and competing, especially in hot weather. Also occurs in sick horses, if there is much sweating, prolonged diarrhoea or excessive urination.

Symptoms. The skin becomes noticeably drier and loses its elasticity, so that a fold of skin taken between finger and thumb does not snap back immediately on release, but takes some time to return to normal. If the horse is working, the sweat will become thicker, and eventually cease altogether.

To avoid work-related dehydration, always ensure that the horse has access to, and drinks, ample water. If he shows a tendency to dehydrate, consult your vet, as electrolytes (page 199) may be needed.

With sick horses, watch for signs of dehydration and report them to the vet.

AZOTURIA

The disease appears to be a more severe form of 'Tying-Up' (see page 126).

Symptoms. Similar to tying-up, but the horse does not improve with gentle exercise. Instead, he becomes extremely distressed, and, if forced to continue moving, may collapse and be unable to get up. If any urine is passed, it will be coffee-coloured.

Treatment. Dismount, slacken girths, cover the horse's loins. Let him rest in a sheltered place, if possible. He may recover sufficiently to be led quietly home, if it is nearby, otherwise he *must* be transported home. Contact your vet urgently. Meanwhile, keep the horse quiet and warm — hot blankets over his loins will give some relief. Offer unlimited water, but no food. Try to encourage him to stale.

Prevention. Azoturia is less likely to occur in horses living out, but if your horse is stabled you should:

1. Make especially sure that he is not receiving more concentrates than his work requires.

2. The night before a rest day, give a bran mash with a handful of epsom or glauber's salts. Cut down concentrates and replace with bulk on the rest day. Turn the horse out in the paddock for at least two hours, or lead him out for half an hour morning and evening.

3. Always work the horse slowly for at least twenty minutes before doing any fast work. Don't gallop him on the day after a rest day.

Once a horse has suffered from either tying-up or azoturia they are liable to recur. Ask your vet's advice, and work in close conjunction with him in your management.

TETANUS

Caused by the tetanus bacillus entering the bloodstream through a wound — usually a small puncture or scratch which has gone unnoticed. *It can be prevented* by inoculation. Riders should also be immunised.

Symptoms. Overall stiffness, standing with nose and tail out-stretched. The membrane in the corner of the eye may protrude or extend over the front of the eyeball. High temperature. Extreme nervousness. Later the jaws lock.

If these symptoms appear, immediate veterinary treatment is the only hope of saving the horse. Meanwhile, keep him absolutely quiet, in a dark place, if possible. Water should be within easy reach, but do not offer food.

RESPIRATORY DISEASES

Since the work required of horses is athletic to a greater or lesser extent, a sound respiratory system is of the utmost importance. Bear in mind the following:

Coughs and colds must never be neglected or the horse worked, particularly at faster paces, until the cause has been identified and the symptoms have subsided. Be most careful of coughs accompanied by a rise of temperature, quickened breathing or thick nasal discharge — all signs of possible lung infection. If in doubt, seek veterinary advice.

Poor management practices increase the risk of respiratory problems, especially:

a. galloping a horse who is completely unfit, or too early in his preparation.

b. working a horse on a full stomach.

c. feeding dusty, musty or unsuitable feedstuffs.

Viral or bacterial diseases, such as equine influenza or strangles can easily lead to pneumonia, roaring or broken wind — see below.

Horses should be inoculated against any influenza virus which is prevalent locally.

EQUINE INFLUENZA

A highly infectious viral disease.

Symptoms. Rise of temperature. Loss of appetite, depression, coughing. Discharge from eyes and nose. Gum and eye membranes may be yellowish or bright red, according to the type of virus.

Treatment. Isolate the horse at once. Keep him warm and quiet, and send for the vet urgently.

If one case occurs, take the temperature of every horse on the property daily. Rise in temperature is often the first symptom.

STRANGLES

A highly contagious bacterial or viral disease, mainly affecting horses under six years old.

Symptoms. Dullness, apathy and loss of appetite, soon followed by a rise in temperature. Nasal discharge, thin at first but becoming thick and yellow, mucous membrane of the eye turns bright red. Sore throat, and difficulty in swallowing. The glands in the throat and jowl region swell up and become hot and tense, and after a few days one or more abscesses form under the lower jaw. Once these burst and drain, the temperature will fall and the horse will be well on the way to recovery, but if they fail to burst, infection may spread through the bloodstream.

Treatment. Isolate the horse immediately you suspect strangles. Keep him warm and send for the vet urgently. Don't bring him into a stable before the vet arrives — most cases do better in the open air and there is less risk of complications. Fomenting the glands may give some relief pending the vet's arrival.

This is a very serious illness, though modern drugs have made it more easily controlled than in the past. It still requires skilled nursing and a long convalescence, followed by careful conditioning if permanent damage to the horse's wind is to be avoided. Work in close conjunction with your vet throughout.

Strict isolation procedures must be observed. Be particularly sure to destroy all swabs and dressings immediately after use.

PNEUMONIA

An inflammatory condition of the lungs, often viral or bacterial in origin.

Causes. Colds or chills. Prolonged exposure or over-exertion. Careless drenching or stomach tubing — liquid entering the lungs. May occur following influenza, strangles etc.

Symptoms. High temperature, rapid, shallow breathing, quick pulse. Cold and shivery, 'tucked up', with head outstretched and dilated nostrils. Any exertion will cause coughing. There is usually a thin nasal discharge at first.

Treatment. Get veterinary help at once. With modern drugs and good nursing, there is every chance of a complete recovery if treatment is commenced promptly. Take the temperature night and morning, and report *any* sudden change.

EMPHYSEMA

Also known as 'broken wind' or 'heaves'. A breakdown of the air vesicles of the lungs.

Causes. See 'Poor management practices' above. Also, bringing the horse back into work too quickly following respiratory diseases, or inflammation of the lungs due to a chronic cough.

Symptoms. Harsh, dry cough, which gets worse with exertion. A distinct 'double beat' can be seen in the flank as the horse breathes *out* — especially noticeable after a gallop. As the disease progresses, any exertion will cause distress, with laboured, gasping breathing.

Treatment. There is no cure, but the following will all help in the early stages:

Damp all feed — be particularly careful as to quality. Linseed oil mixed with the feed several times a week helps to give some relief. Give little or no long hay — use chaff instead.

The horse will usually be best living out, but avoid long, lush grass. If stabled, do not bed on straw.

Shut or tie the horse up so that he eats nothing at all for two hours before any fast work, and don't work him even at slow paces less than 1½ hours after he has finished a feed or been brought in from grass.

If in doubt at any time, consult your vet.

WHISTLING AND ROARING

Different degrees of the same disease. A partial or total paralysis of the cartilage in the larynx. This cartilage should open as the horse inhales, to allow free passage of air. The paralysis usually occurs on the left side.

Whistling is a high-pitched sound, heard as the horse breathes *in*, mainly at faster paces and sometimes increasing with exertion.

Roaring is a much deeper and louder noise. The horse may become too distressed to continue, and the condition can affect the heart.

Causes. Sudden, violent exertion when unfit. May occur following coughs, strangles or any respiratory disease, especially if the horse is put back into work too soon.

Since the tendency to this disease may be hereditary, it is unwise to breed from a roarer.

Treatment. Roaring can only be treated surgically, so consult your veterinary surgeon.

HIGH BLOWING

This is not a disease or an unsoundness. It is a noise caused by an abnormality of the false nostril, which vibrates as the horse breathes out. It occurs mainly in well-bred horses, and is most noticeable when the horse is fresh. High blowers are generally considered to be very sound in their wind.

LAMENESS

(For identifying the lame leg and the cause of the lameness, see page 120.) If there are no obvious signs of injury, the diagrams of seats of ailments on page 243 and 244 may be helpful in finding the trouble spot.

Note also that if the problem is in the foot, the lameness will show more going downhill, whereas if it is in the shoulder (which is uncommon) it is likely to be worse uphill.

FOOT AILMENTS AND INJURIES

(For the structure of the foot, see page 212.)

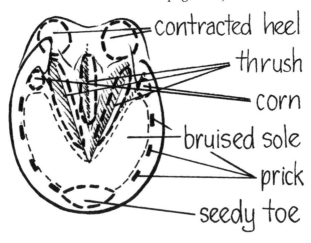

BRUISED SOLE

(See *Manual One*, page 170.)

Further treatment. Examine the foot carefully. A bruise may show as a reddish patch, sensitive to firm pressure with your thumbs, or to gentle tapping with a light hammer.

Tub the foot several times daily, or apply a bran poultice. If there is no improvement after a few days, or if there is a rise in temperature, filling round the coronet or severe pain at any time, consult your vet without delay.

The sensitive sole, or even the coffin bone, may be affected by a severe bruise, which will take time to clear up. If the horse has flat feet or thin soles, consider the use of a leather sole under the shoe to prevent recurrence of the injury. (See page 214.)

CORNS

(See *Manual One*, page 170.) Corns should always be treated by the farrier or vet, as they must be pared out and special shoeing may be necessary. Rest is essential, plus a laxative diet and tubbing or poulticing of the foot if the corn is infected. Deep-seated corns can cause intermittent lameness and are often difficult to detect.

PRICKED FOOT

Even with the best of farriers, pricks do sometimes occur. For immediate treatment, remove the nail, pour tamed iodine (such as Equidine), into the hole, leave nail out.

If unnoticed at time of shoeing:

Symptoms. Lameness, heat round the clench, flinching when tapped, gently, with a light hammer.

Treatment. Remove the suspect nail — signs of black moisture denote a prick. If the symptoms are mild, treat with iodine, otherwise remove the shoe and poultice the foot. If it does not clear up within two days, or there are signs of infection call the vet at once.

QUITTOR

An abcess on the coronet.

Causes. Occasionally direct injury, such as a tread, but more usually infection working up through the foot from a prick, corn or stone bruise.

Symptoms. Heat, pain and swelling round the coronet, with increasing lameness. The swelling will become more localised as the abcess forms.

Treatment. If due to external injury, poulticing should bring relief. Otherwise, consult your vet urgently, as there may be extensive damage within the foot.

SAND CRACK

A crack in the wall of the foot, starting at the coronet and widening as it grows downwards. Does not cause lameness unless deep or infected. (See diagram on page 238.)

Causes. Naturally brittle, especially white, feet. Injury to the coronary band. Rasping the wall. Illness affecting the nutrition of the horn.

Treatment. Consult your farrier in the first place — he may be able to clip the crack, or to burn a groove below it with a hot iron. If the horse is lame, consult your vet. Stimulate the growth of horn by applying a proprietary brand of hoof dressing daily, rubbing it well into the coronet. Cod-liver oil is also a good stimulant.

SEEDY TOE

Separation of the wall from the inner structure of the foot. Starts at the ground surface and works upwards. The cavity is filled with an evil-smelling, cheesy substance.

Causes. Now thought to be due to an organism similar to that which causes foot rot in sheep. More likely to occur in wet conditions. Bad shoeing and lack of foot care may be contributory causes.

Symptoms. Usually none, unless the separation is very large, allowing entry of dirt and small stones, and causing lameness through pressure on the sensitive laminae. Generally found by the farrier when shoeing.

Treatment. The farrier may pack the cavity, after thorough paring, with tow soaked in a proprietary spray such as C.T. 10, Stockholm tar, strong iodine or formalin. Special shoeing may be required. Dress the foot as for sand crack. It is best to keep the horse shod.

THRUSH

An infection in the frog.

Causes. Chiefly standing in dirty bedding in stables, so uncommon in horses living out. Can occur in wet, ill-drained paddocks, or from lack of frog pressure.

Symptoms. Very strong, offensive smell from cleft of frog. There may be a discharge, and the frog will be soft.

Treatment. Should be noted at daily grooming, before it becomes severe. Clean the foot thoroughly, then scrub strong iodine solution, Stockholm tar or formalin into the frog daily with a clean toothbrush.

UNDER-RUN SOLE

Infection from a puncture wound in the foot. Pus cannot escape and spreads under the sole.

Symptoms. Heat and intense pain in the foot. Possibly a rise in temperature.

Treatment. Consult your vet, urgently, if the horse's temperature is up. Meanwhile, tub or poultice the foot to relieve the pain.

REMINDER. If the horse has not been immunised, an anti-tetanus injection is essential for any wound or infection in the foot.

LAMINITIS OR FOUNDER

As this disease mainly affects ponies, it is quite fully covered in *Manual One*, pages 164-165.

NAVICULAR DISEASE

Inflammation and roughening of the navicular bone, also affecting the deep flexor tendon which passes under it.

Causes. Concussion — especially jumping or fast work on hard ground. Poor conformation — upright, boxy feet, contracted heels, upright shoulder and pastern. Poor shoeing. Hereditary disposition.

Symptoms. Intermittent lameness, which may wear off with work at first, but becomes more constant and severe. Pointing a forefoot — each alternately, if both are affected. Heat in the foot.

Treatment. Consult your vet. Although no complete cure has yet been found, palliative measures may relieve the symptoms for some time if the disease is recognised in the early stages. A good farrier can also do much to help.

PEDALOSTITIS

Similar to navicular disease, but the pedal bone is affected. Lameness is usually more severe in the early stages, and does not wear off with exercise.

Treatment. Consult your vet.

BURSAL OR SYNOVIAL ENLARGEMENTS

Soft swellings in the region of a joint, caused by an increased secretion of joint oil, or synovia. Nature's way of relieving irritation and increasing lubrication when the joint is subjected to excessive wear. Rarely cause lameness, unless large enough to interfere with the action of the joint.

Horses with upright shoulders and pasterns and poor hocks are more liable to these ailments, which are aggravated by jumping and galloping on hard ground.

Rest, frequent hosing, massaging with iodine liniment should all help to reduce the swelling. If these are unsuccessful or the horse goes lame, consult your vet.

The principal bursal enlargements are:

Windgalls — occur in the fetlock joints, either of the fore or hind legs.

Thoroughpin — the swelling occurs just above the point of hock, and moves from side to side on pressure with the fingers.

Can be caused by a sudden strain — e.g. pulling up abruptly from a gallop — in which case there will be heat and pain and possibly lameness, but usually the onset is gradual and the symptoms less acute.

Bog spavin — on the inside and towards the front of the hock.

Capped elbow, capped hock. Distinct, but very soft swellings on the point of the hock or elbow.

Both are mainly caused by hard floors and inadquate bedding in stables, so are uncommon in horses living out.

Capped elbow can be used by pressure from the shoe when lying down, or by a kick or blow.

Capped hock sometimes results from kicking in the float when travelling. Use hock boots and/or pad the sides of the float.

Sesamoiditis. Inflammation of the sesamoid bone, and/or the suspensory ligament or the sheath of the flexor tendon.

Swelling occurs low down at the back and sides of the fetlock joint. Can be mistaken for windgalls, but it is much harder and the horse will usually be lame.

Consult your vet as soon as possible. Meanwhile, rest the horse and hose him several times a day. This is a serious ailment, which can cause permanent disability.

BONY ENLARGEMENTS

Splints. (See page 128.)

RINGBONE

Affects one of the pastern bones — high ringbone, the long pastern bone, low ringbone, the short one — and sometimes the joint in between.

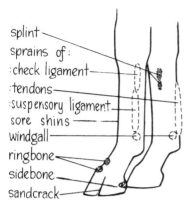

splint
sprains of:
:check ligament
:tendons
:suspensory ligament
sore shins
windgall
ringbone
sidebone
sandcrack

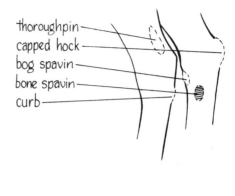

thoroughpin
capped hock
bog spavin
bone spavin
curb

Causes. Concussion, especially in horses of upright conformation, or with very long, sloping pasterns. May result from a blow or sprain or from lack of frog pressure.

Symptoms. Slight lameness at first, which does not wear off with exercise and is more pronounced on hard ground. Lameness will increase, and heat and pain will develop. In high ringbone, the enlargement will become apparent around and above the coronet.

Treatment. Consult your vet. Meanwhile, rest the horse. Hosing or hot fomentations may give some relief. High ringbone can usually be treated successfully, but if the joint is affected or the enlargement is low down inside the foot, the prospects are not good.

SIDEBONE

An 'ossification' (turning to bone) of the lateral cartilages of the foot. (See page 214.)

Causes. Apart from concussion and upright conformation, sidebone can result from a blow or tread on the coronet.

Symptoms. The horse may be quite sound on soft ground, although he may be sore on turning, but will become progressively more lame if worked on hard ground.

Treatment. Consult your vet and farrier, as remedial shoeing could help.

BONE SPAVIN

The enlargement is on the lower inside aspect of the hock.

Causes. Possibly hereditary. Horses with sickle or cow hocks appear to be more susceptible. Overwork, especially in immature horses. Severe exertion, such as jumping in heavy going, particularly if the horse is tired or unfit.

Symptoms. Erratic lameness, especially in the early stages. Usually most severe at the start of work. The hock becomes stiff, and to avoid bending it the horse drags his toe and may swing the leg outwards. The shoe wears at the toe. If the leg is held up with the hock fully flexed for about thirty seconds and the horse then trotted forward immediately, the lameness will be noticeably more severe for the first few strides.

Treatment. Consult your vet and farrier. Shoeing with wedge heels and rolled toes may give some relief. Meanwhile, rest with hot fomentations followed by hosing will help to reduce the pain and inflammation.

SPRAINS

For sprains of the tendons and ligaments between the knee and the fetlock, see page 127. The parts liable to injury are shown below.

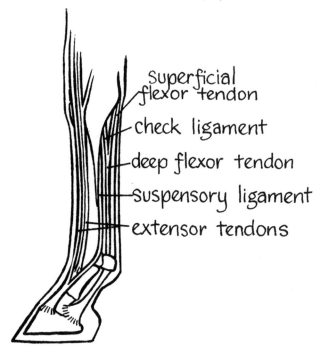

Superficial flexor tendon

check ligament

deep flexor tendon

suspensory ligament

extensor tendons

If the superficial flexor tendon is badly sprained, there will be considerable swelling at the back of the leg, 'bowed' tendon, with heat, pain and lameness.

If both back tendons are ruptured the horse is said to have 'broken down'. He will be in great pain, with much heat and swelling in the leg.

244

Injuries to the deep flexor tendon or the check ligament also involve much pain. The swelling will be on the sides of the leg — high up under the knee if the ligament is affected.

There is usually less swelling if the suspensory ligament is sprained, and it may be on the inside or the outside of the leg only.

Bear in mind that swelling in the knee to fetlock area can also be caused by a kick or a blow from the opposite foot. If a dent remains on pressure from the fingers, the swelling is due to infection, possibly from an injury in the foot, not to sprain.

If a severe sprain should occur out hunting or at a competition where no vet is available, bandage *both* forelegs firmly from knee to coronet, with ample gamgee underneath, to give support for the journey home. Contact your vet on arrival.

CURB

A strain of the ligament of the hind leg. It shows as a bowed swelling on the back of the leg, about a hand's breadth below the point of hock.

Causes. As for sprains. Overwork with a young or unfit horse. Jumping in heavy going. Horses with small, sickle or bowed hocks are more liable to curbs.

Symptoms. Swelling, as above. Usually heat and pain, especially in the early stages. The horse may or may not not be lame.

Treatment. Consult your vet and farrier — wedge-heeled shoes could help to relieve the strain. Do not work the horse, even if he is not lame, without your vet's permission.

SORE SHINS

Inflammation of the periosteum, the membrane of the cannon bone, usually on the forelegs. Most common in young horses, especially if they are jumping or doing fast work on hard ground.

Generally starts with soreness and heat down the front of the cannon bone and a shortening of the stride. At this stage, they should respond quite quickly to rest on a laxative diet and frequent hosing. If neglected and work continued, swelling and lameness will soon follow, requiring poulticing and a much longer rest period.

SELF-INFLICTED INJURIES

Known collectively as 'interfering'.

These include brushing and over-reaching (see *Manual One*, page 170) and speedy cutting, in which the horse hits himself just below the knee. The latter is not often met with, but requires special boots.

In all these cases, check:

1. The horse's condition, and his suitability and fitness for the work required.

2. His shoeing.

3. Your riding. An unbalanced, sprawling horse is much more likely to suffer these injuries, especially in heavy going.

Always use protective boots when lunging, to guard against brushing, and use them on young horses when first ridden, until they have developed some balance and muscle. If brushing is due to faulty conformation or action, boots or bandages may always be needed.

Horses who tend to over-reach should always wear 'bell' boots for jumping and hunting, and should be shod as for 'Forging' below.

Generally, horses are more liable to 'interfering' injuries than ponies.

Forging (sometimes called clicking). This does not cause injury, as the toe of the hind shoe strikes the inside of the toe of the front shoe (not the horse's heel, as in over-reaching), but it does indicate a lack of balance and/or condition in the horse.

It will help to use concave shoes with quarter-clips and the toes set slightly under and bevelled on the hind feet, but check all the above causes and take necessary action.

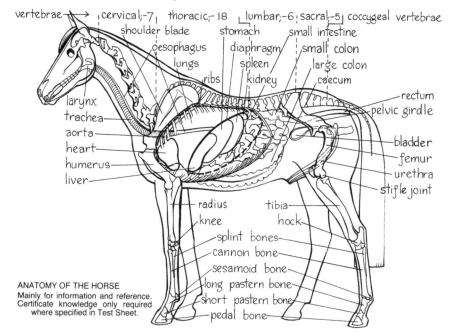

ANATOMY OF THE HORSE
Mainly for information and reference.
Certificate knowledge only required
where specified in Test Sheet.

18
KNOW THE HORSE (A, H)

ANATOMY AND CONFORMATION

You should now be familiar with the terms used to describe conformation, and be able to recognise good and bad points. The next stage is to understand how these factors affect a horse's soundness and suitability for different types of work.

Anatomy

A brief description of the horse's anatomy will help to explain:

1. How the 'machine' functions as a whole.

2. Why certain points of conformation are considered desirable or undesirable.

Points of Interest — Skeleton

1. The large, heavy skull and very flexible neck vertebrae. The importance of correct proportion of head and neck for the horse's balance is obvious. For the horse to be on the bit, the 'bend' should be at the poll, not between the fifth and sixth vertebrae (overbent position).

2. The angle of the shoulder blade, combined with that of the pastern bones, probably affect the horse's 'ride' and soundness more than any other factor. An upright shoulder alone would make the horse short in front and in his paces; coupled with upright pasterns, there would be considerable jar both to his forelegs and to his rider.

3. The solidity of the rib-cage and the vertebrae of the back. This makes it impossible for the horse to 'bend his back' laterally to any appreciable extent.

4. How close the vertebrae of the withers and back are to the surface, showing how easily they can be injured by ill-fitting saddles, and also by heavy or continuous weight on an under-developed spine.

5. The weak area over the loins, between the last rib and the pelvis.

6. The forehand with its solid framework provided by the rib cage and straight but flexible knee joint, is the weight-carrying section of the horse. The hindquarters supply the main driving power — correct angulation of hip, stifle and hock joints is essential for speed, jumping ability and continuing soundness.

Internal Organs

1. The proximity of the trachea, carrying air from nostrils to lungs, and the oesophagus, conveying food from mouth to stomach. Their entrances are very close together, and it is only too easy for the inexpert to make a mistake when stomach tubing.

2. The larynx, where whistling and roaring originate. (See page 237.)

3. The position of the heart, far forward in the chest cavity, and the lungs, which flank it on either side and extend over a surprisingly large area. Hence the need for 'good depth' and sufficient width of chest to accommodate these organs.

4. The situation of the stomach, between liver and spleen, again flanked by lungs and rib cage. When the stomach is distended with food there is little room for the lungs to function to their full extent. If strenuous work is called for, the air is forced into the lungs, but, since expansion is restricted, a breakdown of the air cells may occur (see 'broken wind', page 237).

5. The digestive system as a whole (see page 197).

Muscles and Tendons

A complex muscle system controls all movement (and even stationary stability!) in the horse. Muscles run from bone to bone, crossing and controlling joints. They consist of elastic fibrous tissue, capable of considerable contraction, and requiring a good blood supply, especially during strenuous work.

Basically, each joint has two sets of muscles — flexors, which bend, and extensors, which straighten it. The lower part of limb muscles become tendons, inelastic cords linking the fleshy part of the muscle to bone. Long muscles, particularly in the forearm and thigh, have more power of contraction, producing length of stride, speed, and when combined with short tendons, strength (well let down).

Ligaments are similar to tendons, but run from bone to bone, or wrap round and support joints.

Tendons and ligaments have a very poor blood supply, making healing difficult.

(See back endpapers and page 244.)

ASSESSING A HORSE

This is a question of weighing up the good points against the inevitable weaknesses. To some extent, conformation requirements depend on the work the horse has to do. Faults which may be unacceptable in a show jumper, may matter little for a horse that is only used for quiet riding and the occasional day's hunting or gymkhana.

One rule that applies to all horses is that good temperament is of paramount importance. Any 'performance' horse must have a bold but equable temperament to cope with modern-day demands; the all-rounder, especially if his rider is inexperienced, needs a willing and amiable nature, with a good mouth and manners.

Guidelines:

A show horse or pony must have quality, presence and straight action, and be unblemished and sound. Naturally, the better his conformation, the better his chances! A good front, with well-set-on head and neck, is specially important.

A dressage horse should have presence and move freely and straight. Good balance, with a well-set-on head and neck and strong hindquarters, to assist in collection, are essential.

An eventer should be well balanced, and must be completely sound. Any conformation faults which could affect his soundness are suspect. For example, upright shoulder and pastern, calf knees, back at, or tied in below, the knee, thickened tendons, round fetlock joints, poor feet, straight, sickle or small hocks. Straight action is desirable, though slight dishing could be overlooked.

A one-day eventer does not need quite the quality, substance and ultra-toughness of the three-day event horse, who has to gallop faster and farther over bigger fences, carrying 75kg.

A show jumper must be strong and athletic, built to withstand the continual concussion of landing on hard ground. Short or upright pasterns, poor feet, knees or hocks would be almost certain to lead to unsoundness.

A hunter must be strong enough to carry his rider's weight for a considerable period of time. Although it will make him a less comfortable ride, upright conformation is not so likely to cause unsoundness on the softer ground in the hunting season.

A horse or pony for a novice rider. Generally speaking, the sturdy, rather than the very narrow type of mount, makes it easier for the novice rider to maintain balance and gain a sense of security. Few thoroughbreds are suitable.

TEETH AND AGEING

(For description of dentition, see page 141.)

The incisor teeth are the main indicators of the horse's age. Up to five years, there will always be some milk teeth present, and their replacement by permanent teeth, progressively from centrals to corners, provides an almost infallible guide. Always check both sides — a permanent lateral or corner often comes through on one side before the other.

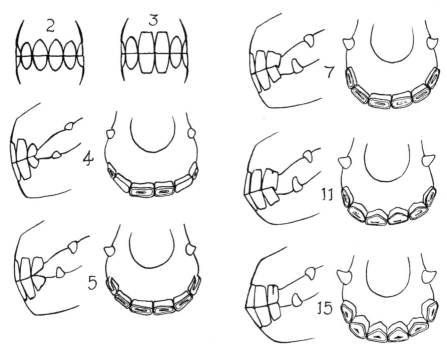

At **two years** the horse has a 'full mouth' of milk teeth (six in each jaw). Check size and colour carefully to avoid confusion with a 'full' five-year-old mouth. Traces of a woolly coat and shorter tail may provide additional clues!

At **three years** permanent centrals have replaced the milk teeth.

At **four years** the permanent laterals are through. Now only the corner milk teeth remain, and the difference is very obvious. Soon after four the tushes begin to show.

At **five years** the permanent corners appear. The horse now has a full mouth of permanent teeth (including tushes), although the corners will have a hollow rounded look.

From now on, the shape, angle and markings of the teeth show gradual changes, which enable one, with practice, to form a fairly accurate estimate of the horse's age.

Markings
1. The infundibulum, 'cup' or 'black mark'. A depression in the

centre of the 'table' — biting surface. Not important to ageing until six years onwards.

2. The 'dental star' appears clearly as a dark line in front of the cup from eight years on, changing shape as the horse ages.

3. 'Galvayne's groove' — a narrow, usually discoloured groove which travels, over a period of years, from top to bottom of the upper corner incisors.

At six years the corner teeth are in wear. The cups are disappearing from the centrals, but the black mark still shows.

At seven years a small hook appears on the outside of the upper corner teeth. There are no cups on the centrals, and they are disappearing from the laterals.

At eight years the 'hook' is disappearing, there are no cups on centrals or laterals, although the black marks are still visible. In front of these, starting with the centrals, another dark line, the 'dental star' can be clearly seen.

At ten years 'Galvayne's groove' can be seen starting from the gum.

At eleven years the 'hook' reappears, usually more pronounced and longer-lasting. The teeth are changing shape, becoming more triangular, and starting to slope forward. The original 'black mark' has virtually disappeared, but the line of the dental star is apparent on all the tables.

Exact ageing now becomes more difficult. The teeth are gradually pushed further out of the gum, making them appear longer, and they protrude more. The tables become rounder, and the dental stars are seen as a dark spot.

'Galvayne's groove' works down the full length of the upper corner incisors, reaching halfway at fifteen years, and the bottom of the tooth at twenty.

Crib biters or horses grazing on pumice or stony ground may wear the centrals and laterals quite badly, and make ageing difficult to assess.

Ageing Terms

'Rising' and 'off'. 'Rising' five, for example, means that the horse is between four-and-a-half and five years: 'five off' means between five and five-and-a-half .

'Aged' means eight years or over — mainly owing to the difficulty of defining the age precisely from then on.

Thoroughbreds' ages are counted from 1 August in the southern hemisphere, 1 January in the northern hemisphere.

Brands

In New Zealand, thoroughbreds, and some other breeds, such as quarter horses and appaloosas carry a 'cipher brand' on the left shoulder, consisting of initials or a hieroglyphic. On the right shoulder two numbers are branded one above the other. The lower of these figures indicates the last digit of the year of birth, e.g. if it is a 1, the horse could have been foaled in 1981, 1971 or even 1961. The teeth should enable you to decide whether he is 4, 14, or 24 without the need of tracing him through the cipher brand.

Hanoverians and other warmbloods have their own ciphers, and the age brand, all on the left side.

BUYING A HORSE

Initial Considerations

1. Type. Try to form a clear idea of the type of horse you need to suit your physique, temperament and lifestyle. He must be capable, at least potentially, of the work required.

2. Age. It takes much skill and experience to estimate the possibilities of a real youngster, seen in the rough and perhaps unable to be ridden. A horse under six needs time, patience and know-how, but will appreciate in value if correctly trained and produced.

From about seven to twelve is the prime of life, and the most expensive horse to buy.

An older horse, if he knows his job, can give you valuable experience, but will depreciate in value and need more care as time goes on.

3. Size. Depends on your height, weight and requirements. There are some useful smaller horses about, but for eventing or other strenuous activities, most adult riders find that 157.5cm (15.2hh) to 167.5cm (16.2hh) provides a good range, depending on build and bone. Very big horses, 170cm or over, require more feed, are harder to get fit, more liable to respiratory problems, and may find normal combination distances difficult.

4. Finance. Good horses are not cheap, and generally, unless you are very discerning or very lucky, you get what you pay for! All the more reason to be selective when buying. Mistakes can be costly.

Trying Out a Horse

Ask your instructor or an experienced friend to accompany you. A second opinion is invaluable.

1. The first impression is most important. See him in hand before he is ridden. Is he the type you have in mind, the right size and up to

your weight? His expression and general attitude can give many clues to temperament. Stand back and consider his balance and proportions — would he fit into the 'square'? Note any major faults in conformation or obvious blemishes or unsoundness.

2. If all seems well so far, see him ridden by the owner, so that you can assess paces and movement, outline, mouth and manners. Watch him at all paces and over fences, according to his present ability. If you intend to ride him on the road, see how he behaves in traffic.

3. Ride the horse yourself. Start quietly, to come to terms, then try him out thoroughly to test his potential for the work required. Is he co-operative? Try to analyse the good and bad points, and then decide whether you (a) want to and (b) would be able to, form a partnership with this horse. When jumping, if possible, build one or two different fences from the ones he knows well, and note his reactions.

4. If you like him, or are unsure, ask your companion to ride the horse, mainly for another opinion on any points you found dubious.

5. Have the horse unsaddled, and study his conformation in detail. See him run up in hand, check straightness of action.

Veterinary examination. Particularly if he is a 'performance' horse, and therefore likely to be expensive, even if green, have the vet of your choice examine him. A veterinary certificate is not a warranty, but it does include a signed statement from the owner, as well as the vet's opinion as to the horse's state of soundness and consequent suitability for the work required, based on a very thorough examination.

Trial. Taking the horse home on trial should not be expected as a matter of right. While any trial in the presence of the owner is reasonable, few owners are prepared to let the horse go away. If you are offered this privilege you should:

a. check whether the horse is insured and will be covered while in your care — otherwise take out a temporary insurance policy yourself.

b. take every precaution for his welfare, in management as well as in riding.

c. notify the owner the moment your mind is made up. One week should be ample.

19

LUNGING, RIDE AND LEAD (A, H)

Lunging is a method of training and/or exercising a horse from the ground. The horse, on a long rein or line attached to a special head-collar called a 'cavesson' moves on a circle round the handler.

Lunging has many uses. Among them are:

1. For the initial training or 'breaking-in' (an unpleasant and inaccurate term) of young horses or ponies:

a. to teach obedience to the aids of voice, rein and whip.

b. to accustom him to saddle and bridle, and to light contact on his mouth through the side-reins.

c. to develop his muscles and improve his balance before he is asked to carry the weight of a rider (see page 172).

2. For retraining horses who are disobedient, stiff or do not accept the bit. A few minutes lunging will settle a horse who is overfresh and above himself. It is invaluable for exercising and, when necessary, disciplining ponies who are too small to carry an adult rider.

3. To improve the training of a dressage horse. It is most useful to be able to observe the horse's outline and way of going from the ground. Many horses benefit from a few minutes lunging prior to riding, to loosen them up and establish paces.

4. For exercising horses who cannot be ridden because of a sore back or other injury.

5. If time is short or it is not feasible to ride the horse for some other reason, twenty to thirty minutes lunging, properly carried out, will provide both work and exercise.

6. For improving the rider's seat and balance. (See page 144.)

Facilities. Only really well-trained horses with experienced handlers may safely and effectively be lunged in the open. For all others, and nearly always for lunging the rider, an enclosure is essential. If you try to lunge an untrained or nappy horse in the open, he will certainly try to pull away at some stage. It is more than likely that he will succeed in getting away from you, and he must *never* be allowed to discover that this is possible.

A lunging enclosure must have:

a. safe, strong fencing, not less than 1.3m high.

b. a level, if possible all-weather surface.

It should be in a quiet situation to avoid distractions, and large enough for a 20m circle.

If no enclosure is available, it may be possible to use a corner of the paddock and erect a temporary fence on the other two sides.

Equipment (See picture on page 259.)

1. Lunging cavesson. This has a padded, jointed steel noseband with a ring on the front, to which the lunge rein is attached, and a jowl strap to keep it in place. It should be as light as possible. A strap from headpiece to noseband, down the front of the face, is not necessary, and can sometimes cause the cavesson to be pulled off.

An ordinary halter with a ring on the front *will not do*, because it cannot be fitted snugly enough to prevent it from rubbing the horse's nose or injuring his outside eye if he pulls out on the circle. Never try to lunge with the rein on the back of the halter — the horse will probably go with his head to the outside, and it will be almost impossible to hold him if he pulls away.

2. Lunge rein. Preferably made of heavy cotton or nylon webbing. Thin nylon webbing tends to cut. Rope is too heavy and difficult to handle, especially when wet. The lunge rein should be about 3cm wide and 9-10m long, so that the horse can work on a 20m circle. There should be a loop on one end and a strong buckle or clip on a swivel at the other end.

3. Whip. Must be long enough to reach the horse on the 20m circle, but light and well-balanced. Leather boot laces can be useful for lengthening.

4. Side-reins. Some trainers prefer elastic, in one form or another, let into the side-reins to make them less rigid; others feel that this encourages the horse to play with the bit excessively and produces a less steady head carriage. A good compromise is to have a short elastic inset backed by leather, so that the expansion is limited.

5. Brushing boots, preferably all round, but certainly on the forelegs. They *must* be used on the hindlegs if the horse shows any signs of brushing.

6. Gloves. Absolutely essential to prevent your hands being burnt by the rein. *Never* lunge without them.

NOTE. Don't wear spurs when lunging — you could easily trip over them or get them entangled with the whip.

Tacking up. The horse would normally be saddled and bridled. Only a snaffle bit should be used, with a drop noseband if necessary. Any other type of noseband would cause discomfort.

The cavesson is fitted so that the noseband is well up on the nose. The noseband goes inside the cheekpieces of the bridle. The jowl strap is lower than a throatlash, and is done up firmly to prevent the cheekpieces from pulling across the horse's eye. The noseband must also be firm to prevent rubbing. Some cavessons may be fitted under the bit as a drop noseband, but this is not recommended.

Side-reins should go under the first girth strap and be attached to the second or third one. This, together with a runner, prevents them from slipping down. Height depends to some degree on the action required. Generally they are fitted fairly high, never below the saddle flap.

Unless the horse is to be ridden on the lunge, the side-reins are attached to the bit rings above the bridle reins, which should be safely secured. Side-reins should be of equal length. The length depends on:

1. Whether the horse is used to them. If not, they should be introduced as for a young horse. (See page 174.)

2. The stage of training. As balance improves it will be necessary to shorten the side-reins to maintain contact (see page 174) but they must always allow the horse to retain his normal outline, and must never be used to force an artificial head-carriage.

3. The pace at which the horse is worked. Side-reins correctly fitted for trot could be restrictive at walk.

NEVER leave the horse standing with side-reins attached, or lead him with them on. They must only be used while actually lunging.

Method of Lunging

When lunging to the left, the rein is held in the left hand, the whip in the right.

A. B. C. and D. are all acceptable methods of holding the lunge rein. E. is dangerous — loop over wrist, uneven coils, rein on ground.

The handler should stand still, pivoting on the left heel, or walk in a small circle, if necessary, and should try to keep the right shoulder in line with the horse's hip. The hand and rein are held across the body, with the elbow bent and close to the side. The whip normally points towards and slightly behind the horse. Horse, rein and whip should form a triangle.

Handling the rein. The rein must always be taut and untwisted, and must *never* be allowed to trail on the ground where the horse could put a foot over it. This applies when leading as well as when lunging. When leading, hold the looped rein in the hand furthest from the horse, and hold the rein in the hand nearest to him, about 30cm from the cavesson. When the horse is halted out on the circle, loop the lunge rein as you approach him, and let it out again carefully as you return to the centre of the circle.

There should be a light, even contact on the lunge rein while the horse is working. It is used, in conjunction with the voice, to steady him, which it does with a series of 'take and give' vibrations rather than a solid pull. Occasionally, quite a sharp tug may be needed, particularly with a trained horse who fails to obey a verbal command.

If the horse pulls out of the circle, a similar technique of rather stronger vibrations is used. This is not usually a persistent problem in a suitable enclosure, but it is extremely difficult to correct in the open.

Handling the whip. This is an aid, rarely used for punishment. It has two main functions, to send the horse actively forward, and to keep him out on the circle. For the first, it is generally sufficient to show or flick it behind the horse, without touching him. If used on the horse, it should be lightly flicked, just below the hocks. To keep the horse out, point or flick the whip towards the girth region. Never lose contact with the rein when using the whip, or step back to keep the rein taut.

When approaching or leading the horse, carry the whip, with the thong coiled up, under the arm furthest from the horse, pointing to the rear. Never drop the whip where the horse could tread on it, or allow the point to drag on the ground. When not in use stand the whip on its stock, not on the point.

It takes practice to learn to handle a whip of the necessary length. Try without a horse at first, pivoting on the spot in both directions, so that you learn to handle the whip with either hand. Then try with another person holding the end of the lunge rein and taking the place of the horse.

Use of voice. This is most important in lunging — the trained horse works mainly on verbal commands.

The principle is that a sharp, rising tone will encourage the horse to go faster, while a lower, drawling tone will steady him. So if, for instance, the horse is walking and you want him to trot, the command could be, 'Ter-r-rot', in two syllables with the emphasis on the second one. To bring him back to walk, it would be a long-drawn out, 'Wa-a-lk'. It often helps to preface the command with the word 'Steady' on downward transitions. It is essential that commands are given in exactly the same way every time — the tone is more important than the actual words. When a command is obeyed promptly, always reward the horse, equally promptly, with a 'Good boy' (or girl). Apart from this, don't talk too much to the horse, he will only be confused by a constant stream of chatter. If a command is *not* obeyed promptly, back it up by the use of the rein, or by showing the whip behind the horse — let him know that you expect to be obeyed first time. Don't forget the praise when he does obey.

When lunging an unknown horse, if he doesn't appear to understand your commands, try different tones or words — he may be used to 'Whoa' rather than 'Halt', for example. Try to find out beforehand what commands he knows, and adapt yourself accordingly. Time enough to teach him yours if you work him regularly.

Working the horse. Lead him into the enclosure, as described. *Be sure to shut the gate.* It is generally better to warm the horse up without side-reins. Start on his best side — usually the left. In this case, take the looped lunge rein in your left hand, the whip in your right. Step away from the horse and towards the rear, and tell him to 'Walk on', guiding him out if necessary with the whip pointing towards his

The 'lunger' shows a well-balanced stance with the weight on the right foot, and a correct and businesslike approach. The young horse shows good activity, balance and bend. Photo: R. Maxwell.

shoulder. Get him out on the 20m circle as soon as possible.

Alternatively, halt the horse on the perimeter of the circle, facing in the required direction, go to the centre yourself and tell him to 'Walk on' from there.

Trot the horse for a few minutes before fitting the side-reins. Always insist that the horse halts out on the circle, without turning in to face you, and go to him, rather than letting him come to you. Allowing him to do so encourages him to stop and turn in when he is working. Don't let him halt directly from the trot, always make him come down through the walk. Change direction frequently.

To halt the horse if he does not obey the voice, move over so that you are level with his shoulder, repeat the command firmly, accompanied by a series of quick, light jerks on the rein. Showing the whip in front of him may help. Failing this, walk him towards the fence at an angle of about 60 degrees, placing yourself far enough forward to block him, not so far as to allow him to whip round. He will be forced to stop, and when he does, go to him and reward him.

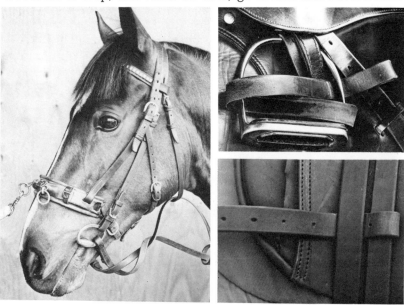

Left: Lunging cavesson, note correct fitting of jowl strap.
Right: Stirrups and side-reins secured.

If you are in the open with no fence nearby, gradually bring the horse on to a smaller circle, talking soothingly to him if he has had a fright, more firmly if you are sure he is just misbehaving. Keep level with, or even in front of, his shoulder, and use whip and rein discreetly as described above. You should be able to stop him as he

259

gets closer to you. But it is asking for trouble, particularly if you are inexperienced, to attempt to lunge in the open until you are certain that the horse is obedient to *your* commands in the enclosure.

About twenty minutes at walk and trot will be enough for most horses — less if they are young, green or unfit. The aims are the same as when the horse is ridden on a circle — controlled impulsion, rhythm, bend, balance, calmness.

At the end of the session, release the side-reins and return them to the saddle dees, give the horse a pat and a titbit, and, if he is hot and you are not going to ride him, lead him round until he cools off.

RIDE AND LEAD

A time-saving method of exercising two horses together whereby one horse is ridden and the other led without a rider. Also useful for exercising a horse which cannot be ridden for some reason.

A horse should be trained to lead from either side, but when leading on the road you *must* keep to the left with the led horse on your left, away from the traffic. (See 'Road Code'.)

Always have a bridle on the led horse. If you anticipate that it may be necessary to tie him up, put on a halter as well, with the rope secured round the horse's neck.

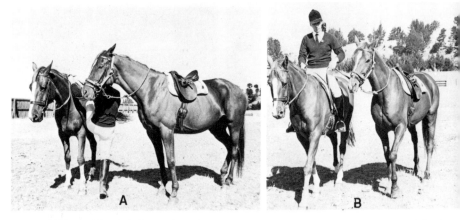

Ride and lead. A. Mounting. Note ridden horse's right rein shortened, and angle of led horse. B. Good control as the rider steadies the led horse.

Hold the reins of the led horse in the hand nearest to him, with a finger dividing them, and the ridden horse's reins in the other hand, with whip, if carried. The led horse's reins are normally held about halfway down, keeping the hand close to your knee. Try to keep his head about level with your knee too. Never allow him to forge ahead, where he might cross in front of you or kick you or your horse, or to

260

hang back. Be especially careful to keep him well up when turning to the right (if he is on your left), and to allow ample room for the led horse when passing through gateways.

If the led horse is very fresh, it may be necessary to shorten his reins to about 30cm. If he tries to pull away, go with him at first and gradually bring him under control. If you are not sure how the horses will go together, practise in the paddock until they are settled. Never go out on the road with horses that are overfresh, traffic-shy, or with one that has never been led from another horse.

The reins are usually held direct to the hand, as shown. If the led horse is inclined to hang back, the far rein may be passed through the ring of the snaffle nearest to you. This prevents the bit from turning backwards in the horse's mouth, but is generally less comfortable for him.

If the led horse is saddled, stirrups should be secured as for lunging (see page 259). If the leathers are loose on the bars, turn up the safety catches to prevent the leathers slipping off, but be sure to turn the catches down again before the horse is ridden. Running martingales must be taken off the reins and secured to the neckstrap. In the case of a double bridle or pelham, lead by the bridoon rein only and secure the curb rein on the horse's neck.

PUTTING UP A RIDER

Legging up. Left side. The rider takes up reins normally, as for mounting, with the whip on the far side of the horse's neck. He stands facing towards the horse, left hand just in front of the wither, right hand on the pommel, left leg bent at the knee. The assistant places his left hand under the rider's knee, right hand under his ankle, and, at an agreed signal, the rider springs up from the right foot, is lifted high enough to clear the cantle with the right leg, and comes down lightly in the saddle. Reverse these instructions for legging up on the right side.

Balancing the rider's weight in mounting. The rider mounts normally, keeping the whip on the nearest side of the horse's neck. The assistant stands on the far side, holding the horse, if necessary, by taking the rein lightly near the bit, and pulling down on the stirrup leather to prevent the saddle being displaced by the rider's weight. He then slips the iron on to the rider's foot. Essential when first mounting a young horse from the stirrup, and almost essential with horses and ponies in gross condition.

20

SADDLERY AND EQUIPMENT
(B, A, H)

Basic information on saddlery and equipment is given in *Manual One*, pages 175-197. To continue:

BITS AND BITTING

The object of the bit is to enable the rider, in conjunction with the other aids, to control the horse without:

a. causing pain or fear.

b. spoiling his paces or

c. forcing him to carry his head in an unnatural or uncomfortable position.

Head carriage (as explained in the riding chapters of this book) depends on conformation, balance, muscular development and training. The well-trained horse, properly ridden and comfortably bitted, should be on the bit — i.e. he should go freely forward, engaging his hocks and seeking a constant, light contact with the rider's hand, and should respond immediately to any alteration in this contact.

There are three main types of bit: the snaffle, the curb, which, with a light snaffle called a 'bridoon' (or 'bradoon') comprises the double bridle, and the pelham.

ACTION OF BITS

The bit, bridle and noseband can act on the following parts of the mouth and head.

1. **The bars of the mouth.** All bits act to some extent on the bars (see page 141). The sharp edge of the jawbone can easily be felt under the thin covering of flesh, which contains a mass of nerves. Constant pressure soon numbs these nerves, rough jerking and sawing at the bit can cause intense pain and deep bruising through to the bone. If mistreatment continues, eventually the nerves, and with them all feeling in the bars, will be destroyed. The horse is then said, quite correctly, to have 'a hard mouth'. This is a man-made thing — no horse was ever born with a hard mouth.

2. **The tongue.** All bits bring some pressure to bear on the tongue.

3. **The lips and corners of the mouth.** Affected mainly by jointed snaffles, and very strongly by gag snaffles.

4. **The nose.** Dropped, flash, Grakle and especially Kineton nosebands all bring pressure to bear on the nose when the horse resists. (See 'Nosebands', page 269.)

5. **The chin-groove.** All curb and pelham bits act on the chin-groove through the curb chain. Dropped, flash and Grakle nosebands act on it when the horse resists.

6. **The poll.** Curb and pelham bits exert some pressure on the poll, and gag snaffles affect it strongly.

7. **The roof of the mouth.** Old-fashioned curb bits sometimes had a high 'port' or central arch, which acted on the roof of the mouth. Fortunately, such bits are rarely seen today.

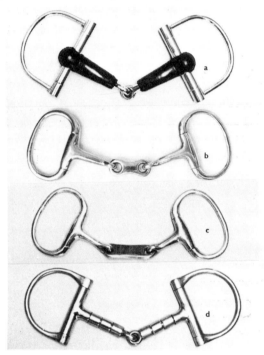

Types of bits. A. A mild, jointed, rubber-covered snaffle. The D-ring cannot pinch the lips. B. French snaffle. Has a smooth, rounded, central plate, which reduces the nutcracker action. Many horses go well in it, especially those with narrow mouths. Both the above bits are allowed for dressage tests. C. Dr Bristol. Has a squared, flat plate. More severe than the French snaffle, due to the angle at which the plate is set. Extremely painful if inadvertently put in upside down, when the edge presses into the horse's tongue. Not allowed for dressage tests overseas. D. Jointed snaffle with rollers — often made of copper. A fairly severe bit, which can sometimes be useful for horses who lean, or who have dry or insensitive mouths. Not allowed for dressage tests. Note: The above two bits should only be used by experienced, self-controlled riders on a temporary basis.

Snaffle

Generally, the mildest bits, though some are extremely severe. The plain snaffle should be the basic bit for riding and training, and nothing else should be used on young horses.

A selection of useful snaffle bits is shown in *Manual One,* page 179, and others are illustrated on page 263.

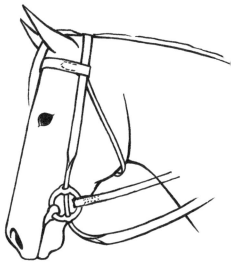

Gag snaffle. When the rein is used the bit slides up the rounded section, exerting a strong upward pull on the corners of the lips and some downward pressure on the poll. Its main purpose is to raise the head. A severe bit, sometimes effective on the heavier type of horse who leans. Should always have a second rein directly from the bit ring which is the 'riding rein', so that the gag can be used only when necessary. See Note above.

Bear in mind that:

a. a thick mouthpiece is milder than a thin one because it acts on a wide area of the bars and tongue.

b. bits with fixed sides, such as an eggbutt or D-ring, cannot pinch the lips (unless the bit is too small) but allow less play in the mouthpiece and may possibly cause more pressure on the tongue. They are not recommended for dry-mouthed horses.

Fitting a snaffle. Hold the bit on either side, so that it is straight in the mouth, if jointed. There should be about 1cm clearance on each side. If too small, the bit will pinch the lips. If too big, a jointed bit will hang too low in the mouth and the nutcracker action will be increased, while any bit will slip about and be uncomfortable.

To check the height of the bit, stand facing the horse, put a finger on each side of the bit and press down lightly. This will show whether the horse is holding the bit up himself. Adjust the cheekpieces so that there is one small wrinkle in the corner of the lip. The practice of fitting jointed snaffles too low is one of the main causes of horses beginning to put their tongues over the bit.

The Double Bridle (curb and bridoon)

The most widely used curb bit is the Weymouth. It is generally a straight-bar bit with a tongue-groove — a shallow arch in the centre to allow room for the tongue. (Not to be confused with the 'port' mentioned earlier.) The mouthpiece may be either fixed or movable where it joins the cheek of the bit. The fixed one is more accurate in its action, and is therefore generally preferred for dressage, while the sliding mouthpiece is a little milder in that it gives the horse an instant's warning before coming into action.

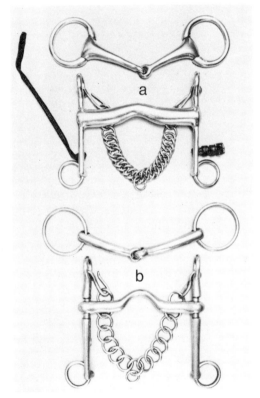

Curb bits and bridoons. A. German dressage bits. Note the egg-butt bridoon, double-link curb chain and lipstrap. B. Weymouth with sliding mouthpiece and single-link curb chain.

The curb bit has a hook at each side for the curb chain, which fits in the chin-groove. The bit works with a lever action on the lower jaw. Since the rein is attached to the bottom of the bit and the curb chain at the top, the mouthpiece forms the fulcrum of the lever. When the rein is tightened, the bit acts on the bars and chin-groove, and to a lesser degree on the tongue and poll. The greater the overall length of the cheek, the greater the leverage and the more severe the action. Extra length above the mouthpiece increases the pressure on the poll.

You can experience the action of a curb bit for yourself by fastening the curb chain fairly tightly, then putting your hand between the mouthpiece and the chain and pulling the lower rings of the bit. It pinches! You should try this before putting any curb bit on your horse, so that you will appreciate just what you are handling.

Action of the double bridle. Before using a double bridle, the horse must be going forward with good impulsion and able to come on the bit in a snaffle, and the rider must have a steady seat and be capable of applying accurate aids and handling two reins. Only in these conditions can the correct action of the bits be attained.

The placing of the head and the impulsion are maintained by the bridoon in conjunction with seat and leg aids, and the curb is used intermittently to obtain increased lightness and flexion of the poll and lower jaw. It is a very delicate instrument. Properly used, it creates a new awareness in both horse and rider of true lightness. (For riding in a double bridle, see page 50.)

Composition and assembly. The double bridle consists of a split-head headpiece, to which the curb bit is attached. The bridoon has its own 'sliphead'. The long strap is threaded through the browband, under the headpiece, from left to right, so that the bridoon buckle is on the right. The cavesson noseband is then threaded under the bridoon strap, from right to left, giving two buckles on each side of the horse's head. Curb chain and lipstrap are attached, to the hook and small ring respectively, on the right-hand side of the curb bit.

A double bridle should be made of fine leather, with stud fittings or sewn — buckles are too clumsy. Reins of plain leather, light and not too wide. The curb rein should be narrower than the bridoon.

Curb chains may either be of large, heavy, single links, or lighter, double links. A strap with links at each end and a ring for the lipstrap are sometimes substituted for the curb chain, or a leather or rubber guard may be used if a less severe curb action is required.

The lipstrap should be of rolled leather.

Leather curb 'chain'. Single and double-link curb chains and lipstrap, see picture on page 265.

Putting on and fitting. Check that the throatlash, noseband, curb chain and lipstrap are all undone. If the bridle is not fitted to the horse, measure it against his snaffle bridle or hold it up beside his head to check that the length of the cheekpieces is approximately correct. Leave the keepers undone, so that it can be adjusted quickly if necessary.

Lay the bridoon over the curb — this keeps the two bits together and enables you to put them into the horse's mouth as one. Then put on the bridle, as with an ordinary snaffle. Check height of bits. The bridoon should make one wrinkle in the corner of the mouth, with the curb now lying just below it, on the bars. Fasten the throatlash and noseband.

Next do up the curb chain, as shown. This is the *only* way to fasten a curb chain so that it cannot twist.

Putting on the double bridle. Inset, fastening the curb chain. Twist the chain until it lies quite flat, then put the nearest edge of the link over the hook. If too long, place the required link over the top of the first one.

To check the tightness of the chain, feel the curb reins gently — the chain should tighten in the chin-groove, bringing the bit into action, when the cheeks reach an angle of 45 degrees.

Finally, thread the lipstrap through the fly-link of the curb chain and do it up loosely. Its purpose is to keep the curb chain in place.

A well-fitted double bridle.

When taking off the bridle, undo the lipstrap, curb chain, noseband and throatlash, in that order. It is especially important to ease the two bits gently out of the horse's mouth.

NOTE. Neither of the bits of a double bridle should ever be used on its own.

Pelhams

A pelham is a bit which attempts to combine the actions of the curb and bridoon in one mouthpiece. It has a curb chain and should have two reins. The disadvantage is that the lever action of the curb can only function if the top rein is released, leaving the rider with no means of maintaining the position of the horse's head. This is why pelhams do tend to make horses overbent, however good the rider's hands, and why they are never allowed for dressage at any level. If both reins are used together, no very definite effect is produced.

There are many different types of pelham, but the usual ones are the mullen-mouth, which can be made of metal, vulcanite or rubber, and the jointed. The latter is not recommended in any circumstances — it combines lever and nutcracker actions, and pinches every part of the horse's mouth.

The mullen-mouth pelham is often used for showing. For this

purpose, despite its theoretical disadvantages, some horses go well in it, especially those with short mouths, and thick tongues, who may find a double bridle rather a mouthful. It can also be useful if the rider is not yet ready to cope with a double bridle.

Pelhams are sometimes used with 'roundings' (a short, rounded strap connecting the two rings) or with forked reins, so that the rider only has one rein. Roundings usually tend to put the pressure more on the curb part of the bit; forked reins depend entirely on the adjustment. Neither should be used for showing, though they can occasionally be effective on small ponies who are rather strong for their riders, or on some horses for hunting or cross country. For older riders, it is better to learn to handle two reins if you use a bit which requires them.

The Kimblewick

This is a curb bit, not a pelham, as it has a curb chain and only has provision for one rein. It is mild as curbs go because it has the shortest possible cheek, but it is still considerably more severe than most snaffles.

The Kimblewick is not allowed for dressage, and should not be used for showing. It can sometimes be effective on the strong, older horse or pony — usually the solid, thick-necked type — for hunting or jumping.

Neither a pelham nor a Kimblewick should ever be used on young horses. Misuse of either on any horse can lead to bit evasions.

(Mullen-mouth and jointed pelhams and the Kimblewick are illustrated in *Manual One*, page 179.)

Bitless Bridles

These are principally used in western riding. They act on the nose, chin-groove and poll — some extremely severely. While they can occasionally have their uses as a temporary measure for horses with mouth injuries, they are not otherwise acceptable for Pony Club work.

AUXILIARIES TO THE BIT — ARTIFICIAL AIDS

Nosebands

Cavesson. Has little effect, other than cosmetic, but is part of correct turnout with a double bridle or pelham. The only noseband that should be used with any curb bit, or to which a standing martingale should be attached.

Fitting. Approximately halfway between the corner of the mouth and the cheek bone. It should be possible to insert two fingers in the front of the noseband.

Dropped noseband. Prevents the horse from evading the bit by opening his mouth wide and crossing his jaws. Discourages him from giving only with the lower jaw and so evading the flexion at the poll, or from rolling his tongue back or putting it over the bit. Helps the bit to act on the bars rather than the corners of the mouth.

Construction. The front strap *must* be fixed, so that it can't slip down on the nostrils, and the back strap must be loose. The length of the front strap is important — if it is too short, the noseband will rub or pinch the lips. The buckle must not come on the lip.

Fitting. Three to four fingers (6-8cm) above the nostril, on the nose bone. Back strap in the chin-groove — if used above the bit, it is liable to cause a rub between bit and noseband. Two fingers width in front.

Correct fitting is vital. Too low, it will interfere with the horse's breathing; too high, it pulls the bit up into the corners of his mouth; too tight, it not only causes discomfort but defeats its purpose. Pay special attention to these details if you use a dropped noseband for cross country.

A standing martingale must not be attached to a dropped noseband. If you need both, use a cavesson as well, or a flash noseband.

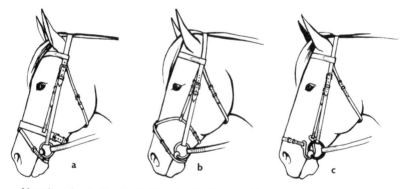

Nosebands. A. Flash, B. Grakle, C. Kineton. For cavesson and dropped nosebands, see *Manual One*, page 177.

Flash (or Hanoverian) noseband — a 'dropped' noseband attached to the centre of a cavesson. Has a similar action to a 'drop', although the pressure comes higher up on the nose. There is no danger of the noseband slipping down on to the nostrils, and a standing martingale may be attached to the cavesson section.

Grakle or crossed noseband. Brings the pressure still higher on the nose, where the two straps cross. Although its action is similar to a 'drop', it is accepted more kindly by some horses. Makes it harder for

270

the horse to cross his jaws. As it cannot affect his breathing, may be safer for cross country.

Fitting. Top strap just under the cheek bone, lower one in the chin-groove. Two fingers in the front, at junction. There should be a connecting strap to keep the two parts of the noseband in place.

NOTE. Any noseband that fits under the bit must be used *only* with a snaffle. There is not room in the chin-groove for both curb chain and noseband, therefore one or the other — usually the curb chain — will be pushed up onto the sensitive branches of the lower jaw, causing great discomfort.

Kineton or Puckle noseband. Has a metal loop on each side which goes between the bit ring and the horse's mouth and an adjustable strap across the nose. Divides the pressure between mouth and nose, according to the length of the front strap. Very severe, not recommended. Does not prevent the horse from crossing his jaws or opening his mouth wide.

Martingales

(For description and fitting of running and standing martingales, see *Manual One*, pages 184-185.)

NOTE. Rubber ring at junction of neckstrap — essential with all martingales, and stops on reins with running martingale.

Objects. To prevent or discourage the horse from avoiding control by raising his nose above the level of the withers, tossing his head about or hitting the rider in the face.

Standing martingale. Correctly fitted, allows the horse to raise his nose to wither height, but no higher. Does not act on the bit in any way, or interfere with the contact from hand to mouth. If too short, the horse may learn to lean against it and it will be dangerous for jumping.

Can be very useful for the rider's safety when retraining a spoilt horse, especially one that is inclined to rear.

Not allowed for A Grade show jumping, or eventing at any level.

Running martingale. Extremely severe if fitted too short, so that the rein is pulled down in a V, especially if used in conjunction with a gag, pelham or Kimblewick. Correctly fitted, it can help to ensure that the contact on the rein always comes from the right direction, and, to cushion the effects of hands that are unsteady or too high while this problem is being rectified.

The only martingale allowed for eventing or for A Grade show jumping.

Market Harborough. The branches of this martingale are about twice as long as those of a running martingale, and end in a clip. They pass through the bit rings and back to Ds specially sewn on the reins. It acts only when the horse raises his head above the desired height and ceases when he lowers it. The effect can be very severe if the horse does not realise this, though a Market Harborough can sometimes work with a spoilt or headstrong horse. Use only with a plain snaffle.

Irish martingale. This consists of two rings joined together by a strip of leather approximately 10cm in length. The reins pass through these rings, under the horse's neck.

Its purpose is to prevent the reins being thrown over the horse's head. It has no influence on his head position.

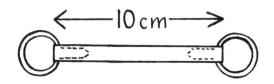

Irish martingale.

No martingale is ever allowed for dressage, and they are totally unacceptable for showing.

If a horse carries his head too high or throws it about, the first thing is to find out why. (See 'Bit Evasions' below.) Merely tying the head down is treating the effect rather than the cause . You are, in fact, preventing the horse from letting you know that something is seriously wrong or painful to him.

Nevertheless, martingales can have their use with spoilt or excitable horses. The essential requirements are to make sure that any martingale is fitted correctly, to regard it as a means to an end, to be used only when necessary and dispensed with altogether as soon as possible.

Chambon, de Gogue. Types of schooling martingales, used *only* when lunging, mainly for retraining horses who are hollow in the back and/or above the bit. Do not use either without expert advice as to suitability for your horse and fitting.

Auxiliary Reins

Side-reins. (See page 255.) Used only when lunging.

Draw-reins or running reins. These are extra (and extra long) reins, which are attached to the girth straps, go through the bit rings and back to the rider's hand. They almost invariably make the horse overbent, and are a forcing aid which is not recommended.

BIT EVASIONS

Causes of Evasion and Resistance

1. **Rider faults** — position not established; unsteady, rough, fixed or unresponsive hands; poor co-ordination of aids; insufficient use of leg and seat for impulsion; lack of understanding and 'feel' for the horse, impatience, bad temper or lack of determination.

Any of these faults will, sooner or later, provoke resistance in even the best-trained horse, no matter what bit is used.

2. **Saddlery.** Bit — too severe, too mild, uncomfortable, ill-fitting. Saddle pressing on or pinching the withers or spine. Misuse of artificial aids, curb bits, trying to force the desired head carriage.

3. **Physical and mental factors in the horse.** Lack of balance and/or understanding in young or untrained horse. Temperament — nervousness, excitability, laziness. Teeth (see page 141). Soreness anywhere, tiredness, poor condition, freshness. Conformation, especially narrow or parrot mouth, badly set-on head and neck, poor natural balance.

Most bitting problems stem, basically, from tension, stiffness or misunderstanding.

Evasion or resistance may be shown in the following ways. In each case, the most common causes are given, but you should always check the above list.

Unsteady Head

(See *Manual One*, pages 112 and 113.) This can also result from sinus trouble or allergy, especially if it occurs more in the summer. If in doubt, consult your vet.

Above the Bit

Above the bit.

Causes. The hands or the bit. Stiffness or discomfort in the back. Temperament or conformation.

Training. For both these evasions, and most others, the circle work outlined in *Manual One*, page 113, is invaluable. Please refer to this. The first object is to persuade the horse, in walk and rising trot, to relax, stretch down and maintain a calm, unhurried pace with the lightest contact on the reins. The rider's lower leg *must* remain quietly on the horse's side.

Next, begin to ride him more actively forward from the inside leg to a soft but definite contact on the outside rein. If he becomes unsteady or above the bit, ask intermittently with a slightly open inside rein for the continued lowering of the head.

As the horse begins to accept all the aids, he will be able to engage his hocks further under his body and his back will become round instead of hollow.

Once acceptance is established, work on half-halts and fairly frequent transitions. Patience and 'feel', with constant praise and encouragement, will be needed.

Walking exercise, first on a long rein, but gradually establishing light contact, is excellent, both for relaxation and correct muscle development.

Pulling

Causes. Rider: allowing the horse to take charge; pulling rather than checking; over-horsed; nervous, hanging on to the horse. Horse: lack of training. Excitement, over-keenness, too much galloping.

Most horses, as they become fitter, take a stronger hold, especially out hunting or across country. In some cases, a change of bit or auxiliary aid may be necessary. Occasionally, a more severe bit, used lightly, may do less damage to a horse's mouth than a mild bit that he ignores. For horses that fight the bit, a milder one will nearly always be the answer. In all cases, training is essential.

If problems of control arise:

1. Consult your instructor. If a change of bit is thought desirable, try to borrow various bits and test the horse's reaction, before buying one.

2. Having found a bit, make sure you understand its action. If it is more severe, use it always with a minimum of force, and only when you must. In jumping, be especially careful that the horse *always* has sufficient rein over his fences.

3. Use a plain snaffle bit for exercising, and, whenever possible, for schooling, and try to educate the horse out of the need for anything else as soon as possible.

Training. The circle work already described is equally valuable for pullers. Depending on the horse's temperament, you may have to be more definite in the initial stage, checking him more sharply if he repeatedly rushes off when offered rein, praising all signs of co-operation.

Work on transitions, including halts, insisting on obedience to upward as well as downward. Practise lengthening and shortening. Make use of stronger 'stopping aids' (see page 53) if necessary. Shorter stirrup leathers could help. Pullers also benefit from long walking exercise and steady trotting, with a minimum of galloping about.

Leaning on the Bit

Leaning on the bit.

The horse is on the forehand, leaning on the rider's hands with a heavy, unyielding pressure.

Causes. Rider: tipped forward; set, heavy hands; insufficient use of seat and leg. Horse: poor natural balance and/or conformation; tired or unfit. Sometimes too mild a bit, especially rubber or metal half-moon.

Training is primarily concerned with improving balance. First, check your position. Make use of basic dressage and gymnastic jumping exercises. Transitions, lengthening and shortening, serpentines, demi-pirouettes when ready, should all help.

If due to the horse's poor natural balance and conformation, improvement may be slow and limited.

Behind the Bit

The horse is not 'onward bound', seeking contact with the bit, but drops behind it, trying to avoid all contact. He will usually, but not always, be overbent.

275

Overbent

Overbent — head behind the vertical, bend too far down the neck, hocks not engaged.

Causes of both these faults. Rider: fixed, unresponsive hands; insufficient use of seat and leg. Too severe a bit. Forcing aids.

Training. Ride the horse strongly forward in rising trot, asking him to accept a light but definite contact on the bit. Practise transitions, demanding prompt obedience to the 'upward' aids. The downward transitions must be ridden with great care, the hands being especially tactful. Sit tall, and steady yourself with a hand on the pommel, if necessary, to help you to make the best use of your seat.

Lengthening and shortening the stride will increase impulsion. Trotting poles, work on undulating ground and an occasional good gallop can all help this type of horse to go forward more enthusiastically.

Head Tilting

Head tilting.

Causes. Rider: uneven hands; crossing inside hand over the neck. Horse: one-sided; evading even contact; sore teeth or mouth; stiffness or discomfort in the back.

Training. Check for sharp molars and/or wolf teeth. Check rider's hands and co-ordination of aids. Immediate recognition should make

276

correction of this fault fairly easy, but since it is usually a 'discomfort' evasion, the cause must always be ascertained. Suppling exercises, such as serpentines and riding in position (see page 44) will help.

Tongue over the Bit

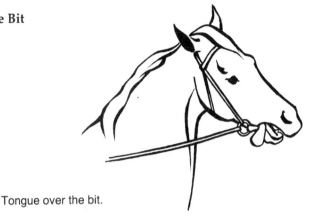

Tongue over the bit.

Causes. Bit uncomfortable or ill-fitting, especially a jointed snaffle that is too big or fitted too low. Faulty 'mouthing' practices with young horses. A narrow mouth or thick tongue.

Correction. Try different snaffles to find the most comfortable one. Fit it as high as possible without unduly wrinkling the corners of the mouth. A drop noseband may help.

Once established, this is a difficult habit to cure.

This section is for reference only for B Certificate candidates, who should be able to discuss bit evasions of which they have had experience.

SADDLES

STRUCTURE

The Tree

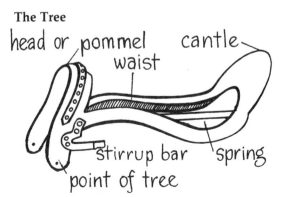

Saddle tree.

The tree is the foundation of the saddle. If it is wrong, it may cause discomfort to horse and rider, and it will be impossible to sit correctly in it. The shape of the tree will vary according to the type of saddle, but it must always have:

a. a deep seat, with the lowest part in the centre and the cantle higher than the head.

b. a good waist, neither too broad nor exaggeratedly narrow.

Materials. Most modern trees are made of moulded, laminated plywood, which is both lighter and stronger than the solid wooden trees in older saddles. Constant research is being carried out to find a material which combines lightness and resilience with strength, durability and good weight distribution. Fibreglass has been used, not always successfully. Flexible trees, made in some cases of composition nylon, appear to be giving good results.

There are basically two types of tree, spring and rigid.

A spring tree has two strips of flexible, tempered steel running lengthways from head to cantle. This makes it resilient and more comfortable for the rider. It is a matter of opinion as to whether it enables the seat aids to be transmitted more clearly to the horse.

Disadvantages. 1. Weight distribution. Some spring tree saddles concentrate the rider's weight on too small an area, especially if they are very narrow in the waist. This can give the horse a sore back if the saddle is used for long periods. It is advisable to use a sheepskin numnah to help to cushion the weight.

2. Fragility. The 'springs' are easily broken, and it is rarely possible to get them repaired.

A rigid tree does not have the springs and is generally of stouter construction. Usually gives better weight distribution, especially with heavy riders.

Trees are available with narrow, medium or wide heads, to suit horses of different conformation. For those with exceptionally high withers, a 'cut-back' head may be necessary.

Stirrup or safety bars are attached to the tree. They may be either hand forged (the safest method) or cast, and should be stamped accordingly. 'Recessed' bars are set on the underside of the tree, to reduce the bulk under the rider's leg.

Most stirrup bars have a hinged end (the thumbpiece) which can be turned up to prevent the stirrups coming off when a saddled horse is being led. It must always be down when riding, so that the stirrup leathers can come off in an emergency.

Stuffing

May be made of wool, horsehair, felt, foam plastic or similar material. It must be smooth and evenly distributed on both sides, sufficient to give a clear channel through the gullet and keep all weight off the horse's spine.

Stuffing may need adjustment to fit the individual horse. New saddles usually require repacking after a few months' use.

Panels

Nearly all full-size, modern saddles have a Continental panel.

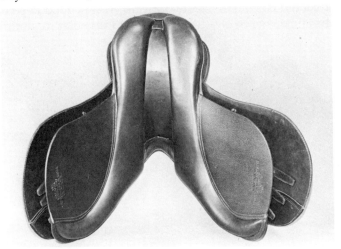

Continental panel.

A half panel reaches about a third of the way down the saddle flap, with a large sweat flap under the girth straps. It provides no support for the rider's leg, and is not recommended for jumping.

Full panels are rarely seen now. Being stuffed throughout, they tend to keep the rider's leg too far away from the horse.

Flaps

The shape is governed by the type of saddle, the tree and the panel. The length must suit the rider.

Girth Straps, Tabs or Points

Long girth straps are used on most dressage saddles, to avoid having girth buckles under the rider's leg. They are also used quite frequently on general purpose saddles, but are not usually necessary on jumping saddles.

When short straps are used, there should be three. The front one is sewn to a separate piece of webbing, which goes round or across the tree, and the back two are sewn to one web, attached to the tree on either side. It is best to use the first strap, and alternate the other two. Always use buckle guards.

General Purpose

A well-designed general purpose saddle, which fits both horse and rider, is suitable for most Pony Club activities. The depth of seat and length of flap should allow a reasonably long leather for dressage, while it should be cut sufficiently forward, with a good knee roll, to allow the stirrups to be shortened by about four holes for jumping.

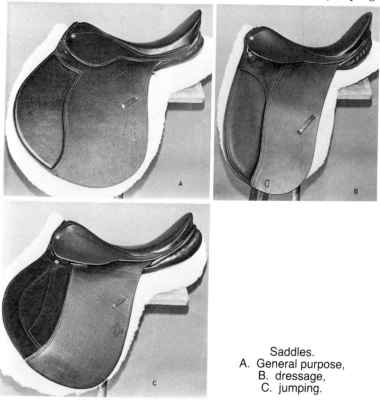

Saddles.
A. General purpose,
B. dressage,
C. jumping.

Dressage

This saddle should enable one to ride with a 'long' leg, while still retaining a bend in the knee, a balanced, central position, allowing full use of seat and leg aids for more advanced dressage.

The seat is fairly short, waist not too narrow, and the flaps straight and long, with knee rolls. The stirrup bars should be set further back than in a jumping saddle.

The best type of saddle to use for showing, as the straight flap shows off the horse's shoulder, but it is useless for jumping.

Jumping

In jumping, the horse's centre of balance is further forward, and the saddle should help the rider, with shorter stirrups, to remain forward and in balance. It should be comparatively long in the seat, cut well forward, with a substantial knee roll for maximum support, and the stirrup bars should also be set further forward.

Some jumping saddles have an exaggeratedly narrow waist. This, particularly with a spring tree, tends to concentrate the rider's weight over too small an area of the horse's back, and may cause problems if the saddle is used for long periods.

Jumping saddles are unsuitable for dressage or showing.

FITTING A SADDLE

Horse

1. The saddle must sit straight on the horse's back. Check from behind and slightly above.

2. There must be a clear passage through the gullet.

3. The weight must be distributed evenly on the lumbar muscles on either side of the spine. There must *never* be any weight on the spine itself.

4. The front arch must not pinch or press on the withers. When mounted and leaning forward in the saddle, you must be able to insert at least two fingers (three, with a new saddle) edgeways between the wither and the pommel. Check that the width is correct for the horse — too wide, the saddle will come down, too narrow, it will pinch the withers.

5. The saddle must not interfere with the action of the horse's shoulders. Check for correct width of tree. You should be able to insert the flat of the hand between the panel and the horse's shoulder.

6. Stuffing. Fundamentally, the saddle must be the right size and shape for the horse, but it still won't fit if the stuffing has become flat or uneven. The correct amount and placing of stuffing can make all the difference when fitting individual horses.

It is best to check the fitting without a numnah.

Rider

1. Should feel comfortable and well-balanced, not too close to the pommel, or slipping to the rear. When sitting in the centre, you

should be able to put your hand flat between your seat and the cantle.

2. The waist must not be too wide, especially if you have short legs, as it prevents you from getting down in the saddle. Neither should it be too narrow, which can be uncomfortable for you and the horse.

3. Flaps should suit your length and thickness of leg, especially the thigh. The knee should fit snugly into the knee roll.

Measuring a Saddle

The measurement is made straight across (not following the dip of the seat) from pommel to cantle. A cut back saddle is measured from the metal stud on one side of the pommel to the centre of the cantle. Standard sizes are 38cm (15''), 40.3cm (16'') and 42cm (17'').

Buying a Saddle

It is essential to try any saddle before buying, to be sure it fits both yourself and your horse. It is preferable to try the saddle without a numnah, but this cannot be done with a new one. Use a towel or thin blanket, and make sure the lining does not come in contact with the horse's back. Also, to avoid marking the saddle, you should not attach stirrups when trying it. Use buckle guards.

New saddles always need 'breaking in', and feel rather stiff at first, but the leather should not be very thick and hard. Notice the attachment of girth straps.

Cheap saddles are rarely satisfactory, as the money is saved by using inferior materials, either in the leather or the tree, or by poor quality workmanship.

When buying a used saddle, check the stitching, girth straps, stuffing and, above all, the tree. A saddle with a broken tree can cause severe injury to a horse's back:

Checking the Tree   *Below:* Checking: A. the front arch and B. the waist of the saddle for a broken tree.

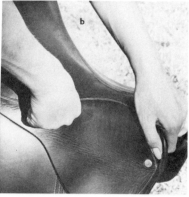

282

1. Pommel. Any movement or squeak indicates a broken tree.

2. Seat region. This should feel equally flexible on both sides if it is a spring tree, but if it is broken it will move more slackly, possibly only on one side, and there may be a grating sound.

3. Cantle. The shape is usually altered, and movement can be felt.

NOTE. Always check any saddle if it is dropped, or the horse falls or rolls on it.

A good saddle is an investment tnat will last a lifetime and will retain its value, if it is properly cared for. It will add tremendously to your pleasure and achievement in riding.

Stirrup irons, leathers and girths. (See *Manual One* pages 182-183.)

Surcingle. (See *Manual One*, page 184.) While a surcingle should never be used merely to reinforce poor girths or girth straps, it can help to stop the saddle lifting, relieving the girths of some of the sudden extra strain when the horse makes a big effort. Used mainly on cross country, or in show jumping over bigger fences.

Check: 1. That the stirrup irons are heavy and of the correct size.

2. That the surcingle fits on top of the girth, otherwise it will pinch or slip back.

3. When using elastic type girths, be sure that the surcingle also has elastic.

Breastplates

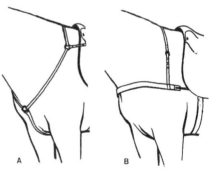

A. Hunting-type breastplate. The neckstrap should allow the width of a hand at the withers. It is attached either to the D's or to the girth-straps above the buckles. The ring at the breast should be backed with leather to prevent rubbing. B. Racing-type breastplate (or breast-girth). Great care is needed in fitting. If too high, the horse's breathing will be affected, if too low, it interferes with the action of the shoulders.

Uses. For horses whose conformation allows the saddle to slip back. Sometimes needed even on a well-made horse as he gets fitter, particularly if he tends to run up. May be essential in cross country, or when riding on hills.

The hunting-type breastplate sometimes has an attachment for use as a running martingale. Since there is little or no provision for adjustment, and it is almost invariably too short, this is not advisable.

CARE OF SADDLERY

Cleaning. (See *Manual One*, pages 195-197.)

Transport to shows, etc. A special bag can be bought to contain the complete saddle and bridle. This keeps it clean and tidy; useful even when you have a lock-up chest.

Saddle covers. Waterproof covers protect the saddle when lunging or leading a horse in wet weather.

Long-term storage. Tack should be cleaned and soaped, and then covered with a layer of dubbin or vaseline. Wrap in newspaper or cotton material, not plastic, nylon or wool (attracts silverfish). Store in a dry place, and check for mould or brittleness whenever possible.

BANDAGES AND BOOTS

Bandages — Uses and Types

Travel and stable. For protection against knocks and treads, for extra warmth when travelling or stabled, especially for a sick horse. Made of wool, flannel or stockinette, 10cm wide, preferably 3m in length (needed for the hind legs of a big horse).

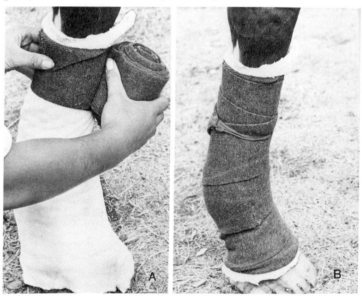

Putting on a travel bandage.
A. Starting the bandage. B. The finished article.

Putting on. Wrap a layer of cotton gamgee or similar material round the leg from the knee or hock to cover the coronet. It must be flat and have a good overlap.

Hold the bandage with the roll towards you and be sure to bandage in the same direction as the overlap of the gamgee. Leave a short 'tail', which is turned down after one circuit and covered by the next, before moving down the leg.

Cover about two thirds of the bandage each time, and keep the tension *light* and *absolutely even* throughout. Continue down to the coronet, and return as far up the leg as the bandage will allow — it must come at least halfway up the cannon bone. If the bandage is too short, it will be necessary to start lower down, especially for a travel bandage, where it is essential to protect the coronet.

Tie the tapes on the outside of the leg, using a reef knot or bow, and tucking the ends in carefully. Never tie the tapes tighter than the bandage, or on the back or front of the leg.

The gamgee should protrude above and below the bandage, otherwise circulation may be impeded. It should be possible to insert a finger comfortably in the top of the bandage.

Veterinary. For keeping a poultice or other dressing in place — applying pressure to control swelling in sprains, etc.

Travel-type bandages are best for applying a poultice (see page 123). Other dressings, depending on the site and nature of the injury, normally require crepe or stockinette. The usual principles of bandaging always apply — ample padding and even tension, but some areas need special techniques. If in doubt, ask your vet.

For pressure bandages use crepe, elastic or stockinette, 7-10cm by 2.30m approximately. In some cases, two bandages may be needed. They are applied over gamgee from knee or hock to coronet. Ask your vet to show you how much pressure is required. While they must be firm, great pain and damage will be caused if these bandages are too tight. Normally, both legs should be bandaged.

Exercise/work, support. For protection, bandages are generally less efficient than boots, they take more time and skill to apply, and are dangerous unless properly secured. For support, opinions vary as to whether bandages can actually support tendons and/or ligaments, or whether they are even desirable. Do not use unless absolutely necessary, preferably on veterinary advice.

Made of crepe, cotton or stockinette — other materials are also available: 7cm by 2.30 approximately.

Putting on. Apply as for a travel bandage, but in this case from close up to the knee or hock to the fetlock joint. It is not normally desirable to go over this joint, as it is liable to restrict its action. The bandage should be firm, but not tight. Bandage both legs.

Methods of securing. 1. Tapes. Adequate for exercise, provided they are tied with a reef knot and well tucked in. Either insulating tape or velcro strip. Adequate for most purposes — must never be tighter than the bandage.

2. Stitching — the only safe method for cross country. Oversew each layer of bandage, as well as the end.

NOTE. Nearly all leg bandages must have gamgee or other padding underneath. Stitching gamgee along the cut edges prolongs its life and enables it to be washed.

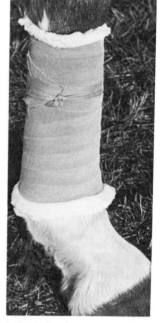

A good working bandage, which comes well onto, but not over, the fetlock joint.

Removing bandages. Unfasten and unroll the bandage from hand to hand — do not roll up as you go. Keep bandage and gamgee clear of gritty surface. Rub leg briskly with palms of hands — especially important after pressure or support bandages.

Tail bandage. Used to protect the tail when travelling, and to shape a pulled tail. Materials and size as for an exercise bandage.

Putting on. Thoroughly damp the tail, not the bandage, which may shrink. Unroll about 30cm of bandage and place it under the tail, keeping it as high as possible and making sure all the hairs are lying flat. Hold the end of the bandage with one hand, angled slightly up to form a very short 'tail'. After one turn of the bandage, fold this 'tail' down and bandage over it. Continue down the tail, covering about two thirds of the bandage each time, or using a herringbone pattern. Go to about 3cm from the end of the dock, then come up again about halfway.

Tie with tapes on the outside, using a reef knot or bow and tucking the ends in neatly. The tapes must not be tighter than the bandage. Bend the tail back into a comfortable position.

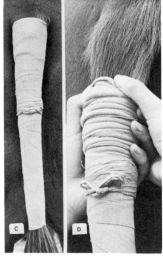

Tail bandage. A. & B. putting on,
C. the finished article, and
D. taking off.

Removing a tail bandage. Hold firmly on either side at the top, and slide down. Do not unroll unless the tail is plaited, in which case it is better to use a tail guard.

Rolling a bandage. Curl the tapes together, roll the bandage over them. Keep the tension firm and the spare end over your shoulder, off the ground.

Apart from cleanliness, bandages should be washed regularly to maintain their elasticity.

Applying bandages correctly takes much practice. Poor bandaging does far more harm than good. Never leave any bandage on longer than necessary. Exercise bandages should be removed on return from work; most veterinary bandages should be removed every twelve hours, maximum twenty-four, and tail bandages after four or five hours maximum. For very long trips, use a tail guard.

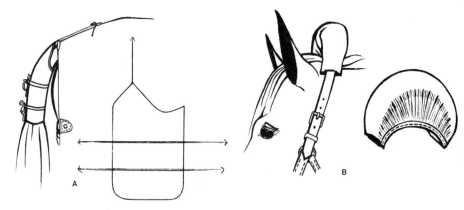

A. Tail guard. Diagram shows shape of guard, which should fit snugly up to base of tail. B. Poll guard.

Boots — Uses and Types

Travel. For protection against knocks, treads and draughts. An alternative to bandages — quicker to put on, more durable, but more expensive. Made of canvas, plastic, sometimes leather, and should have a thick lining. Must be long enough to cover the leg from knee or hock to below the coronet, and should overlap slightly on the outside.

Knee caps protect knees when travelling — essential in trucks with floor-grids or where loading is carried out on bitumen. Usually made of felt or canvas with a leather pad.

Hock boots — invaluable for horses that kick in the float.

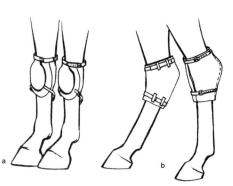

A. Knee caps. Top strap should be fairly firm, bottom strap loose, to allow for bend of knee. The only type of boot where the straps point forward. B. Hock boots. For horse fully dressed for travel, see picture on page 108.

Some travelling boots are now made to cover the whole leg from above the knee or hock. A good fit is essential.

Working boots. To protect the horse against self-inflicted injuries — brushing, speedy-cutting, over-reaching or just hitting himself — and against injuries from hitting fences.

Brushing boots should always be used, at least on the forelegs, when lunging, on young horses when first ridden, and on any horse who, through poor action or other causes, obviously needs them. May be made of leather, felt, plastic, neoprene or other synthetic material, with a strong pad on the inside, shaped to cover the fetlock joint.

Tendon boots — as above, with the addition of a narrow pad down the back to protect, and possibly support, the tendons.

Shin boots have padding in front, for protection when jumping.

Linings, if any, should make for a more comfortable fit. Felt, leather and foam plastic are all good, providing they are kept clean and soft. Rubber or some synthetic materials may rub or cause the leg to sweat, in which case it may be necessary to use some material between boot and leg, but this is not desirable.

Fastenings. Velcro is quick to use, suitable for travelling, lunging and everyday riding. Buckles are safest and strongest and are used on the sturdier type of boot needed for jumping. Foreleg boots usually have four buckles, hind leg boots five. Clips are not always reliable.

Putting on. With the boot slightly too high, fasten centre straps first, slide down into position before fastening the others. Buckles should always be on the outside of the leg, straps pointing to the rear. Tension should be even, and just firm enough to keep the boot in place. To remove, start from the bottom strap.

Fetlock boots. Generally used on the hind legs, for horses who brush. Made of leather, felt or synthetic material with a strong leather 'cup' to protect the joint.

Yorkshire boots. Easy to make, cheap and effective fetlock boots, consisting of a piece of felt or other heavy material with a tape sewn across the centre. Tie above the fetlock and turn over for double thickness.

Rubber rings are sometimes used for horses who brush on the coronet.

Over-reach boots. Used on the forelegs to guard against over-reach injuries, especially when jumping. Usually made of rubber and pulled on over the hoof — hard work if well-fitting! Dangerous if too big. Should never be left on after work. Other types have buckles (preferable) or velcro — easier to fit but more expensive.

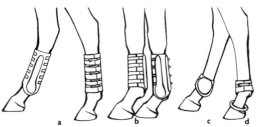

a   b   c   d

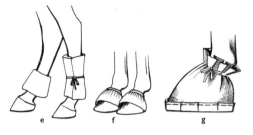

Boots. A. Brushing, B. tendon, C. fetlock, D. rubber ring (see page 289), E. Yorkshire, F. over-reach (bell boots), G. poultice.

Care of working boots. Remove and clean thoroughly immediately after use, as mud or sweat will dry hard and make the horse sore. Since they are subject to much moisture, leather boots should be oiled quite frequently to keep them soft. Check all stitching, buckles, straps, keepers and other fastenings regularly.

Veterinary boots. Poultice boot — used for applying a poultice, usually bran, to the foot. Ice boot — has compartments into which crushed ice may be inserted.

CLOTHING

Covers. (See *Manual One*, pages 184, 193, 196.) Usually made of canvas, they come in a variety of weights and textures — heavyweight, wool lined, medium weight, wool or jute lined and lightweight, unlined. As stated in *Manual One*, a good fit is essential if the cover is to remain in place without rubbing. Heavyweight covers should have a small piece of lambskin sewn in over the withers, and possibly in front to prevent the buckle from chafing. Unlined covers, or sheets, are rarely waterproof in continuous wet weather.

Neck covers. Materials as for covers. They should be well-fitting, attached to buckles on the cover by straps, and buckled under the neck. If the neck is clipped, a lined neck cover should always be used when living out in cold weather. In summer, a light sheet and neck cover will prevent bleaching, which is unsightly in a show horse.

Woollen rugs. Light but warm — used as day rugs for stabled horses, for travelling and at shows. Should be kept in place by a roller — see below. A 'dress' rug, often embellished with the owner's initials.

Quilted nylon/cotton. There are various types available, lined or unlined. They are wind- and shower-proof, warm and very light. Useful for travelling and at trials, etc. Often have a wide surcingle-type fitting, which does not put pressure on the spine.

Anti-sweat sheet. Made of open cotton mesh. May be used on its own after exertion in warmer weather, or under a sheet, rug or cover in cold conditions. Also useful when travelling or for stabled horses who 'break out'.

Summer or fly sheet. Made of any light material. Used in stable, yard, travelling or at shows, to protect against flies, dust and draughts.

Night rugs. Made of jute or similar, with woollen or other lining. Used for stabled horses to avoid soiling the day rug when the horse lies down.

Blankets. Usually heavy, striped wool. Used instead of an extra rug for a clipped, stabled horse. Fold the front back *under* the day rug, but *over* the night rug, to keep it in place.

Rollers and fillet strings. Any rug or sheet, apart from the quilted type, as described, requires a roller and a fillet string. The roller is made of leather or canvas — well padded to keep pressure off the spine. It should not be done up too tightly — if necessary, use a breast girth (attached to Ds on the front of the roller) to keep it in place. A fillet string is made of plaited cotton or similar, and fits loosely under the tail to stop the sheet or rug from blowing up.

Surcingles, whether sewn on or not, put pressure on the spine. If a thick soft pad can be placed underneath, they may suffice for short periods.

Rugging Up

(For putting on and taking off a cover, see *Manual One* pages 193-4.) For rugs and sheets, put on as for cover, then: if outside, place fillet string under tail, put on roller (with pad if required), check both sides to see that it is far enough forward and then do up the front buckle. Make sure there is no pressure round the horse's neck and shoulders, and no wrinkles under the roller. In stables, the front buckle may be fastened before putting on the roller and breast-girth if used. Taking off. Reverse the procedure. Fold the rug(s) and lay over rail or stable door, or on a clean area — *not* in the manger.

Cleaning and Storage

(For care of covers, see *Manual One*, page 196.) Rugs and blankets should be shaken, brushed and aired regularly, and may be sponged to remove stains. An occasional wash or dry cleaning is desirable — best to remove leather straps, otherwise oil well afterwards. Sheets should be washed as necessary. Prompt repairs are always cheapest!

When storing, see that all clothing is clean and repaired. Any covers or rugs with wool content are liable to damage by moths and silverfish. Sprinkle insect powder inside covers, and use mothballs or crystals for rugs and blankets. These are best kept in an airtight chest or in large plastic bags.

REQUIREMENTS FOR THE RIDER

(See *Manual One*, pages 184 and 186.)

Headgear. The NZPCA ruling is that an approved helmet is 'compulsory for *all* riders in Pony Club jumping activities'. This includes practice. The helmet must comply with NZSS8601, or NZSS8602 Medium Protection Helmet, British S4472, Australian S2063, or equivalent. NOTE: NZSTD 8602 Lightweight Protection Helmet will *not* be allowed for Cross-country or Show-jumping activities. Hunt caps are suitable for flat work.

A helmet or cap *must* fit snugly. The safety harness is an essential part of the helmet. Don't drop your helmet, or paint it! After a fall, check for damage — if cracked or dented, it must be replaced.

The basic Pony Club uniform is suitable for all everyday activities, and for most gymkhanas or shows run under Pony Club rules. For other shows, for horse trials and for hunting, the dress may vary. Be sure to check what is required. General guidelines:

Jodhpurs and breeches of various colours are available. Light shades are worn for showing or hunting, darker ones are practical for every day. Many people wear jodhpurs with long boots and this is quite in order.

Boots. Jodhpur boots are quite correct for pony riders on all occasions. Long boots, vinyl or rubber, are practical, waterproof and easy to clean, but hot. Leather boots are very expensive, but do give a good feel and add stability to the leg position. New boots should *just* catch you behind the knee, otherwise they will be too short when worn in. Leather boots require trees.

Jackets. Tweed or plain dark material is always correct for pony riders. For others, it is generally accepted that a black jacket — with black boots — is worn on formal occasions such as hunting, bigger shows and more advanced dressage.

A shirt (not a blouse) should be worn for smarter occasions. It should be of a light colour, with a neat collar. The tie should be pinned down. A stock is only worn with black or really dark jacket, and is correct for hunting. A jersey is normal wear for cross country.

Good turnout is often marred through neglect of the finishing touches: a hairnet or plaits for girls; gloves; well-fitted (and clean) spurs — if worn; and, of course, your Pony Club badge. A discreet buttonhole is permissible at top shows, but fancy jewellery is never in keeping. Earrings must not be worn.

21
SITTING CERTIFICATES

Many people find examinations rather a frightening prospect. Because of this, some candidates, who really have the knowledge and ability to pass, fail because they are unable to do their best on the day, and to convey their knowledge to the examiner. Thorough preparation and a clear idea of what to expect can do much to boost your self-confidence.

Preparation

1. Study all the Test Sheets up to the one you are sitting. Revise especially carefully any subjects in which you were weak in previous tests.

2. Read the appropriate chapters of *Manual One* and *Manual Two*.

3. Get together with other candidates for practical work and for question sessions, preferably with an instructor. Practise doing even the simplest things quickly and neatly, with someone watching and commenting. This is invaluable — often candidates do not realise the mistakes they are making. Some C+, B, A, and H candidates fail on C or even D requirements — for example, incorrect tying-up.

The question sessions should help you to order your thoughts so that you can answer clearly and speak up for yourself in front of others.

Be sure to attend any practice sessions or mock examinations that may be arranged.

4. Make sure your horse is capable of carrying out all the work required.

5. Practise working independently with one or two others in an arena. When meeting on opposite reins, pass left hand to left hand.

6. Gain all the experience you can of riding, assessing, ageing and handling unknown horses of every type, temperament and stage of training; ride them on the flat as well as over fences. Practical experience in stables is helpful for B Certificate, and essential for A and H.

7. Attend a test day as a spectator. You will not be allowed close enough to hear much, but you will get a good idea of the procedure, especially on the riding side.

Do not enter tests just to find out 'what it's all about' or on the spur of the moment, because 'everyone else is'.

On the Day

1. Be punctual. It is a requirement for A Certificate that you should be on the ground at least thirty minutes before starting time, and if you are late for any test you may not be examined.

2. If your horse requires a lengthy work-in, allow time for this before the test starts. Always ask where you may work your horse.

3. Turnout:

Your horse should show the results of regular grooming. He must be in good condition, fit enough for the quite hard work required, especially for A Certificate, and well shod. The horse does not have to belong to you, but you are responsible for his condition, turnout and the way he goes on the day. For B and A certificates the horse should be plaited.

Tack must be spotless, sound and correctly fitted. The tale that your badly fitting saddle is 'going to the saddler next week' will not help you at all! You will be given an opportunity to change saddles between the dressage and jumping phases, if you wish.

Bridle. A plain snaffle, with a drop, Grakle or flash noseband, if needed, is recommended for all work in B and A certificates. If you think your horse goes especially well in a double bridle, by all means use one for the dressage phases of A.

Martingales are not acceptable for work on the flat in B or A and they should not be necessary for jumping if your mount has been correctly trained along Pony Club lines. If you use a martingale, a pelham or Kimblewick, or any other gadget, you must be prepared to explain why you think it is necessary, and what you are doing to retrain the horse.

Breastplates, boots, bandages are allowed in all phases.

All work on the horse — grooming, plaiting, etc., and on the tack — must be your own.

Dress. Pony Club uniform is perfectly acceptable for all tests. However, many A Certificate candidates prefer to wear a black or tweed jacket and long boots. An approved helmet must be worn for all jumping phases. You should wear gloves. Don't forget your Pony Club badge.

Whips. You should carry a whip. A long whip is recommended for the dressage phases, especially at A level. It should not, of course, be used for jumping.

Spurs are optional. Always take them off when changing horses, unless the horse's owner wears them, and advises you to do so.

For H Certificate, a jersey is more practical than a jacket, as there is very little riding. Remember your cap for the 'ride and lead' phase and gloves for lunging.

4. During the test, listen carefully to instructions. If you are told where to work your horse, stay in that area. The further away you go, the harder it is for the examiner to see you and assess your work.

Be sure you know what you are supposed to be doing, which fences to jump, etc. If in doubt, ask, and keep asking until you are certain.

When not actually working yourself, watch the other candidates — you may be asked to comment on some aspect of their performance, and, you may be riding that horse yourself in a few minutes! In either B or A Certificate, but *not* in C+ Certificate, you will be required to change horses during the test.

5. Questions. If you are not sure of the meaning of any question, *ask for it to be clarified.* Think for a moment before you answer, and emphasise the most important points first.

Listen to other candidate's questions. You could be asked if you have anything to add, or whether you agree with their answers. Don't hesitate to say if you don't agree.

At A and H levels, you are often given a situation to think about and asked to express your opinion. For instance:

Outline the last month's preparation for a horse before the first event of the season. (This can easily lead to a general discussion on a variety of aspects.)

6. Examiners. The best possible day for an examiner is a day when everyone passes! While every effort is made to create a good atmosphere in which you can give of your best, you must realise that the examiner has to find out in a very short time how much you know of a particular subject. He, or she, has to decide if what you have done and said is on sound lines, and shows practical experience to the level of the test. Candidates who don't answer freely, or who appear to resent further questioning, make assessment much more difficult.

Pass or fail, accept the verdict gracefully. If you fail, find out just where you went wrong so that you can learn from this experience and do better next time. Whatever happens, be sure that the time and effort put in to training for these certificates will not be wasted. You will be a far more knowledgeable person than you would have been without this training.

THE FORM OF THE TESTS

(C+ Certificate see page 300.)

B Certificate

The riding side is divided into four phases:

1. Inspection of turnout of horse, tack and rider, and riding in the open. You may be asked to work on a large circle with one or two

other candidates, in which case the examiner will tell you when to change pace or direction, or to work your horse quite independently. Either way, the examiner will want to see you riding at all paces. The object at this stage is to assess your general appearance, ability and partnership with your horse — whether you look really 'at home' on a horse and would be a credit to Pony Club wherever you might be seen.

2. Dressage, in a lettered arena. This is a test of knowledge as well as performance. You could be asked to execute drill movements in conjunction with others, and to carry out any of the dressage movements listed on the test sheet. Nobody expects perfection, but you must be able to comment on the way your horse is going, and whether he is achieving what is required. You must know the aids for each movement, and, when things go wrong, be able to recognise the fault, and possibly improve matters after discussion with the examiner.

3. Jumping — up to 90cm. This could include trotting poles and jumping exercises, as well as different types of fences to be taken at specified paces. There may be separate show jumping and cross country courses, or one course combining some of each. The examiners are looking for a balanced and secure jumping position, with good contact and sympathetic control over the horse. Questions may be asked on simple fence construction and distances between elements in combinations and exercises.

4. Riding a different horse — usually one of the other candidates' horses. You will be asked to ride the horse at all paces and over one or two jumps and then to assess it briefly. Be prepared for such questions as: Does he have good paces? Which is his best side? Does he come on the bit? What are his best and weakest points? How does he compare with your own horse?

In addition, there will probably be a horse to be ridden (but not jumped) in a double bridle.

Horse management. Never think of this section of any test as 'theory' — it will be as practical as possible. You must be prepared, for example, to put down a bed, use a body brush, put on a tail bandage, dress or foment an imaginary wound. You should be able to carry out these tasks efficiently, safely and confidently — giving the impression that you have done them many times before. Certainly there will be questions, but there, too, your answers must reflect practical experience. You can expect at least one task or question connected with each section of the test, with a greater concentration on one or two aspects.

B Certificate examination takes two to two-and-a-half hours overall. The whole test must be passed on one occasion.

For some people, B Certificate seems unattainable — for others, it is a stepping stone on the way to still higher things. It *is* attainable to anyone who has a good average Pony Club mount and is prepared to put in the necessary work. It *should* be attained by all who are interested in area trials and other forms of competition, or who want to take more responsibility for the care and conditioning of their horse, in a way that cannot be done at C level. It is a required qualification for Inter-Pacific selection (see page 11) or, of course, to sit A or H certificates.

A Certificate

The riding side consists of five phases:

1. Inspection of turnout and riding in the open. Turnout as for B Certificate, but more polished in every sense of the word. You will then be asked to work your horse independently in the open for approximately ten minutes before going into the school. The examiners are looking for a clear method or pattern of work. There is a definite element of showmanship in A Certificate — try to make it all look easy, enjoyable and logical.

2. Dressage — may be in a long or short arena, and include working with others, either independently or as a ride, or on your own. You may be asked for any or all of the movements on the test sheet.

Emphasis is placed on the rider's position and application of the aids and the way the horse goes, his balance, suppleness and enjoyment of the work. Again, perfection is not expected, but by this time you must know what you are trying to do and how much you are achieving, and be aware of your own and your horse's strengths, weaknesses and problems. You should be able to discuss your present and future training programme.

You may be required to change horses in this phase.

3. Show jumping. A straightforward course including at least one combination — emphasis on a firm seat, style and polish. Fences will be approximtely 1.10m (maximum 1.15m). Gymnastic jumping may be included.

You should now have sufficient balance, suppleness and experience to be able to adapt your position according to circumstances and the horse you are riding.

Be prepared for questions on any aspect of the jumping course, the fences, or on training methods.

4. General riding and cross country. You will be required to ride on the flat and over a variety of fences at any pace. In gallop, and in cross country, a forward position would normally be maintained, but you could sit more upright on the approach to the fence.

You will ride your own horse for one of phases 3 and 4, and this phase will be taken first. For the other phase, you will change over and ride one or more other horses.

5. Training a green or awkward horse. Here you will ride the horse provided and may be asked to age it, and to assess its conformation, present performance and potential. You should be able to discuss its good and bad points and suggest a training programme for the next few months. You could also be asked questions on any aspect of the initial handling and training of young horses.

Horse management. The examiner must feel confident that you could safely be left in charge of somebody else's horse, whether stabled or at grass, for at least two weeks, and that the horse would be returned in as good or better condition and training. The form of the examination is similar to B Certificate, but you must show a greater depth of knowledge and experience in all subjects. For instance, you must not only have knowledge of the different types of clips, but have had experience in actually clipping horses. This includes assembly and care of the clipping machine. Tasks set will be in line with the more advanced nature of the test. As mentioned, there will be greater emphasis on discussion, both with the examiner and with the other candidates, than on direct question and answer.

In the general knowledge phase, you may be asked about the structure of Pony Club and the running of your own club or branch. You should have ideas and opinions about Pony Club and other horse activities and training methods and the ability to express yourself in a fluent and interesting way.

An A Certificate examination takes approximately three hours for two candidates, but as more people than this are generally involved, it is likely to be spread over a longer period.

A Certificate is the highest award of Pony Club — a peak that is reached only by a minority, worldwide. It is not a test of advanced, specialised knowledge, but of practical experience over a wide range of subjects. Obviously, at this level, any ingrained faults which would inhibit further progress cannot be overlooked. Successful candidates should feel that they have achieved excellent foundations, from which they can continue to learn and to enjoy whatever areas of equitation appeal to them.

H Certificate

This is a test entirely of horse management. It is most valuable, particularly for the many associate members who take great pride in their horses, but who do not have the opportunity or ambition on the riding side to attain A Certificate.

There are two elements in H Certificate which are not normally examined in a practical way in A Certificate — lunging and 'ride and lead', both used here as methods of exercising.

Lunging. You will be given a trained lunge horse, saddled and bridled, and a selection of tack — boots, cavesson, side-reins, etc. You will be asked to prepare the horse for lunging, lead him out to the enclosure provided, and there work him on the lunge as you would do if you were exercising him in this way. The examiner is looking for safe handling throughout, with control over the horse, whip and lunge rein, and an understanding of the use of side-reins and the general principles of lunging.

Ride and lead. you will be given two horses in adjacent yards or boxes, one saddled up, the other bridled. The requirement is to bring both horses out, mount one horse while holding the other, then 'ride and lead', as directed by the examiner. Control and safety are again paramount, and questions may be asked about this method of exercising, especially on the road.

There is really little difference in the range and depth of knowledge needed for H Certificate and for the horse management section of A Certificate. The difference lies in the time factor. Both examinations take approximately three hours, of which, in A, half is spent in riding. With twice the time available, it is obvious that the H test can be deeper and more detailed.

H Certificate holders are not required to sit the horse management section of A. For this reason, many people find it best to concentrate on H after gaining their B Certificate. While working for H, they are training themselves and their horses, and acquiring the necessary experience for the riding phases of A Certificate.

Qualifications and Organisation for B, A and H Certificates

To sit your B Certificate,you must:

1. Hold C Certificate (C+ is optional).
2. Be 15 years of age, and under 21.
3. Have participated in five working rallies during the twelve months preceding the application to sit the examination.
4. Bring a pony/horse (one only) trained to a reasonable standard in all phases of the work required.

If, for some reason, you wish to sit your B Certificate in another club, you must have the permission of your district commissioner.

Should you fail in the test, three months must elapse before trying again.

There is no fee for B Certificate, but examiners' travelling expenses may have to be met, and candidates levied accordingly.

To sit A or H Certificate, you must:
1. Hold B Certificate.
2. Be 17 years of age and under 21.
3. Have participated in five working rallies during the previous year.
4. For A Certificate, bring a horse to the examination trained to a reasonable standard in all phases of the work required.

Examination dates and venues are fixed twelve months ahead by the NZPCA Committee of Management.

Applications must be received by the association three months prior to the selected date. Application forms are available from the association secretary. They must be signed by the district commissioner and lodged by the candidate's club.

The fee for these two examinations is set from time to time by the Committee of Management.

In A Certificate, if you pass all phases of either the riding or the horse management sections, you will be awarded a 'partial pass' and will not have to sit that section again. H Certificate holders only have to sit the riding section of A to obtain a full pass.

If you fail either of these examinations, six months must elapse before you may attempt the whole test again, or complete a partial pass.

C+ Certificate

This test is examined in much the same way as B Certificate, although, since C+ marks a half-way point between C and B, the standard expected is in accordance with that level.

Sections 1 and 2, work in the open and dressage, are similar to B, but check the dressage requirements for C+ carefully. They are not nearly so demanding. However, you must know what you are doing, and why, and be able to discuss your pony's work with the examiner.

Section 3, jumping, up to 75cm. You should show that your position is becoming well established and that you understand the importance of good contact. Trotting poles, a course of fences, with a double, and a variety of cross-country obstacles may be included — also walking a course.

You will also be asked to show control at a gallop.

You are *not* expected to change ponies, or to ride in a double bridle, in this test.

Pony management. You must show increased knowledge and practical application of the care and conditioning of your pony, with all its associated factors — again, check the test card carefully.

C+ takes one and three-quarters to two hours overall.

RECOMMENDED READING

New Zealand Pony Clubs Association Manual One and **Manual Two** cover the full range of Pony Club teaching. Practical and theoretical examination for all certificates will be formulated solely on the contents of these two books, according to the test sheet at each level.

Other books which may be of interest:

British Horse Society's Equitation Country Life Books, in association with the BHS. 1983. Training of rider and horse to advanced levels, dressage and jumping.

British Horse Society and Pony Club Manual of Horsemanship produced for the BHS by Threshold Books Ltd. 1980.

Lt-Col W. S. Codrington, TD, MRCVS *Know Your Horse* J. A. Allen & Co. Ltd. 1972. Veterinary.

Christopher Coldrey *Courses for Horses* J. A. Allen & Co Ltd. 1978. Valuable for riders and for those building courses.

Anthony Crossley *Training the Young Horse — the First Two Years* Stanley Paul & Co. Ltd. Basic to advanced elementary dressage.

E. Hartley Edwards *The Book of Saddlery and Equipment* Lansdowne. 1981. Expensive, but very comprehensive, with excellent colour pictures.

E. Hartley Edwards *Saddlery* Country Life Ltd. 1971.

W. J. W. Froud *Better Show Jumping* Thomas Nelson & Sons Ltd. 1975.

Elaine Knox-Thompson and Suzanne Dickens *Guide to Riding and Horse Care* Lansdowne. 1984.

Elaine Knox-Thompson and Suzanne Dickens *The Young Horse* Collins, 1985. Lunging, backing, training up to four years.

Ron and Val Males *Foaling — Brood Mare and Foal Management* Ure Smith. 1977.

Sally O'Connor *Practical Eventing* Whittet & Shepperson, Richmond, Virginia, USA. 1980.

Alois Podhajsky *The Complete Training of Horse and Rider* George C. Harrap & Co Ltd. 1967. Basic to very advanced dressage.

Mary Rose, FBHS *Horsemaster's Notebook* George C. Harrap & Co Ltd. 1977. Comprehensive on horse management.

R. H. Smythe, MRCVS *The Horse — Structure and Movement* J. A. Allen & Co Ltd. 1972. Conformation.

INDEX

Illustrations are shown in bold type.
See also the index to *Manual One.*

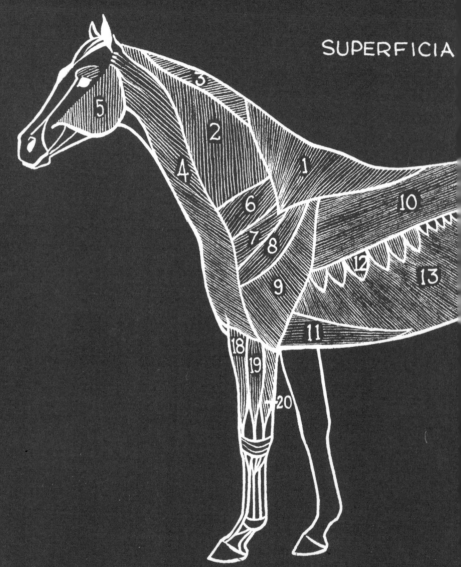

SUPERFICIA